**PERGAMON INTERNATIONAL LIBRARY**
of Science, Technology, Engineering and Social Studies
*The 1000-volume original paperback library in aid of education,*
*industrial training and the enjoyment of leisure*
Publisher: Robert Maxwell, M.C.

# A Social Geography
# of England and Wales

## THE PERGAMON TEXTBOOK
## INSPECTION COPY SERVICE

An inspection copy of any book published in the Pergamon International Library will
gladly be sent to academic staff without obligation for their consideration for course
adoption or recommendation. Copies may be retained for a period of 60 days from receipt
and returned if not suitable. When a particular title is adopted or recommended for
adoption for class use and the recommendation results in a sale of 12 or more copies, the
inspection copy may be retained with our compliments. The Publishers will be pleased to
receive suggestions for revised editions and new titles to be published in this important
International Library.

# PERGAMON OXFORD GEOGRAPHIES

*General Editor:* W. B. FISHER

A Pergamon Journal of Related Interest

**REGIONAL STUDIES**

**Journal of the Regional Studies Association**

EDITOR: **J. B. Goddard, Department of Geography, University of Newcastle-upon-Tyne, England**

This journal aims to provide a forum for the exchange of ideas and information in the area of regional planning and related fields. It is international in character, aiming to circulate and disseminate the studies and results of regional research. Contributions reflect the application of systematic methods to the solution of problems of regional planning and cover such subjects as: machinery of regional economic planning; regional economic development; economic growth in developing countries; metropolitan regional planning and models of regional and urban development.

# A Social Geography of England and Wales

by

**RICHARD DENNIS**

and

**HUGH CLOUT**

Department of Geography, University College London

**PERGAMON PRESS**

OXFORD · NEW YORK · TORONTO · SYDNEY · PARIS · FRANKFURT

| U.K. | Pergamon Press, Ltd., Headington Hill Hall, Oxford OX3 0BW, England |
| U.S.A. | Pergamon Press Inc., Maxwell House, Fairview Park, Elmsford, New York 10523, U.S.A. |
| CANADA | Pergamon of Canada, Suite 104, 150 Consumers Road, Willowdale, Ontario M2J 1P9, Canada |
| AUSTRALIA | Pergamon Press (Aust.) Pty. Ltd., P.O. Box 544, Potts Point, N.S.W. 2011, Australia |
| FRANCE | Pergamon Press SARL, 24 rue des Ecoles, 75240 Paris, Cedex 05, France |
| FEDERAL REPUBLIC OF GERMANY | Pergamon Press, GmbH, 6242 Kronberg-Taunus, Hammerweg 6, Federal Republic of Germany |

First edition 1980

**British Library Cataloguing in Publication Data**
Dennis, Richard
A social geography of England and Wales — (Pergamon Oxford geographies)
1. Anthropo-geography — England
2. England — Social conditions
3. England — Historical geography
I. Title    II. Clout, Hugh Donald
309.1'42      GF551      79-41690

ISBN 0-08-021802-4 (Hardcover)
ISBN 0-08-021801-6 (Flexicover)

*Printed and bound in Great Britain by*
*William Clowes (Beccles) Limited, Beccles and London*

# Contents

# Preface

RECENT years have witnessed a growth of interest in 'social geography'. There has been social geography based on human ecology, social geography based on behavioural psychology, social geography based on political economy. This book draws on each of these traditions, adding to them a strong historical element that reflects its authors' training and research interest in historical geography. Although several books in the general field of social geography have appeared recently, none has combined this historical approach with an empirical emphasis on England and Wales. In addition, one of our objectives in writing *A Social Geography of England and Wales* has been to place selected aspects of English society in a theoretical context; so several sections of the book, especially in Chapters 1, 2 and 11, focus on geographical and sociological theory and only in passing refer to England and Wales. Readers may already be familiar with at least the outlines of these concepts, but we would urge them to follow our arguments through these sections, since frequent reference is made to them in the more empirical parts of the book. Much of the book is based on undergraduate courses that we have taught to first- and second-year students at University College London.

Throughout the book we have used 'England' or 'English' as shorthand for 'England and Wales' or 'English and Welsh', except where a specific example from Wales immediately follows. We have used the term 'British' where we are contrasting societies and academic schools of thought on this side of the Atlantic with those in North America, and where it seems to us that the Scottish or Irish experience parallels that of England and Wales. As far as possible our detailed illustrations relate to England and Wales, but some statistics, particularly in the field of housing, are produced for Great Britain or the United Kingdom. This is unfortunate, given the unique organization of the housing market in Scotland (e.g. the greater importance of council housing, long history of tenement dwellings, and different procedure for buying a house) and the peculiar situation pertaining in Northern Ireland since the late 1960s; but it is unlikely that the inclusion of data for Scotland and Northern Ireland significantly distorts the figures for England and Wales. We have also cited Scottish or Irish evidence where the best published research relates to these areas and we can see no reason why the situation in England and Wales should be any different.

Many of our examples, especially on the housing market and inner-city problems, are drawn from London and the south-east of England. In part this reflects the emphasis in the literature and the ready availability of data on London. In addition, we both live and work in London, we have personally experienced the operations of London's housing market, between us we have lived in a wide variety of London environments, and we have participated in teaching courses on the geography of London. Few of the capital's experiences do not also apply in some degree to Birmingham, Liverpool, Manchester or other large cities. London's problems may be more complicated than those of other cities, but its principal differentiating characteristic is size and that, in itself, is another good reason for concentrating on London.

In the references at the end of each chapter we have listed all the works to which we make explicit reference, together with selected additional reading including books and papers that refer to places other than those we discuss in the text. As far as possible we have avoided citing unpublished articles or working papers to which students may not have easy access.

As is customary in a work of joint authorship, we would claim corporate responsibility for what follows, but those who know us will have little difficulty in guessing who wrote what. To satisfy those who do not know us, Richard Dennis prepared the first drafts of Chapters 2, 5–9 and 11, Hugh Clout Chapters 1, 3 and 10, while Chapter 4 was a joint effort from the beginning. But all of these chapters have subsequently been rewritten in the light of our criticisms of each other.

Finally, our thanks go to our students, the results of whose labours appear scattered through the following pages: to Teresa Filippi, Claudette John and Annabel Swindells for translating our handwriting into typescript, and to Christine Daniels and Richard Davidson of the Cartographic Unit, University College London, for preparing the maps and diagrams.

University College London,                                    RICHARD DENNIS
October 1979.                                                      HUGH CLOUT

# 1
# An Introduction

**Through the Looking-glass**

OF all the varieties of geography, 'social geography' is probably the most elusive and poorly defined. Several generations of geographers, qualifying their interests as 'social', have attempted to describe and justify their viewpoints and methods of enquiry. A veritable mountain of literature in many languages may be amassed and forms valuable quarry for students of geographical methodology. However, there has been little agreement on the detailed content and characteristics of social geography. Quite distinctive national brands flourish in different countries, as do different approaches and foci of interest which have been developed by eminent social geographers and their students. The problem of definition is compounded if one turns to that international corpus of geographical writing in search of inspiration. 'Social geography' as it appears to be practised and taught in Great Britain is not synonymous with *géographie sociale* in France, *Sozialgeographie* in Germany, *sociale geografie* in the Netherlands or with 'cultural geography' in North America. Lewis Carroll expressed a similar dilemma in *Through the Looking-Glass*. "When *I* use a word", Humpty Dumpty said, in a rather scornful tone, "it means just what I choose it to mean – neither more nor less." Alice questioned "whether you *can* make words mean so many different things" but Humpty Dumpty believed that the real question was "which is to be master – that's all." Most social geographers sit with Humpty Dumpty on the wall and their collective writing prompted Anne Buttimer (1968) to report that "social geography lacks definite boundaries and has neither a central unifying concept nor even an agreed content. Instead, there are scattered individual efforts to analyze the changing social patterns of the modern world" (p. 139).

Just what comprises the detailed substance of social geography remains a matter of debate but most so-called social geographers would probably agree that their specialism forms part of a larger field of human geography. Many would probably also confess their belief that spatial variations in Man's occupation of the Earth's surface and in his utilization of its resources are produced in response to influences exercised by society as well as to economic forces and physico-geographical conditions. As a result, the social geographer defines the 'environment' in which Man lives, and which he in turn modifies, in rather a different way from that proposed by many of his colleagues. He acknowledges the importance of 'physical' resources like land and water for human survival and recognizes the power of the various economic systems within which mankind operates but in addition he argues that all Earth's inhabitants are members of groups or societies which influence their personal aspirations, their perceptions and ultimately their behaviour. Social relationships are thus advanced by social geographers as forming a kind of missing link or an area of mediation between the natural milieu and the processes of economic production. It is argued

1

that individuals have a large measure of choice in organizing their lives but they do not have complete freedom since they are influenced by the attitudes, value systems and traditions shared by the groups into which they were born or otherwise came to belong.

Groups exist at varying scales and exert differing degrees of influence. Everyone belongs to a family or a household and this kind of primary group, together with the village community or the town gild, exercised the most significant institutional influences on our predecessors in pre-industrial times. The family remains the fundamental group in the modern world but traditional rural communities have disappeared and new socio-economic 'classes' have emerged in association with the processes of modernization and industrialization. Greater personal mobility has served to bring together people of different spatial, cultural and social origins. Often the result has not been a 'melting pot' situation but a complicated social and spatial mosaic which cannot, of course, be analyzed with reference to each individual human being but may be elucidated by reference to the groups to which they belong. The situation is remarkably complex because each individual will belong simultaneously to several groups (e.g. primary educated/manual worker/working class/Roman Catholic/Irish/Socialist/council flat dweller; or secondary educated/clerical/lower middle class/Muslim/Pakistani/Conservative/owner-occupier; or university educated/professional/ middle class/Protestant/English/Socialist/private tenant). The range of possible permutations is enormous but the study of groups is accepted by social scientists as the manageable scale of investigation to elucidate the diversity of mankind.

To describe, analyze, explain and trace changes in the variety of the human condition is not essentially the geographer's task but rather that of the sociologist. Instead, the social geographer is interested in using his academic looking glass to examine the spatial mosaics that have been produced in town and country alike in response to the social processes that serve to structure and power the increasingly complex societies to be found on the surface of the Earth. Unlike the work of other social scientists the social geographer's field of enquiry has an explicit territorial base which is constantly exploited and refashioned by members of human groups which have differing degrees of access to resources, education, financial capital and political power. The mosaics that confront the social geographer are expressions of that inequality. They are also manifestations, albeit partially modified ones, of social conditions in times past. For example, all forms of settlement and types of housing in contemporary Britain were built at some time in the past when social conditions were, in varying degree, different from those of today. British society is changing continuously but the built environment, by definition, can only be modified at a slower pace. Such discordance forms a fascinating point of enquiry for the social geographer.

So let us ask again 'what is social geography?' Three definitions from practitioners of the art in different parts of the world will help clarify our ideas.

(i) Joseph Hadju (1968) puts geographic space in pride of place in his analysis of German *Sozialgeographie* and then elaborates the concept of the social group. The work of German social geographers "sets out to interpret the cultural landscape and the forces which give it its ever-changing character. These forces are often to be found in the social group or groups which are active in the region. The social group can have as its common factor birth, income, occupation, ethnic origin, religion, distinct customs, or occupational techniques" (p. 409).

(ii) From her deep acquaintance with French and North American styles of geography, Anne Buttimer (1968) summarizes social geography as "the study of the areal (spatial) patterns and functional relations of social groups in the context of their social environment;

the internal structure and external relation of the nodes of social activity; and the articulation of various channels of social communication" (p. 142).

(iii) After scrutinizing this and other international literature, the British geographer Emrys Jones (1975) concludes that social geography involves understanding "patterns which arise from the use social groups make of space as they see it, and the processes involved in making and changing such patterns" (p. 7). He believes that to establish "a better ordered society" and to "eliminate what are universally regarded as social ills based on inequality" (p. 9) represent the final goal of social geography, but he does not specify the new social order that such an objective implies. Patterns of social groups and processes operating in society, together with concepts such as the 'social group' and 'social space', form central themes in Professor Jones' collection of *Readings in Social Geography* (1975) and, together with social planning, provide the basic structure for his *Introduction to Social Geography* (1977) written in collaboration with John Eyles.

Many radical social geographers in Britain and North America agree with Jones' objective of improving as well as describing the state of society, but concentrate on particular types of social process and social group. They stress the political and economic essence of all social patterns, and especially the relationship between social groups and 'classes' defined in terms of control over the means of production. To them, social inequalities reflect the unfair distribution of scarce resources such as employment, housing, education and health care but, in turn, the distribution of resources reflects the state of the class struggle and the ideology of those in power. According to this interpretation, even apparently 'social' factors are economically determined and socio-spatial structure is a function of the dominant mode of production, whether feudalism, capitalism or socialism (Harvey, 1973; Gray, 1975; Peet, 1977, 1978).

Undoubtedly, social geography has become more 'relevant' and social geographers politically more aware in recent years, and this trend permeates the later chapters of this book. There is, perhaps, more economics than we anticipated when we began to write the book, indicative of our sympathy with some radical, if not Marxist, contributions, but the independent role of culture and the freedom of the individual to make locational decisions remain central to our view of the subject. Our approach to the social geography of modern England is essentially descriptive and inductive, but we feel it necessary to begin with a theoretical chapter in which England's experience over the last few hundred years can be placed in a wider context. By virtue of our training, spatial experience and research interests we are acutely aware of the role of the past in the present with respect to social and spatial differentiation in England's towns and countrysides and, more controversially, to the survival of attitudes and prejudices that we believe to be both anachronistic and inappropriate to the times in which we live. As a result, we pay considerable attention to the social geography of England in the past. So many of our landscapes and our class-based social distinctions are rooted firmly in processes of modernization and industrialization which occurred during the nineteenth century that we devote Chapters 4 and 5 to that vital formative phase in our social history. British society is now essentially urban and we think it appropriate to include four chapters on the social geography of contemporary towns and cities. Several ecological and economic models of urban structure have been transported from North America to Great Britain without the critical treatment that they deserve. The strengths and weaknesses of these and other more appropriate models are examined in Chapters 6 and 7. Variations in housing type and quality form intriguing reflections of fundamental differences in British society and are analyzed with reference to a theory of housing classes in Chapter 8. Residents of the inner areas of many British cities now experience substantial social problems which are compounded in areas of multiple deprivation. Such problem areas offer plenty of scope for practising social geography as an applied social science (Chapter 9). In addition, urbanism as a way of life has been dispersed far into the countryside where it has provoked fundamental social and spatial changes related to commuting, retirement migration and tourism (Chapter 10).

The dynamism of modern society must be mirrored in the concepts and techniques adopted by social geographers in the future. Certainly their subject has advanced considerably beyond the largely 'neutral' enquiries that attracted Pahl's righteous indignation more than a decade ago (1965, 1967). In compiling the present book we have not tried to write a 'complete' social geography of England and Wales. We would not dare to do so. The choice of themes reflects our own interests more than anything else. As a result, a number of issues, including religious, ethnic and linguistic differences in modern Britain, have had to be excluded. We make no apology for such omissions since many of these matters are discussed by Jones and Eyles (1977) and by the contributors to Jones' (1975) collection of readings.

### References and Further Reading

Valuable and wide-ranging discussions of the nature of social geography, together with lengthy bibliographies, are presented in:
Jones, E. (1975) *Readings in Social Geography*, Oxford University Press, Oxford.
Jones, E. and Eyles, J. (1977) *An Introduction to Social Geography*, Oxford University Press, Oxford.
Buttimer, A. (1968) Social geography, in *International Encyclopedia of the Social Sciences*, vol. 6, Macmillan and Free Press, New York, pp. 134–45.

Writings in *géographie sociale* and *Sozialgeographie* are analyzed by:
Buttimer, A. (1969) Social space in interdisciplinary perspective, *Geographical Review*, 59, 417–26.
Buttimer, A. (1971) *Society and Milieu in the French Geographic Tradition*, Association of American Geographers, Chicago.
Hadju, J. (1968) Toward a definition of post-war German social geography, *Annals of the Association of American Geographers*, 58, 397–410.

Two stimulating onslaughts on the limitations of past writings in social geography are launched by:
Pahl, R. E. (1965) Trends in social geography, in R. J. Chorley & P. Haggett (eds.), *Frontiers in Geographical Teaching*, Methuen, London, pp. 81–100.
Pahl, R. E. (1967) Sociological models in geography, in R. J. Chorley & P. Haggett (eds.), *Models in Geography*, Methuen, London, pp. 217–42.

Radical approaches to social geography are discussed by:
Gray, F. (1975) Non-explanation in urban geography, *Area*, 7, 228–35.
Peet, R. (1977) The development of radical geography in the United States, *Progress in Human Geography*, 1 (3), 64–87.
Peet, R. (ed.) (1978) *Radical Geography: alternative viewpoints on contemporary social issues*, Methuen, London.

and classically exemplified in:
Harvey, D. (1973) *Social Justice and the City*, Arnold, London.

# 2

# Theories of Industrialization and Urbanization

## Approaches

OUR objective in this chapter is to provide a basic introduction to some theories about the social and spatial consequences of the modernization of societies, as a prelude to considering their application in pre-industrial and industrializing Britain. Social scientists have adopted several different approaches in explaining changes in social structure and their consequences for social geography. For example, Marxist interpretations of social structure, in terms of the economic relationships between different classes, have attracted increasing attention from geographers in recent years (e.g. Harvey, 1973; Peet, 1977, 1978). Marxists view societal change in terms of continuous advances in the technology of production which produce discontinuous change in social structure, much as 'catastrophe theory' invokes the concept of the threshold whereby a continuous process periodically generates entirely new states of being. In the same way as the continuous heating of water suddenly produces the change from water to steam, so it is argued that there are historical discontinuities where continuous technological change produces a transformation from, for example, a society based on reciprocity to one based on redistribution or market exchange. Marxists emphasize the *dialectical* nature of change: discontinuities arise because the existing social and economic structure is incompatible with new developments in the means of production.

It is an interpretation that accords well with recent trends in geographical thought. The systems approach, stressing the interrelatedness of everything, is reflected in the links that are identified between technology, economy, society and politics. Most classical economic theory analyzed static relationships between different variables, assuming a state of equilibrium, but more recently geographers have preferred to study change in terms of dynamic relationships. As Muir (1978) has noted, the Marxist emphasis on the dialectical nature of change seems to be compatible with the development of a dynamic, process-oriented, behavioural geography. Day and Tivers (1979), in a critique of catastrophe theory, cite Lenin's observations on the dialectical nature of change:

"We cannot understand a particular society in terms of some set of institutions in and through which individual men and women are organized, but we must study the social processes which are going on, in the course of which both institutions and people are transformed." These words are so uncontroversial that they could have been written by any geographer, Marxist or non-Marxist! In fact, the generality of dialectical theory is one of its shortcomings. How do we define the elements that are supposed to be in contradiction with one another, and the transformation that is supposed to emerge? "What Marxists do is arbitrarily to select any two dissimilar phenomena which it may suit them to represent as contradictions or oppositions, term them respectively the thesis and the antithesis, resolve them into a third phenomenon described as the synthesis, and label the whole process as dialectical" (Carew Hunt, 1963, quoted in Muir, 1978).

Despite superficial similarities, Marxist analysis is incompatible with much behavioural geography, for while the latter stresses the individuality and unpredictability of man, Marxism emphasizes technological and economic determinism. It may, therefore, be an inappropriate framework for the study of change at the local or individual scale, but an appropriate framework for the study of major societal change, as in the example cited above: the transformation from reciprocity, through redistribution, to market exchange (Harvey, 1973).

Reciprocity denotes a state of equal exchange, as might occur in a tribe in which decisions are agreed communally and land and goods are held in common. If the result of hunting and gathering, or of primitive cultivation, is to produce a surplus, then that surplus is shared equally among all the members. Services rendered by one member to another are reciprocated by equivalent services rendered in return. In this type of society no individual has overall control, and no individual has the opportunity to gain overall control by economic means. In a redistributive society, one group has the authority to expropriate any surplus, either in the form of excess production or as forced labour, and to utilize the surplus according to its own values. Feudal societies, including societies in which the priesthood assumes a dominant role, are usually characterized by redistribution. Market exchange economies correspond to *laissez-faire* capitalism in which there is an economic and social hierarchy, but where social mobility is possible by exercising an appropriate strategy in selling one's labour or one's product. Interestingly, Marx and Engels in *The Communist Manifesto,* and Engels in *The Condition of the Working Class in England,* take a very different view of social mobility in feudal and modern societies. In pre-nineteenth-century history, they perceived a complicated arrangement of society into numerous orders, and it was possible for workingmen to rise above their class; but nineteenth-century society was a two-class society of bourgeoisie, in control of the means of production, and proletariat, with no means of production of its own. Because the lower-middle class of craftsmen and gildmasters had been "crushed out" (Engels, 1969 edition, p. 51), there was no opportunity for workingmen to escape from the proletariat. Of course, it was essential for Marx and Engels to offer this interpretation to justify their conclusion that the proletariat was now sufficiently united to form a powerful, independent and revolutionary movement. The reality was rather different, as we shall argue later.

But whatever the details of social change, if we assume that most modern societies have passed through all three stages of economic organization, our interest will necessarily focus on the means by which a reciprocal society becomes a redistributive society, or redistribution is replaced by market exchange, and on the socio-spatial consequences of each type of economic system. Marxists would then argue that the structural characteristics of each type of society made it inherently unstable, and instability could be resolved only by the transformation of the system into a new form. For example, problems of inflation and unemployment are claimed to be inherent in capitalism. Engels identified successive and, potentially, successively worsening crises in the expansion of capitalist industrial production, since the means whereby one crisis is overcome only means that the next crisis will bite deeper and prove more difficult to defeat. So the problems of capitalism cannot be 'cured' by applying policies consistent with the overall ideology of capitalism. The ultimate downfall of capitalist society and its replacement by a new form of social organization is thereby guaranteed. Harvey (1973) considers such internally consistent policies to be 'status quo' or 'counter-revolutionary' and repeats Marx's dictum that our object should be to change the world as well as to understand it.

It will be apparent that neither industrialization nor urbanization can occur in a reciprocal society in which there is no opportunity for the concentration of the surplus. Concentration is essential for the large-scale, long-term investments associated with the building of cities or the establishment of factories. Both these processes become possible in a redistributive economy but function most efficiently under market exchange.

Alternatively, we may focus more directly on the social consequences of agglomeration or technological change, without considering the mediating role of economic structure. For example, Sjoberg has emphasized the role of technology in shaping the class structure of societies and their consequent spatial organization, distinguishing between pre-industrial and industrial cities on the basis of their technology (Sjoberg, 1965). The pre-industrial city was dependent on animate and human sources of power: 'factories' were merely agglomerations of manual workers with no powered machinery and no economies of scale. Given certain disadvantages of collecting large numbers of similar workers under one roof — the possible development of class consciousness and trade unionism, the problems of daily journeys to work on foot, the cost of providing factory buildings — it was usually preferable for entrepreneurs to distribute raw materials to and collect finished goods from labourers working in their own homes, as in the domestic textile industry. With the introduction of inanimate power in both production and transportation, the factory became both possible and necessary. Economies of production were associated with increasing specialization, for example by dividing the production of textiles into a series of linked, but separate, processes so that each worker was responsible for only one stage of production. Inevitably, some processes required more skill than others and received different levels of reward. Hence the development of status consciousness within the labouring classes, the desire to establish one's status in the eyes of others and the development of residential segregation by socio-economic status.

The frequent association of industrialization with urbanization makes it difficult to distinguish the social consequences of the two processes. Urbanization introduces rural-urban migrants to a scale and density of human interaction to which they are quite unaccustomed. Attempts to create order out of chaos and nullify the disconcerting effects of a vast army of unfamiliar faces may take the form of segregation in voluntary societies or homogeneous social areas in which the individual maximizes contact with the people he wants to meet, and avoids contact with those he fears or with whom he has nothing in common. This is a principal theme of Louis Wirth's (1938) influential theory of 'urbanism as a way of life', but it can be traced much earlier in literature (Williams, 1973).

## Traditional and Modern Societies

When the pre-industrial city is compared with pre-industrial countryside, clear differences in social organization and interaction are apparent. For example, William Wordsworth in eighteenth-century London and Descartes in seventeenth-century Amsterdam both commented on the impersonality and anonymity of city life, implicitly contrasting it with the more intimate nature of rural society familiar to most of their contemporaries. Interestingly, neither adopted the stance of most subsequent commentators, of lauding the rural life-style while castigating urban society. Descartes wrote that "I could spend my entire life here without being noticed by a soul. I go for a walk here through the Babel of a great thorough-fare as freely and restfully as you stroll in your garden". Wordsworth, in Book 7 of *The Prelude,* observed that:

"Even next door neighbours, as we say, yet still
Strangers, nor knowing each the other's name"

But despite such variations within pre-industrial society sociologists have usually been more interested in the contrast between pre-industrial society as a whole and modern urban-industrial society (Burke, 1975).

It is argued that traditional society was centred on the family or kin-group: relationships between individuals were based on their inherited or ascribed status as members of particular families. By contrast, the important unit in industrial society is the individual, making decisions rationally in his or her own self-interest and forging purposeful relationships. Status in modern society is earned rather than inherited and individuals may be socially mobile, changing their status through time. In traditional society, where your status was universally recognized and accepted, there was no need for status symbols to designate your place in the social structure. With the collapse of traditional society, status symbols became more important. Some symbols are merely elaborations of features that have always existed but previously had no special significance: differences in style of speech or dress between people of differing status. For the geographer, more significant forms of symbol are con-cerned with interaction (whom you mix with, what societies you belong to, which church you attend) and residence (whom you live next door to). The selectivity and compart-mentalization of modern social life imply that each person has a number of roles that are acted out in different situations. You have different roles as a member of a family, a member of a college, a supporter of a local football team or a member of particular special-interest groups, and there may be little overlap between the people you encounter in each situation. Your fellow football supporters may hardly be aware of your other 'life' at college: they are unlikely to meet your non-football friends unless you introduce them. Urban-industrial society, therefore, is made up of 'secondary relationships' which form loose-knit social networks. Our image of traditional society is of 'primary relationships' which together comprise strongly connected social networks. In a primary relationship you encounter the same person in a variety of situations and you cannot maintain contradictory images in different roles. In a strongly connected network your friends know one another inde-pendently of knowing you (Fig. 2.1). The extremes of traditional and modern society are often labelled with the terms 'community' and 'association', the closest English translation of Ferdinand Tönnies' ideas of *gemeinschaft* and *gesellschaft.* Berry (1973) has sum-marized the differences between traditional and modern societies as outlined by a long line of social scientists from Herbert Maine writing in the 1860s to Georg Simmel and Max Weber at the beginning of the twentieth century. Traditional societies were based on primary social relationships which touched on every aspect of a common experience of life and depended on sentiment, custom and the recognition of hereditary rights. Modernization involved the increased significance of reason and rationality, the substitution of specialized and often impersonal secondary relationships, the emergence of the individual as a decision-maker.

There is some confusion whether the two extremes of 'traditional' and 'modern' represent polar types of society at the present day, or extremes on a time continuum. It is clear from Frankenberg's (1966) overview of communities in Britain that there are no completely

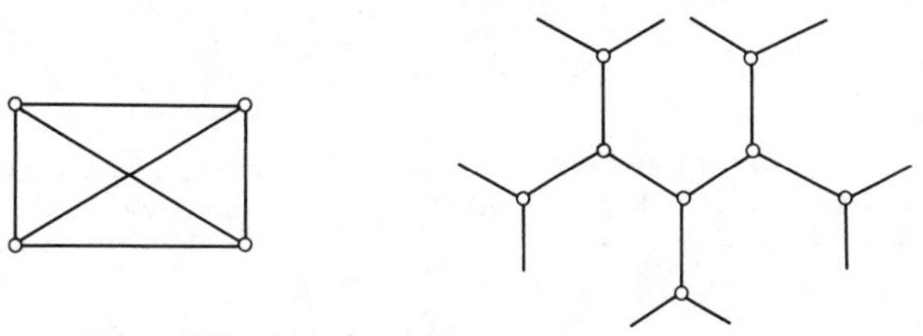

FIG. 2.1. *Close-knit and loose-knit social networks.*

traditional societies in Britain today. The closest equivalents, which Frankenberg designated 'truly rural', lay in the poorest and most remote areas of the British Isles: County Clare on the west coast of Ireland and parts of mid-Wales. But even these areas have experienced the effects of tourism, telecommunications, government aid and the mass media since they were described by sociologists more than twenty years ago. It seems, therefore, that we have been contrasting the rural past with the urban (and increasingly, the rural) present. Some of the quantitative rural–urban differences observed by Mann (1965) seem to be declining (Table 2.1) and it is likely that this trend is paralleled by an increasing similarity in the attitudes and behaviour of rural and urban inhabitants. In fact, differences between regions, and especially between 'metropolitan' and a range of 'provincial' cultures, reflected in such diverse phenomena as Welsh and Cornish nationalism, Geordie independence and even the 'Mersey Beat', may now be more important than differences between neighbouring rural and urban areas (Mellor, 1977). There is a danger in attributing any of these changes through time merely to the fact of time passing, assuming that such grandiose terms as 'development' or 'evolution' are sufficient in themselves to explain social change. It is preferable to focus on explanations that relate social and spatial changes to specific processes subsumed under the general headings of urbanization and industrialization.

## Urbanism as a Way of Life

In 1938, Louis Wirth produced a paper entitled "Urbanism as a way of life" in which he recognized the impersonal nature of life in modern society, characterized by secondary relationships, a reliance on meeting people through formal societies and special-interest groups, a retreat into segregated social areas, which functioned as both status symbols and means of reducing undesirable contacts, and — for an unfortunate minority — a condition of 'anomie' or normlessness, which was frequently expressed in family breakdown, mental illness or a resort to crime. Wirth attributed these characteristics to the effects of size, density and heterogeneity. He argued that the greater the size of a city, the greater the total volume of interaction between its inhabitants. Even if each resident is more gregarious than in rural society, the chances are that he or she will be less dependent on particular individuals. Contacts become impersonal, superficial and transitory. The size and high density

TABLE 2.1. *Rural—urban differences* (after Mann, 1965; Registrar General's Decennial Supplement, 1967; Registrar General's Statistical Review, 1973)

(i)    *Sex Ratio*

| | No. of females per thousand males | | |
| --- | --- | --- | --- |
| | 1931 | 1951 | 1973 |
| Urban | 1107 | 1107 | 1068 |
| Rural | 1017 | 983 | 1015 |

(ii)   *Standardized Mortality Ratios: all causes of death*

| | Male | | | Female | | |
| --- | --- | --- | --- | --- | --- | --- |
| | 1950—3 | 1959—63 | 1973 | 1950—3 | 1959—63 | 1973 |
| Conurbations | 104 | 105 | 105 | 100 | 102 | 101 |
| Urban areas, 100,000+ | 105 | 103 | 103 | 102 | 100 | 101 |
| Urban areas, 50—100,000 | 100 | 99 | 100 | 98 | 97 | 99 |
| Urban areas under 50,000 | 100 | 99 | 99 | 102 | 101 | 100 |
| Rural districts | 90 | 91 | 91 | 97 | 98 | 97 |

(iii)  *Standardized Mortality Ratios: deaths from ischaemic heart disease: a specific example of declining rural—urban differences*

| | Male | | Female | |
| --- | --- | --- | --- | --- |
| | 1959—63 | 1973 | 1959—63 | 1973 |
| Conurbations | 105 | 102 | 104 | 99 |
| Urban areas, 100,000+ | 104 | 103 | 103 | 104 |
| Urban areas, 50—100,000 | 100 | 100 | 96 | 100 |
| Urban areas under 50,000 | 100 | 103 | 99 | 102 |
| Rural districts | 89 | 91 | 93 | 96 |

(iv)  *Deaths from Suicide*

| | Male | | Female | |
| --- | --- | --- | --- | --- |
| | Ratio of local rate to national rate | | Ratio of local rate to national rate | |
| | 1959—63 | 1970—2 | 1959—63 | 1970—2 |
| Conurbations | 1.11 | 1.08 | 1.15 | 1.17 |
| Urban areas, 100,000+ | 1.03 | 1.04 | 1.06 | 1.00 |
| Urban areas, 50—100,000 | 0.99 | 0.95 | 1.12 | 1.15 |
| Urban areas under 50,000 | 0.96 | 0.87 | 0.92 | 0.88 |
| Rural districts | 0.84 | 0.99 | 0.69 | 0.82 |

Note:   The Standardized Mortality Ratio shows the number of deaths registered in the year(s) of experience as a percentage of those which would have been expected in that (those) year(s) had the sex- and age-specific mortality of a standard period and area operated on the population under consideration.

of cities mean that such contacts occur frequently. To impose some sort of organization on their social life and to filter out unwanted contacts, people with similar backgrounds, needs or interests (e.g. ethnic or behavioural minorities, socio-economic or occupational groups, adherents to the same religious denomination, or families at the same stage in the life cycle) congregate in the same parts of the city, or join clubs that facilitate their meeting, something which rarely happens by chance. The heterogeneity of the city's population – the mixture of peoples of different origins, colour, language or religion – implies the lack of a common set of values. This provides a further reason for the employment of status symbols such as residence, and for segregation to avoid meeting people you do not understand.

Wirth's theory seemed to provide an acceptable explanation for the social and spatial arrangements that we find in big cities, but it was less obvious why modern society as a whole, including areas outside cities, should have adopted urbanism as a way of life. In Wirth's theory it is size, density and heterogeneity that are held responsible for the reorganization of society, yet rural areas may have no higher populations than before, experience no influx of alien groups, but still assume urban life-styles. In fact, the conditions that Wirth specified were unique to the type of city in which he lived and worked. Wirth was a professor at the University of Chicago and few cities grew as quickly as Chicago in the early twentieth century. Few contemporary cities shared the same densities, particularly of daytime population working in the skyscrapers of the Loop (Chicago's central business district); and few cities were so dependent for their growth on immigration, from almost every European country, as well as from Asia and from other parts of the United States. In the 1970s most urban population growth in the developed world is the result of natural increase within cities. Even the smaller numbers of migrants are likely to share the same culture as existing city-dwellers: they will have read the same news stories, watched the same networked television programmes and eaten the same convenience foods. Another feature of contemporary cities is their declining physical density, as both residents and workplaces are removed from congested and often decaying inner-city areas.

Berry (1973) has suggested that the characteristics of 1970s society, on which a new social theory should be based, are its increasing scale, increasing mobility and declining density. Whereas size measures the number of participants in an individual's social network, scale denotes the extent of networks. Although the size and density of cities have not increased, higher levels of personal mobility, telecommunications and computer linkages mean that contacts can be maintained over longer distances. While physical density – the number of potential contacts per unit area – declines, interactional density – the number of actual contacts per person – increases. Many of these contacts are neither primary nor secondary, but 'tertiary', in the sense that only the roles interact by advanced technology and the identity of the individuals playing those roles is irrelevant. Curiously, the consequence of more freedom from the tyranny of distance has been to accentuate residential segregation in American cities, although social interaction is no longer confined to neighbours in the same area, but extends to like-minded people living in other areas of the same type, possibly in other cities.

There are additional grounds for criticizing Wirth's theory. Once people are segregated into homogeneous areas alongside their social or cultural equals, there is nothing to prevent the development of primary relationships of a *more* satisfying nature than in rural society. We often forget that primary relationships may involve conflict rather than concord in rural societies in which people with contrary personalities cannot avoid one another. In traditional society, because of the small size of the population, its low density and immobility, you have no choice in making friends. In cities you can choose from a much wider range of contacts, so that friendships may be even more intimate than in the country (Mann, 1965).

Several case studies have illustrated the continuing existence of 'urban villages' and close-knit social networks within cities. The studies of social life in Bethnal Green in East London, carried out by the Institute of Community Studies, identified communities in which neighbours were often kin, many residents worked locally and most had lived in the area all their lives (Young and Willmott, 1957). Many of the closest-knit communities are associated with extreme circumstances. Ethnic minorities may be forced into ghettos by discrimination by the host society, but they may also choose to live together so that established immigrants can help new arrivals to come to terms with city life, find a job and somewhere to live. Other communities are built around resistance to a common threat, as in the emergence of community action groups in Tolmers Square and Covent Garden in central London. Both areas were threatened with redevelopments which would replace working-class residences with offices or upper-class apartments (Clout, 1978). Herbert Gans' study of 'urban villages' in the West End of Boston, U.S.A., showed that the residents became most aware of their community once its physical manifestation was threatened by the bulldozer (Gans, 1962). It seems, therefore, that the closest-knit urban communities are associated with the need for security, self-defence and self-identification, especially when faced with the threat of authority or a rival group. Boal has referred to such situations as 'communities of conflict' and has exemplified them in his own research in Belfast where, even before the escalation of violence in the late 1960s, Protestants and Catholics were segregated in adjacent areas of the city, each territory or 'turf' clearly delimited in the eyes of its residents (Boal, 1969, 1972).

Although 'urban villagers' do not lead the impersonal, anonymous lives that Wirth hypothesized, it remains true that in many segregated social areas the life-style is characterized by individualism and privatism. A private and impersonal life-style may be encouraged by the physical layout of suburbs: low density housing, front gardens and tree-lined roads which hinder observation of street life from sitting-room windows; high-rise flats where there is no street outside the window and no passing traffic; culs-de-sac and vehicle—pedestrian segregation which also reduce the amount of street life, whether observed or not. But the impersonality of suburban life may also be attributable to the newness of suburban environments. At first residents maintain friendships with neighbours from their previous addresses, but despite the use of private cars these contacts will probably diminish in intensity and frequency through time, to be replaced by more intimate relationships with other families in the same suburb.

Wirth argued that those who failed to opt for a segregated social area or special-interest group experienced 'anomie': a condition in which individuals recognize no absolute rules of behaviour or belief, and identify with no particular social or cultural group. These people were also segregated — into areas that nobody else wanted: areas with the worst housing and the least amenities, usually inner-city districts developed as suburbs in the nineteenth century and later abandoned by all who could afford the move to more modern housing in newer and more distant suburbs. Whereas the residents of each suburb shared a common outlook on life and a common life-style, all that the segregated residents of the inner city had in common was their isolation. The failure to adjust to urban life was reflected in high crime rates and pathological disorders. For example, inner-city areas contain disproportionately large numbers of schizophrenics. However, Berry (1973) cites evidence that, for cities taken as a whole, rates of mental illness are no higher than in rural areas. Either this confirms

that even rural areas have adopted 'urbanism as a way of life' or it casts doubt on the hypothesis that the conditions of urban life are innately productive of social disorganization,
implying instead that urban residents who have developed social pathologies only later concentrate in inner-city areas. Certainly we cannot claim that high population densities, in
terms of persons per unit area, are responsible for psychological disorders. More important
than gross population density is density measured in terms of persons per dwelling or per
room and neither of these variables is necessarily at its maximum in the inner city. Rural
slums may be equally overcrowded.

Gans (1968) has recorded the diversity of inner-city residents, not all of whom
correspond to Wirth's stereotype. In Wirth's model nobody lives by choice in such a disorganized area as the inner city, but according to Gans both 'cosmopolites' and the
'unmarried or childless' live there by choice. The former are attracted by the cultural
facilities and night-life of the city centre, the latter find it more desirable to live near their
work and rent their home from a private landlord than to get encumbered with a mortgage
and a garden in the suburbs. To these Gans adds a third group of 'ethnic villagers' who live
in the centre partly by tradition and partly to be near their work, often in services with
unsocial hours: for example, restaurateurs and transport workers. In central London the
Chinese in Soho and Greek and Indian populations in Fitzrovia (around the Post Office
Tower) fall into this category. Only two inner-city groups identified by Gans conform to
Wirth's ideas: the 'deprived' – usually poor, coloured or emotionally disturbed – and the
'trapped' – often elderly people who failed to move out with their neighbours and now
cannot afford to move. Gans (1968) concluded that:

> "These five types all live in dense and heterogeneous surroundings,
> yet they have such diverse ways of life that it is hard to see how
> density and heterogeneity could exert a common influence" (p. 101).

We might argue, therefore, that the problem families and disordered personalities of the
inner city are not problems or disordered because of their heterogeneous, high-density
environment, but have drifted into that area because they have been rejected by other groups
and the inner city is the only area that will accommodate them.

Rather than imagine Wirth's form of urbanism as the only way of life in modern society
we should view it as only one among a range of alternatives. There are some faceless and
impersonal suburbs, and some areas of multiple deprivation; but there are also 'urban villages'
inhabited by a cohesive working class, by ethnic and religious minorities, or by particularly
pressured minority groups; and there are even some people who enjoy the fast pace, variety
and unpredictability of urban life. For example, Jacobs (1961) highlights the advantages of
diversity and heterogeneity in inner-city neighbourhoods as one way of combating the
imminent 'death' of great American cities.

Given the variety of objections it is strange that Wirth's theory dominated urban sociology
for so long. The reason may lie in its ideological context. Wirth's theory was judged to be
anti-urban since it held the city responsible for the development of segregation and pathological behaviour, neither of which have featured in many prescriptions for utopia. For
example, the design of Mark I New Towns in Britain after World War II incorporated groups
of socially balanced neighbourhoods, each neighbourhood containing members of different
socio-economic classes in the same proportions as in the town as a whole, and each provided
with a mixture of public and private housing, accommodation for old people and services
suitable for everybody to use. In the nineteenth century 'settlement houses' in poor areas of
cities housed a local upper class who emerged daily to set an example to the poor and act as

leaders of the local community (Glass, 1955). But these methods of making cities as 'un-urban' as possible have always been second-best. The forerunners of new towns were garden cities and suburbs (e.g. Letchworth, Welwyn and Hampstead) where a maximum of country-side was introduced into the city in the form of low-density housing, tree-lined roads, parks, private gardens and easy access to the real countryside. Urban merchants and gentry have always had their country seats and in this century the ownership of second homes in the countryside has become a reality for many more of the population. Middle-class suburbani-zation since the eighteenth century can also be seen as an anti-urban reaction.

Western religion, too, has cast cities in a predominantly evil role, from the very first biblical reference to a city, in which its construction is implicitly condemned as contrary to the will of God (Genesis 4, 16–17: Cain went away from the Lord's presence . . . and built a city), through the incident of the Tower of Babel, the wickedness of Sodom and Gomorrah and later of Nineveh (in the Book of Jonah), to the dilettante attitudes of sophis-ticated Athenians to the preaching of St. Paul. Throughout, the city is depicted as the seat of man's rebellion against God, although ultimately God creates the new Jerusalem (in Revelation 21 but foreshadowed in Ezekiel) to reimpose his authority on Man's misdeeds. Despite this final act of reconciliation, the biblical narrative is predominantly anti-urban and, in this context, it is less surprising that an academic anti-urban theory found wide-spread acceptance.

## Social Area Theory

Whereas Wirth developed his theory in Chicago, the classic inter-war industrial city, the principal alternative adopted by urban geographers — social area theory — originated in the city that epitomizes post-war, post-industrial society: Los Angeles. The social area theorists — Shevky, Bell and Williams — began with a theory of social differentiation which described changes through time in the structure of society as a whole, and which was mirrored in changes in urban structure. The main trend through time was the increasing scale of society as each inhabitant contacted more people, but in less intimate ways. Thus far the argument resembles Wirth's theory of the effects of increasing size and density, but thereafter social area theory probes more deeply into the consequences of industrialization and specialization (Shevky and Bell, 1955; Theodorson, 1961; Timms, 1971).

Increasing scale has three major forms of expression:

(1) Changes in the range and intensity of relations. New demands arise for new and different skills as manual productive occupations decline in importance and more of the labour force is employed in clerical, technical, supervisory, management and service activities, and as production is separated from marketing. Meanwhile, the production process is increasingly differentiated and jobs within industry become more specialized. A complex ranking system emerges as different degrees of skill receive different levels of financial reward and are accorded different levels of prestige. This elaboration of socio-economic differentiation is associated with increasing residential segregation of socio-economic groups. The implication is that in pre-modern cities, particular areas were not associated with particular socio-economic classes whereas in modern cities each residential area will be occupied by only one socio-economic class.

(2) Functional differentiation. Changes in the structure of productive activity are not confined to specialization but also include changes in the role of the family as the unit of

economic activity. Under the domestic system all the members of a family worked at home in different aspects of the production process: the wife and children of a domestic handloom weaver might be engaged in related aspects of textile production such as spinning, combing or teasing. In early industrial society it was still common for several members of the same family to work at the same factory: father as skilled worker, children as unskilled operatives and 'machine minders'. But later it became more likely that different members of the family would work in different places and make acquaintances at work who would be unknown to the rest of their family. Consequently, the family ceased to function as the unit of either production or social interaction. The individual became a more important decision-maker than the family, and many individuals now lived outside family situations, either as lodgers or one-person households or sharing accommodation with friends rather than relatives. Previously, women were employed only within the home, on domestic duties or assisting the household head in his productive work, or as servants in somebody else's home. Now more women entered paid employment outside the home in shops, factories and offices. Another consequence was for working wives to bear fewer children (and, perhaps, for employed single women to value their independence and delay marriage and childbirth, again producing a fall in the fertility rate). In contemporary urban society we should there-fore find lower levels of fertility, higher levels of women in the labour force and fewer single-family households than in traditional society. However, not everybody embraces these trends with equal enthusiasm. Rather, the effect of modernization is to increase our choice of life-style so that within the city we should find residential segregation in terms of female employment, fertility and family structure. Some areas contain large proportions of women in the labour force, low fertility rates and relatively few nuclear families. Other areas are more traditional.

(3) Complexity of organization. This dimension is equivalent to Wirth's arguments about the heterogeneity of urban society. Industrialization and the prospect, if not the reality, of a house and a job attract a variety of different migrant groups, each of which takes up residence in a particular area of the city.

Whereas Wirth's theory generated segregation, privatism and anomie as responses to urban size, density and heterogeneity, social area theory concentrated on segregation according to several different criteria — social rank (or economic status), urbanization (or family status) and segregation (or ethnic status), respectively associated with the three types of social change that have been outlined — and associated segregation with industrialization and the changing role of the family as well as with urbanization. The implication is that even large cities in non-industrial, family- or tribe-dominated societies will not show residential segre-gation along the lines postulated by social area theory. This implication has been confirmed by several researchers employing techniques of social area analysis and factorial ecology (Timms, 1971).

Social area analysis is the method by which social area theory was operationalized. Each sub-area of a city (e.g. each block, enumeration district or census tract) was classified according to its performance on each of the three dimensions of economic status, family status and ethnic status, using appropriate census variables as surrogates for the three dimensions. Economic status was assessed using information on the proportion of the employed population engaged in manual work and the proportion of adults with no experience of further or higher education. Family status was measured using three indices:

(1) women-at-work as a percentage of all adult females;

(2) the fertility ratio;

(3) single-family dwellings as a percentage of all dwellings.

Finally, ethnic status was expressed in terms of the proportion of the population that belonged to minority ethnic groups. These values were standardized so that in any particular city each index ranged in value from 0 to 100 (Theodorson, 1961). But for the purpose of assessing the modernity of different cities standardization is undesirable, since we would expect one vital difference between cities to be concerned with their range of values. In a residentially undifferentiated city every sub-area would contain a mixture of economic classes, family types and ethnic groups. Each area would therefore register index values close to the index averages for the city as a whole, whereas in a segregated city values would vary more widely between sub-areas. In a pre-industrial city we would also expect the city-wide averages for each index to differ from their values in an industrial city. For example, in pre-industrial cities we would expect fewer women in the labour force, fewer migrants, fewer people with higher education and higher fertility rates than in modern cities, but all these comparisons are lost in the process of standardization.

To the extent that the three dimensions occurred at all in pre-industrial cities, we should not expect them to have been independent. For example, migrants were usually of the same economic status, the proportion of women at work (e.g. washerwomen, servants) was inversely correlated with educational attainment and positively correlated with the proportion of manual workers, and fertility was also correlated with economic status. In the fully developed industrial city the pattern of correlation should be as shown in Table 2.2(a), but Herbert (1972), in a partial test of the theory in Newcastle-under-Lyme, Staffordshire, found the correlations indicated in Table 2.2(b). Either Newcastle-under-Lyme is a very peculiar place or social area theory is inadequate for British situations! However, tests of the theory in North America confirmed that the six variables could be grouped into three factors and that the patterns of intercorrelation were as hypothesized by Shevky and Bell (Van

TABLE 2.2. *Expected and observed patterns of correlation between variables included in social area analyses*

(a) Expected Correlations

|  | Occn | Edn | Fert | W-at-Wk | SFD | Eth |
|---|---|---|---|---|---|---|
| Occupation | 1 | + | 0 | 0 | 0 | 0 |
| Education |  | 1 | 0 | 0 | 0 | 0 |
| Fertility |  |  | 1 | − | + | 0 |
| Women at work |  |  |  | 1 | − | 0 |
| Single-family dwellings |  |  |  |  | 1 | 0 |
| Ethnicity |  |  |  |  |  | 1 |

+   denotes high positive correlation
−   denotes high negative correlation
0   denotes no correlation

(b) Correlations observed by Herbert (1972) in Newcastle-under-Lyme

|  | Occn | Edn | Fert | W-at-Wk |
|---|---|---|---|---|
| Occupation | 1 | +0.81 | +0.41 | +0.27 |
| Education |  | 1 | +0.32 | +0.30 |
| Fertility |  |  | 1 | +0.08 |
| Women at work |  |  |  | 1 |

Arsdol *et al.*, in Theodorson, 1961). These tests provide an unusual example of the use of factor analysis to test social area theory. More commonly factor analysis has been applied inductively, as a descriptive device without any underlying theory, in the practice of factorial ecology (Johnston, 1976).

In factorial ecology a wide range of variables is mathematically reduced to a small number of 'factors' or 'components' which summarize the most important variations in the original data set. The correlation between each variable and each factor is known as a factor loading and factors are often given names that reflect the variables with which they are significantly correlated (i.e. those variables with the highest loadings on each factor). For example, Herbert (1972) undertook an analysis of Cardiff using twenty-six census variables that yielded information on the age-sex structure, housing quality and tenure, occupational and educational status, birthplace and migration history of residents living in each of the city's 334 enumeration districts. The twenty-six variables could be reduced to only two components which between them accounted for over half of the variance included in the original data. On the basis of the loadings shown in Table 2.3, the first component could be called 'Housing Occupance and Tenure' while the second also identified different housing conditions. However, many American studies have produced results that coincide with social area theory: a first factor labelled 'socio-economic status' on which occupational, educational, income, housing-cost and car-ownership variables have high loadings; and a second factor labelled 'family status', associated with variables measuring fertility, female employment and family structure. A third factor, 'ethnic status', has also been identified in many studies, linked with variables that describe the levels of poverty, overcrowding and poor housing as well as the percentages of immigrants or members of minority groups in each area (Johnston, 1976). The differences between British and American analyses signify the distinctive role of the housing market in British cities, a subject to which we will frequently have to return.

The statistically more objective approach to urban structure provided by factorial ecology has been used by several authors to test the hypothesis that there are several independent dimensions in modern cities, whereas in pre-modern cities (in either the contemporary Third World or nineteenth-century Britain or North America) these dimensions were not independent of one another. For example, there was a gradual separation of socio-economic and family status into independent axes in the expanding industrial town Wolverhampton between 1851 and 1871 (Shaw, 1977), while a study of Toronto, Ontario, designated the

TABLE 2.3. *Census variables with high loadings (correlations) in principal component analysis of Cardiff (after Herbert, 1972)*

| High loadings on Component 1: | |
|---|---|
| persons per room | +0.91 |
| % aged 0–14 | +0.87 |
| % aged 65+ | −0.85 |
| % renting council housing | +0.86 |
| High loadings on Component 2: | |
| %foreign-born | +0.70 |
| % without exclusive WC | +0.69 |
| % overcrowded | +0.67 |
| % renting private unfurnished | +0.66 |

city as 'disorganized' in 1860 but organized according to the postulates of social area theory by the end of the nineteenth century (Goheen, 1970).

In Cairo, in 1960, the three most important factors were associated with socio-economic status, transience (as measured by the presence of single male migrants) and social disorganization (linked to population density, divorce and unemployment). But the variables with high loadings on the first factor also included female employment and fertility, variables linked to 'Urbanization' or 'Family Status' in social area theory, thus reflecting the lack of separation of socio-economic and family status. Cairo had progressed some way from the single-factor structure of feudal cities, but had not achieved the independence of socio-economic, family and ethnic status dimensions that characterizes modern American cities (Abu-Lughod, 1969). Similarly in Calcutta, Berry and Rees (1969) identified a family status factor, but no distinction between socio-economic and ethnic or religious variables. Again the conclusion was that the city lay somewhere between the pre-industrial and the industrial, but would eventually evolve into the form of a modern industrial city.

Spatially, all these nineteenth-century and Third World cities contained a mixture of land uses and population groups in each small area, superimposed on a basic contrast between centre and periphery (Sjoberg, 1960). It could be argued that the segregation of urban population into large areas of uniform status occurs only when a system of ranking by skill and income has developed, when public transport provision allows people to live apart from their work, and when the supply of different kinds of housing is geographically differentiated according to the varying requirements of families of different size, stage in the life cycle and ability to pay. These conditions were not totally fulfilled in mid-nineteenth-century cities, where status ranking was emerging but neither transport provision nor the operation of the housing market was sufficiently modern to facilitate the spatial expression of status. Nor are they fulfilled in African or Asian cities, where status is still associated with religion and caste and more people work where they live.

Although empirical studies appear to confirm the tenets of social area theory, several criticisms have been levelled against the theory itself. Firstly, it is not clear why three interrelated aspects of increasing scale should generate three independent dimensions of segregation. Secondly, there are some very tortuous and unconvincing lines of reasoning involved in moving from the postulates about industrial society (change in the range and intensity of relations, functional differentiation, complexity of organization) to the specific variables concerned with occupation, education, etc. Thirdly, there is little indication why the effects of industrial society on each *individual* or family should have an *ecological* expression in terms of the characteristics of each area. For example, the reaction of individual women to the changed circumstances of industrialization may be to delay marriage or to put their career first, and so reduce the fertility rate in society as a whole, but that does not explain why *areas* should be differentiated in terms of fertility. One critic, Udry (1964), went so far as to describe social area theory as "two quite distinct theories which are accidentally articulated to the extent that they happen to share the same operational measures" (Timms, 1971, p. 140). Udry suggested that "we consider these two separate but co-ordinated theories: one a theory of increasing scale; the other, using the same axes and variables, but not deducible from the first, a theory of sub-area differentiation. The two theories are logically co-ordinated through the proposition that as a society increases in scale, its sub-areas are functionally differentiated" (Udry, 1964, pp. 408–9). But the co-ordination remained no more than a proposition and was not empirically verifiable.

Some of the theoretical objections to social area theory have been countered by

McElrath (1968), who distinguished four aspects of 'modernization' concerned with changes in:

(1) the distribution of skills, i.e. specialization and class structure;
(2) the organization of society, i.e. individual and family roles;
(3) the aggregation of population, i.e. rural—urban migration;
(4) the distribution of resources in society, i.e. urban agglomeration.

These four types of change were expressed in four dimensions of social differentiation: social rank, family status, migrant status and ethnic status. At face value, McElrath's model appears little different from social area theory. He emphasized the impact of industrialization, indicated by the first two categories of modernization, as something distinct from urbanization, which was subsumed under the last two categories, but the only difference between McElrath's and Shevky's dimensions of differentiation lay in the former's subdivision of 'ethnic status' into two dimensions confusingly labelled 'ethnic status' and 'migrant status'. The former was defined by the existence of culturally distinct minority groups, the latter by the origins of all migrants and the effects of selective migration on the age-sex structure of different areas.

In fact, the differences between McElrath and the social area theorists were more fundamental. McElrath acknowledged the interrelated nature of his four aspects of modernization and did not suggest that each aspect was uniquely linked to only one dimension of social or residential differentiation. Instead, he argued in two stages. Firstly, modernization allowed the separation of an individual's roles and generated a class society, articulated by processes of individual and group social mobility. Secondly, this social differentiation generated residential differentiation, through the desire for normative, within-group, social interaction among a geographically immobile population and through the operation of the housing market. However, the effect of the latter was often to delay the translation of differentiating factors at the individual level into the differentiation of residential areas. This lag effect was clearly illustrated in the lack of coincidence between social structure and residential patterns in mid-nineteenth-century cities, a subject to which we will return in Chapter 5.

### Marx and Engels on Residential Differentiation

McElrath employed the concept of a class society as an intermediary between modernization and residential patterning, but notions of class and class consciousness figure more prominently in Marxist interpretations of residential differentiation. We began this chapter by outlining a Marxist scenario of changing modes of economic integration. It is appropriate to conclude by returning to the writings of Marx and Engels on the formation of classes in industrial society and its consequences for the development of social areas.

In *The Condition of the Working Class in England,* first published in Germany in 1845, Engels showed that the Industrial Revolution inevitably led to the concentration of the population in urban areas. His arguments on "the centralizing tendency of manufacture" closely resemble those of twentieth-century economic geographers (e.g. Pred, 1977), although Engels also stressed the counterattraction to entrepreneurs of being able to offer lower wages in the countryside. Nevertheless, "every new factory built in the country bears in it the germ of a manufacturing town" (Engels, 1969 edn, p. 56). More important to Engels were the social consequences of industrialization, some of which we sketched earlier in this chapter. He contrasted the pre-industrial period, in which workingmen could hope to become master craftsmen and gradually rise into the middle class, with the new industrial society in which the population was "reduced to the two opposing elements, workers and capitalists" and "he who was born to toil had no other prospect than that of remaining a toiler all his life" (p. 51).

It was a short step for Engels to move from the division of society into classes to its division into social areas. He foreshadowed Wirth and replicated the anti-urbanism of many nineteenth-century critics, noting that "The very turmoil of the streets has something repulsive, something against which human nature rebels. . . . The brutal indifference, the unfeeling isolation of each in his private interest becomes the more repellant and offensive, the more these individuals are crowded together, within a limited space" (pp. 57–8). The segregation of rich and poor was a consequence not of each group *choosing* to live apart but of the rich's capacity to contain the poor within areas where they could be exploited and ignored socially. Poverty was assigned a separate territory "removed from the sight of the happier classes" (p. 60). Of Manchester, Engels observed that "a person may live in it for years, and go in and out daily without coming into contact with a working people's quarter or even with workers . . .", but more generally "this hypocritical plan" was "more or less common to all great cities" (pp. 79–80). It was a curious paradox that in an unplanned, unregulated centre of *laissez-faire* capitalism, the end-product suggested an extreme degree of premeditated social planning.

The graphic language that Engels employed may lead us to accept his argument too uncritically. For most places, and for most of the nineteenth century, his division of society into two opposing classes was a gross oversimplification of reality. Given that the 'proletariat' comprised the vast majority of the population, it is important to explore the alignment of social groups and the organization of social areas within the working class. In fact, there is no simple connection between class consciousness and residential location. Working-class consciousness may arise from living cheek by jowl with the rich and recognizing the inequalities in society, or it may arise from being segregated from the rich and identifying with one's neighbours. Arguing in the opposite direction, class consciousness may be so strong that it makes class segregation on the ground unnecessary, or it may provoke people of the same class to live close to one another to facilitate social interaction.

Engels' interpretation is important because it stresses aspects of economic determinism that are neglected in the permissive and choice-oriented theories of Wirth and the social area analysts, who imply that people *choose* to live apart in segregated areas or together in communities. Much recent 'social geography' in Britain finds its roots in Marxist political economy and, it could be argued, is more 'economic' than 'social'. Consider, for example, the symposia organized by the Social Geography Study Group of the Institute of British Geographers (reported in *Area* 9 (1977), 166–7; 10 (1978), 61–3, 140–1, 249–51; 11 (1979), 16–18) on such topics as public expenditure cuts and land, property and financial investment.

While a Marxist approach to social geography has much to commend it, particularly in analyzing the structure of early industrial society, in which the distinction between employer and employee was more clearly drawn than it is today, several shortcomings must be noted. Firstly, it ignores distinctions of religion, culture and ethnicity that are independent of class, but fundamental to the way in which people live and make decisions. This brings us back to the point we made in Chapter 1 about the multiplicity of groups to which any individual belongs: based on education, occupation, religion, nationality, politics and housing. But for Marxists everything is subsumed under class. To Marx, 'culture' was for most people a mere training to act as a machine (Marx and Engels, 1973 edn, p. 67). Even concepts of nationality were class-based: "the working men have no country" (p. 71). Secondly, the approach ignores the processes of choice by which people distribute themselves *within* class-defined areas, presumably because there is no way in which economic determinism can account for differences between people who are economically identical. Yet in any society in which the great majority of the population are supposed to belong to one class, this means that most location decisions are simply disregarded. Thirdly, the approach ignores the complexities of class definition in a mixed economy in which the 'petty bourgeoisie' has not been eliminated as Marx predicted, and in which a whole army of state- or privately-employed managers occupies a middle ground between 'bourgeoisie' and 'proletariat'.

The theoretical perspectives that we have considered in this chapter all focus on the effects of urbanization, with or without provision made for the distinction between urbanization and industrialization. Given this starting point, it is fitting that for most of this book we will be examining the social geography of England and Wales in terms of the processes and the consequences of urbanization, beginning in the following chapter by considering the organization of society in pre-urban, pre-industrial times.

## References and Further Reading

Different kinds of 'traditional' society are discussed in:
Burke, P. (1975) Some reflections on the pre-industrial city, *Urban History Yearbook*, 13–21.
Frankenberg, R. (1966) *Communities in Britain*, Penguin, Harmondsworth.
Sjoberg, G. (1960) *The Preindustrial City*, Free Press, Glencoe, Illinois.
Young, M. and Willmott, P. (1957) *Family and Kinship in East London*, Routledge & Kegan Paul, London.

The contrasts between 'rural' and 'urban' and between 'traditional' and 'modern' are considered by:
Berry, B. J. L. (1973) *The Human Consequences of Urbanisation*, Macmillan, London.
Gans, H. J. (1968) Urbanism and suburbanism as ways of life, in R. E. Pahl (ed.), *Readings in Urban Sociology*, Pergamon, Oxford, pp. 95–118.
Glass, R. (1955) Urban sociology in Great Britain, *Current Sociology*, 4(4), and reprinted in R. E. Pahl (ed.), *op.cit.*, pp. 47–73.
Mann, P. H. (1965) *An Approach to Urban Sociology*, Routledge & Kegan Paul, London.
Mellor, J. R. (1977) *Urban Sociology in an Urbanized Society*, Routledge & Kegan Paul, London.
Sjoberg, G. (1965) Cities in developing and in industrial societies: a crosscultural analysis, in P. M. Hauser & L. F. Schnore (eds.), *The Study of Urbanization*, Wiley, New York, pp. 213–63.
Williams, R. (1973) *The Country and the City*, Chatto & Windus, London.
Wirth, L. (1938) Urbanism as a way of life, *American Journal of Sociology*, 44, 1–24.

The variety of communities within urban areas is illustrated by:
Boal, F. W. (1969) Territoriality on the Shankill–Falls divide, Belfast, *Irish Geography*, 6, 30–50.
Boal, F. W. (1972) The urban residential sub-community – a conflict interpretation, *Area*, 4, 164–8.
Clout, H. D. (ed.) (1978) *Changing London*, University Tutorial Press, London.
Gans, H. J. (1962) *The Urban Villagers*, Free Press, Glencoe, Illinois.
Jacobs, J. (1961) *The Death and Life of Great American Cities*, Random House, New York.

Social area theory and factorial ecology are discussed by:
Herbert, D. (1972) *Urban Geography: A Social Perspective*, David & Charles, Newton Abbot.
Johnston, R. J. (1976) Residential area characteristics: research methods for identifying urban sub-areas, in D. T. Herbert & R. J. Johnston, (eds.), *Social Areas in Cities Volume I*, Wiley, London, pp. 193–235.
McElrath, D. C. (1968) Societal scale and social differentiation: Accra, Ghana, in S. Greer *et al.* (eds.), *The New Urbanization*, St. Martin's Press, New York, pp. 33–52.
Shevky, E. and Bell, W. (1955) *Social Area Analysis*, Stanford University Press, Stanford, California.
Theodorson, G. A. (ed.) (1961) *Studies in Human Ecology*, Harper & Row, New York.
Timms, D. W. G. (1971) *The Urban Mosaic*, Cambridge University Press, Cambridge.
Udry, J. R. (1964) Increasing scale and spatial differentiation, *Social Forces*, 42, 403–13.

and exemplified by:

Abu-Lughod, J. (1969) Testing the theory of social area analysis: the ecology of Cairo, Egypt, *American Sociological Review,* 34, 189–212.

Berry, B. J. L. and Rees, P. H. (1969) The factorial ecology of Calcutta, *American Journal of Sociology,* 74, 447–91.

Goheen, P. G. (1970) Victorian Toronto, 1850 to 1900, *University of Chicago Dept. of Geography Research Paper,* 127.

Shaw, M. (1977) The ecology of social change: Wolverhampton 1851–71. *Transactions Institute of British Geographers,* New Series, 2, 332–48.

Economic aspects of urbanization are summarized by:
Pred, A. (1977) *City-Systems in Advanced Economies,* Hutchinson, London.

English editions of *The Condition of the Working Class* and the *Communist Manifesto* are:
Engels, F. (1969) *The Condition of the Working Class in England,* Panther, London.

Marx, K. and Engels, F. (1973) *Manifesto of the Communist Party,* Progress Publishers, Moscow.

Recent publications by radical geographers include:
Day, M. and Tivers, J. (1979) Catastrophe theory and geography: a Marxist critique, *Area,* 11, 54–8.

Harvey, D. (1973) *Social Justice and the City,* Arnold, London.

Peet, R. (1978) *Radical Geography,* Methuen, London.

while a critique of radical geography is offered by:
Muir, R. (1978) Radical geography or a new orthodoxy?, *Area,* 10, 322–7.

# 3

# Pre-Industrial England

## Introduction

SOCIAL geography is concerned with the unequal role of social groups and institutions in the use of geographic space. By definition, the social geography of any period is in part a legacy of earlier conditions and it is therefore important to look back into history, not only to provide datum planes against which contemporary society may be delineated and compared, but also to understand how features of settlement and social organization that we have inherited, albeit in modified form, came into existence under very different conditions from those we experience. This chapter will be concerned with social institutions and their use of space across the broad span of time before mechanized manufacturing made a significant impact on the processes of economic production. This definition is of necessity vague since the so-called 'industrial revolution' was an immensely complicated phenomenon, affecting different regions and different trades with varying degrees of intensity over an enormous stretch of time.

In theory, this discussion should embrace the origins of peopling and settlement and also examine the workings of feudal society with its hierarchy of groups of different legal status, ranging from the king, through great territorial lords, lesser barons and knights, freemen, those who were semi-free, villeins and bordars (who were tied by work service to a lord), to the unfree, or serfs, at the base of the system. Such societal differences provide an essential starting point for any understanding of early medieval landholding, tenure, settlement types and the degree to which communities were involved in trade or manufacturing. For example, settlements in free areas were much more likely to be recharged with migrants from elsewhere than were villages where an unfree and hence immobile peasantry predominated. Similarly, free settlements were much more able to supply towns with any agricultural surpluses they might generate. Freemen dominated in flows of townward migrants and they also served as itinerant pedlars and seasonal migrants. None of these possibilities was open to the unfree. Under feudal conditions all land was held from the king, with a complex array of landholders beneath him, from great lay and ecclesiastical lords, through many smaller lords to tiny peasant owners. The medieval landscape derived its logic from local variations in the relationship between these groups in society and whether landlords managed their own farmland or arranged for others to do so according to various forms of social and economic obligation.

In practice, we shall pay little attention to medieval conditions and for an understanding of the workings of feudalism and the nature of life in England and Wales prior to Tudor times readers should refer to works on social and economic history and historical geography (e.g. Dodgshon and Butlin, 1978). Pre-industrial Britain did not, of course, lack manufacturing activities but these were essentially manual in character and rural in location. Not until the nineteenth century did the equations manufacturing equals urban, farming equals rural begin to offer even an approximate description of socio-economic life in England. The period under consideration is great and so is the diversity of conditions from place to place; hence what follows can be no more than a series of caricatures.

## Families and Households

The dimensions of life were small in pre-industrial England and due attention must be paid to the family, the household and the community as key institutions in establishing rules or norms governing the organization of life and the use of space. The horizons of many of our predecessors were limited in the extreme and the geography of their daily, if not total, life was tightly circumscribed. Of course there were exceptions to that rule and these became increasingly numerous with the passage of time, although local rather than national conditions still dominated the lives of most country folk and perhaps also town dwellers in early Victorian England. Nonetheless pre-industrial England contained market towns by the score, around which the use of rural space became increasingly organized, and also one truly great city, which commanded an ever growing catchment for food and labour and served as a vital link to insert England into a wider commercial world. Each of these environments, countryside, town and metropolis, will be examined in turn.

It is fashionable to extol the virtues of the 'good old days' when England was inhabited by groups of loving and caring people who worked out their problems in the context of their own families with help from their neighbours in the community. Yet in many respects nostalgia is a matter of fiction rather than fact and important researches over the past twenty years have shown that many popular images of the past are fuelled as much by imagination as by the transmission of accurate recollections. The basic institution of pre-industrial society was, of course, the biological family but not exactly the kind of family that is sometimes imagined. In an age when 'shanks's pony' was the only means of locomotion for the great majority of people, most but not all of our predecessors sought their marriage partners in their home community or in those that immediately surrounded it. Eversley (1966) has estimated that marriages between persons living in the same parish plus those involving a partner living within a five-mile radius accounted for 80 per cent of all marriages during the seventeenth century. Virtually all marriage partners would be included if the radius were extended up to fifteen miles. An interesting study in early Victorian Dorset displayed a very similar situation, with most marriage partners living less than four miles, or one hour's walking time, apart (Perry, 1969). This appeared to be the maximum distance over which a regular courtship routine would operate for members of the rural working class until they gained access to other forms of transport much later in the nineteenth century.

Marriage in pre-industrial England did not normally occur very early in life. Evidence from the diocese of Canterbury during the seventeenth century shows that the commonest age of first marriage was 24 years for men and 22 years for women (Laslett, 1971). Other calculations raise or lower the figures by a year or two. For example, Smith (in Dodgshon and Butlin, 1978) cites the average age of marriage in ten sample parishes as 27 years for men and 25 for women between 1550 and 1599; and 28 and 27 respectively for 1700–1749. By comparison, figures for all marriages (including re-marriages) in the 1960s were 28 or

29 years for men and 25 or 26 years for women. But the span of life in pre-industrial England was substantially shorter than that of today, with life expectancy at birth being little more than 30 years during the seventeenth century. However, those who survived childhood might reach the age of 50 or so. Thus, a couple marrying in their middle twenties might expect to have 25 years of married life ahead of them before one partner was claimed by death. This pattern was, of course, frequently interrupted much earlier by mortality arising from disease, famine, war or complications in childbirth. Widows, widowers and orphans were present in many families in times past, but so too were stepmothers and stepfathers since re-marriage was common. Some of our ancestors lived out their three score years and ten but they were rare and were viewed as veritable 'patriarchs'. From the late sixteenth to the early eighteenth centuries life expectations at birth fluctuated within the range of 35 to 40 years. Harvest failures and outbreaks of disease provoked short-term fluctuations on the graph. Given the relatively late age of marriage and relatively early age of death it is not surprising that few children knew both of their grandparents in pre-industrial times. For biological and social reasons multi-generation families were rare. At marriage, couples sought homes of their own in which to raise their families. Marriage might even be postponed until a cottage became available. For a grandparent to live with the nuclear family was the exception rather than the rule but might occur because of the ill-health of one marriage partner or of the older person. The demographic structure of English settlements in times past was much younger than that of today. Children were everywhere but rates of infantile and juvenile mortality were high and only a small proportion survived to reach a marriageable age.

In addition to the family as a social institution it is important to recognize the significance of the household. The former was a biological and legal unit, whilst the household was a functional unit that would expand or contract temporarily as families at different levels in the social structure became aware of shortages or surpluses of labour. In this age before widespread adoption of farming machinery a family might be short of hands to run the house and the farm. Maidservants and farm labourers would be hired according to need, would live in and become part of the household. That kind of arrangement was still to be found in many parts of the countryside in Victorian times. Likewise a craftsman might need more labour than his wife and children could provide for the making and selling of goods and once again outsiders would be received into the household. Laslett (1971) gives the example of a typical bakery in sixteenth-century London that would comprise as many as thirteen or fourteen people, including the master baker and his wife, four paid journeymen, two apprentices, two maidservants, and the master's three or four children. Toward the other end of the socio-economic spectrum landless families or those living on smallholdings might be unable to survive from their own meagre resources and would welcome the opportunity of sending a son or a daughter to be housed and fed in a household other than their own. Indeed, young apprentices and servants were often viewed as 'extra sons and daughters' by their masters. The word 'family' was used frequently to describe what was, strictly speaking, a 'household'. In such a way many young people were bound to their masters in farming or craft work, rather than to their parents, until their apprenticeship was over or they were released at marriage.

It is hardly surprising that there were important differences in household size at the various levels in the social structure. Laslett (1971) quotes the reply sent by a Kentish curate to the Archbishop of Canterbury in 1676. The mean size of household in his parish was 4.45 persons, but for the gentry the figure was 9.0, 5.8 for yeomen, 3.9 for tradesmen, 3.2 for labourers, but only 2.1 for 'poor men'. Other settlements displayed statistical variations from these averages but the message of social differentiation was clear enough. In addition, it is likely that poorer families had fewer children born to them than richer families. Poor men and their wives lived harsher and less nourished lives than their richer counterparts. Their married life would normally be shorter and their chance of having many children would be proportionately smaller. In any case, rates of infantile mortality were particularly severe among the poor. Between one-quarter and one-third of households in any settlement in pre-industrial England would contain servants and a similar proportion would have children that were in service and therefore living away from home. Few families were outside this important process of give-and-take.

## The Community

Reciprocity formed an essential element at the next level of social organization in pre-industrial England, namely, that of the community. There were, however, important variations in the ways whereby families and households shared space and collaborated in the exploitation of resources. In the countryside, a fundamental distinction existed between areas in which communal rules governed agricultural activities, inheritance of land and many other aspects of life, and other regions which were far more individualistic in terms of their social and economic organization.

In general terms, areas of arable farming and mixed husbandry in lowland England contained nucleated settlements and scattered strips of ploughland (Fig. 3.1). They were organized according to communal regulations, with one manor, one village, one church being the simplest equation, although there were exceptions with perhaps two manors being found in a single village. Manor courts controlled the organization of farming and other aspects of the yearly round. Such gatherings and the village ale-houses were the preserve of the men, with the women and young children of the community appearing in public only at church services and at market. Otherwise their place was in the home. With the passage of time traditional rules of communal organization became eroded as external commercial pressures came to be felt or as manors were poorly administered or sold off and sub-divided. However, at its most basic level, the day-to-day running of the lowland community and its yearly round of ploughing, seed time, harvest and other crucial events was controlled by rules. Primogeniture was the normal means whereby property was transmitted between generations. Food production was the main occupation in these areas with relatively rich environmental resources. Scope for alternative employment was limited, although these predominantly agricultural settlements supported an important quota of craftsmen in this age of relative self-sufficiency.

The community comprised the lord (or lords) of the manor, the priest, well-to-do family farmers, tenant farmers, craftsmen and the landless, many of whom worked as hired labourers. Areas of communal heath and waste provided valuable resources for villagers, allowing them to graze cattle, sheep, pigs and geese. Rights of use were claimed for exploiting other resources from the commonlands and these included undergrowth, peat, bracken, furze, gravel, stone, coal and many more commodities. Hares, fish, wood pigeons, birds' eggs, nuts and wild herbs could also be obtained from the commonlands and were put to good use to enhance the meagre diets of the poorer peasants and landless labourers. All these rights, or alleged rights, were administered with varying degrees of attention according to communal laws. To our eyes these laws may appear petty and repressive but it may be argued that they

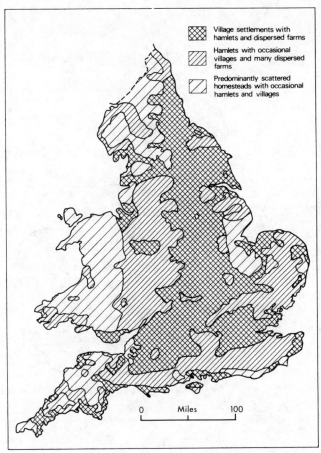

FIG. 3.1. *Basic aspects of modern rural settlement in England and Wales (after Thorpe, 1964).*

were necessary in times past when food and all other resources were relatively sparse and the intrusion of communal rules was accepted by the majority as a way of life. Manorial lords sought to ensure that regulations were enforced and that in-migration and division of land between a growing number of tenants was held in check. The threat of large numbers of poor folk becoming squatters on the commonland was seen as an evil to be avoided at all costs. Very similar fears underlay the existence of the 'close' villages that were widespread in many parts of England during the eighteenth and nineteenth centuries.

By contrast with this kind of social arrangement, conditions in upland Britain were less obviously 'organized'. Settlement tended to be in hamlets and isolated farms rather than in nucleated villages (Fig. 3.1). Co-operation involved kinsmen and small groups of neighbours rather than the large village communities found on the lowlands. Land was partitioned among all or many sons, unlike the rule of primogeniture in lowland England. Bread grains for local needs were grown in closes or small, irregular common fields but this activity formed only one component in the rural economy of upland Britain in pre-industrial times. Environments that were harsh for arable farming offered important alternative resources in the form of

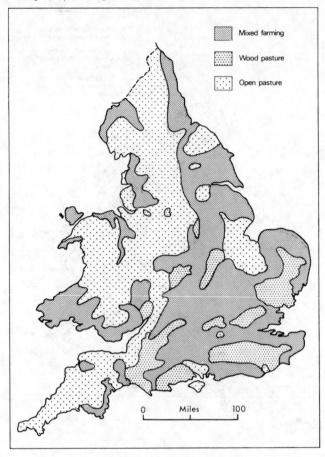

FIG. 3.2. *Farming types in England and Wales in the sixteenth century (after Thirsk, 1967).*

grazing land and minerals (Fig. 3.2). Regulation of pastoral activity on heaths and moorlands formed a significant and rather exceptional example of co-operative organization but the commonlands were highly vulnerable to erosion by miners, quarrymen and squatters who were anxious to carve out smallholdings for their own exclusive use. Thus, unlike lowland England, rural communities in the uplands were characterized by rather weak social organization and a wide range of employment. Many by-employments were found, with miners and spinners working smallholdings and agriculturalists taking on temporary work in mines and quarries during slack periods of the year or indulging in domestic industries in their farmhouses when hands might otherwise be idle.

The pattern of mining, potting, tiling and iron-smelting activities in the sixteenth and seventeenth centuries closely reflected the natural environment, but in order to understand the distribution of textile manufacture and many other craft activities it is necessary to recognize that some areas generated surplus reserves of labour which actively sought alternative employment to supplement what was offered by farming. Craft activities in pre-industrial times were found predominantly in upland Britain and, to a lesser extent, in the 'wood-pasture' environments of the lowlands. Cloth-making flourished in the West Country, Westmorland, Cumberland and Furness by 1500 and in the following hundred years the manufacture of coarse cloths spread to West Yorkshire. By this time the knitting industry was firmly established in north-west Yorkshire, with goods being sent to London and exported to the Low Countries. Simpler operations tended to be 'put out' among cottagers, but weaving, dyeing and other final stages of processing were usually performed by families that spent little time working the land, except perhaps for lending a hand at times of harvest and haymaking (Everitt, 1967; Thirsk, 1967).

Agricultural activities in the wood-pasture areas of lowland England, such as the Kentish Weald and south-central Suffolk, were apparently not sufficient to employ the local labour force full time and these areas also supported cloth industries (Patten, 1972, 1978). Growing and working flax and hemp, the working of wood and a host of other activities added diversity to rural economies and societies. Such forms of employment absorbed local labour and thereby allowed higher densities of population to be supported than would have been possible from farming alone. Indeed, labourers migrated from areas of arable farming to wooded (or formerly wooded) districts such as the Weald which displayed some of the highest densities of population in any part of England during the seventeenth century.

In pre-industrial times, farming and craftwork, family, household and community co-existed harmoniously and supported one another. The dissolution of that harmony represented one of the most distinctive indices of the 'industrial revolution' and marks a major contrast between our lives and those of our predecessors. As Everitt (1967) has noted, it was an evil day for rural workers when industries left the countryside and moved to the towns. Important though the concepts of community, locality and self-sufficiency undoubtedly were they should not be overplayed in our view of pre-industrial society. It is true that as late as the sixteenth century some settlements in northern and south-western England remained sufficiently isolated to be almost entirely beyond the realm of commercial exchange but such cases became increasingly rare with the passage of time. Poor transport conditions rendered movement of foodstuffs and manufactured goods difficult and expensive but trading went on nonetheless. Certainly by the seventeenth century some parts of south-east England and East Anglia had developed agricultural systems that were largely orientated to meeting the needs of London. Communal rules and regulations were gradually disregarded in such areas and farming acquired more individualistic forms. This was encouraged in an equally dramatic way by the impact of successive enclosure movements, often associated with a conversion from arable to livestock husbandry, over many parts of the country (Dodgshon and Butlin, 1978).

Self-sufficiency was far from complete in another important respect, since temporary labour had to be brought to many parts of pre-industrial England from other areas in order to bring in the grain and hay harvests. Seasonal labour migration was a vital aspect of farming in times past because of the uneven seasonal spread of farm workloads and the fact that agricultural labour was distributed imperfectly in relation to work peaks. Indeed seasonal migration was to become even more pronounced after 1750 when many by-employments were wrecked by the early impact of factory industrialization. Migrant labourers moved from grass and wood-pasture areas to help out in neighbouring arable regions at corn harvest time and there were also examples of reverse flows as labourers moved to help with hay gathering. In any case, the timing of harvest activities varied in detail and this encouraged workers to migrate from area to area. The migrants also included cottage-based craftworkers from the Midlands and Yorkshire, who took their turn in the fields of eastern England, and smallholders who moved from parts of Britain, such as the Scottish highlands, the Welsh hills and eventually western Ireland, where resources were limited and over-population was endemic.

Undoubtedly there was much local migration in operation in pre-industrial England and the volume intensified with every decade that passed. Smith (1978) concludes that "the population of Tudor and Stuart England was highly mobile – a condition stemming from the interplay of certain basic characteristics of society" (p. 221). These included the institution of service, whereby adolescents worked away from the parental household, and the facts that production was increasingly for exchange rather than for direct consumption, that migration at marriage was certainly taking place, and that because "England was composed of relatively small settlements . . . the sphere of individual lifetime activity was often wider than the community of birth" (p. 222). By the late seventeenth century there were few parishes, save perhaps in some of the most remote regions, that remained largely self-sufficient and many of these were soon to be affected by seasonal if not permanent out-migration. However, as Laslett (1971) has explained, "to be a social unit conscious of itself, and removed, distinct from others, it was not necessary for the village community to be cut off from interchange with its companions. On the contrary, it was in perpetual negotiation with its neighbours, and this was an essential of its individuality" (pp. 82–3).

## Urban Life and Institutions

Pre-industrial patterns of contact involved links between villages and towns as well as between one village and its surrounding rural settlements. Yet in the sixteenth century it is likely that the greater part of England's agricultural produce was still not being marketed to satisfy urban needs. That situation was to change markedly in succeeding centuries. None-theless, fairs and markets in England may be traced from Saxon times onwards and by far the majority originated in the twelfth and thirteenth centuries, the great age of borough making, when Bristol, Boston, Stamford, Winchester and St. Ives (Huntingdonshire) held fairs that were of international importance. In the thirteenth century there were probably more than 1,500 market settlements in England but by the year 1500 the number of market towns had declined to about 750 (Everitt, 1967 and in Clark, 1976). Each centre had regular market days each week and also held fairs less frequently. These fairs remained a significant feature in the economic and social organization of England certainly until the eighteenth century but their international character declined. The operation of 'the open market' was carefully organized and stood in contrast with the private buying and selling that escaped the eyes and ears of the market officials. Pre-industrial towns depended also on supplies of migrants from the countryside for their very survival, since rates of urban mortality were extremely high and would have precluded population growth. Certainly London was to continue to rely on the arrival of country folk for its growth until well into the eighteenth century. Thus in many parts of England, town and country were functionally intertwined long before the appearance of mechanized industrialization. With the passage of time many of those links became stronger with, for example, London and other large cities drawing their food supplies from ever-broadening hinterlands within which agricultural production became increasingly market orientated (Fisher, in Clark, 1976).

The origins of English towns, whether ancient or medieval, need not detain us here. What is of particular importance to the social geographer is the distinctive legal status of towns and the existence of social institutions, such as gilds, which helped to distinguish towns from rural settlements. Urban charters defined the rights, freedoms and privileges of townsfolk, making them and the communities to which they belonged quite different from rural groups. Pre-industrial towns were normally bigger than villages, though not necessarily so. Many were walled and most contained market places, market crosses, shops and shambles. But in some visual respects they were similar to villages and, in Patten's (1978) words, "were deeply penetrated by the countryside.... Ploughland, meadow, orchards, farms and gardens marched boldly into the back streets of even the biggest towns, whose streets were often full of livestock and of people bringing foodstuffs from field to consumer" (p. 17). Many townsfolk, like their country cousins, responded to the call for help to get the harvest home.

According to Clark and Slack (1972, 1976) every pre-industrial town displayed at least one of the following characteristics: a specialist economic function; a marked concentration of population; a sophisticated political superstructure; and a community function which extended beyond the immediate limits of the town. The lowest order of urban centre had strong rural overtones and exhibited only a couple of the above characteristics. Then came perhaps one hundred or more middle-order English towns, which possessed all four characteristics; and, finally, seven major cities which played "a dominant, quasi-metropolitan role in their regions" (Patten, 1978, p. 21). These were Bristol, Exeter, Hull, York, Norwich, Newcastle and, of course, London. But for all their size and distinctiveness pre-industrial towns in England were demographically and economically frail, being ravaged by fires, plague and the devastations of war.

Sir John Clapham (1957) estimated that in 1500 only 10 per cent of England's population lived in places of more than 5,000 inhabitants and by 1750 the figure had risen to 20 per cent. Throughout pre-industrial times most boroughs and even cathedral cities contained fewer than 5,000 residents. Taking a different kind of definition, Gregory King estimated that England's market towns and provincial cities contained about 870,000 people in 1688 (16 per cent of the total). A further 4,100,000 people (74 per cent) were country folk and the remaining 530,000 (10 per cent) were Londoners. London was a giant, with the next most populous cities (Bristol, Norwich and York) housing only 25–30,000 people apiece. London had in fact achieved that kind of dimension as early as the fourteenth century. The capital was indeed exceptional in terms of its rate of growth since Patten (1978) insists that change rather than rapid growth was "the diagnostic characteristic apparent within individual towns and within the urban system" of England which altered "relatively little and slowly in its main lineaments" between 1500 and 1700 (p. 16). Even London in the early eighteenth century "wore something of a rural smock: although the area within the walls was densely populated the newly colonized suburbs were still more country than town" (Clark and Slack, 1972, p. 6). Trees surrounded the new Georgian squares to the west of the City and the royal parks and surrounding open fields provided a markedly rustic fringe.

In pre-industrial England gilds were distinctly urban institutions which existed to organize manufacturing and trading activities, guarantee quality, control prices and safeguard privileges, especially to protect each member's share in the total business of the town or the gild's particular occupation. Indeed in some towns there were several and sometimes many gilds which served the interests of specialist groups. For example, the city of Chester contained at least 25 gilds in the sixteenth century and even in a smaller country town like Lincoln there were half as many (Clark and Slack, 1976, p. 28). Apprenticeship and eventual membership of a gild gave a man status and privileges that were jealously guarded. Traders and other foreigners were attracted to pre-industrial towns and whilst some outsiders, such as Dutch, Walloon and Huguenot refugees in Norwich, were readily assimilated, others occupied special quarters. The presence of Hanseatic merchants in London forms the classic example. These 'Easterlings' had occupied their 'Steel Yard' alongside the Thames since the tenth century and were trusted traders until the mid-sixteenth century when complaints were voiced and the 'Liberty of the Steel Yard' was seized by the Crown. The special privileges of the Hansards were revoked and in 1598 they were ordered to abandon the Steel Yard and leave the Kingdom of England. Jewish traders formed another group of outsiders whose presence added social diversity to the pre-industrial town. Jews first came to England with William the Conqueror and remained until 1290 when all 5,000 were expelled and crossed to France and Flanders after their property had been confiscated. In the preceding 200 years communities of Jews had come into existence in London and in many provincial towns, such as Oxford, where they gained unpopularity for the terms under which they made loans to students. Not until the time of Cromwell were Jews permitted to return, with a mere 400 being in England in 1690 and 26,000 in 1790. Monasteries, convents and other large religious communities with their distinctive precincts, provided yet another element of social and spatial differentiation in pre-industrial towns prior to the Dissolution.

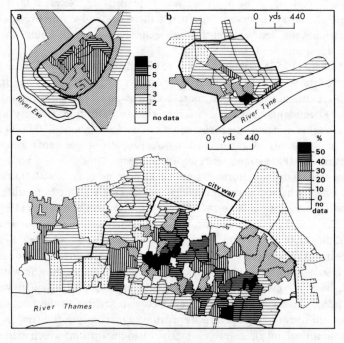

FIG. 3.3. *Distribution of wealth in (a) Exeter, (b) Newcastle, and (c) London in the seventeenth century; showing average number of hearths per taxed household in Exeter in 1671– 2, and in Newcastle in 1665 (after Langton, 1975); and percentage of 'substantial households' in each London parish (after Glass, 1966). For the most part 'substantial households' are defined as those with a personal estate of not less than £600 or real estate not less than £50 per year and thus liable to surtax under an Act of 1694.*

A most fruitful area of academic enquiry has involved attempts to explain the internal organization of such settlements. In his classic study entitled *The Preindustrial City* (1960), Sjoberg examined a wide range of archaeological, documentary and contemporary Third World evidence and argued that pre-industrial cities did not display the same kinds of spatial patterning that are to be found in industrial settlements and have been generated in response to essentially economic processes. He contended that the operation of activities of a religious, political, administrative and essentially social nature were crucial in ordering the use of urban space in pre-industrial times. According to his thesis, a small and powerful elite controlled such spheres of activity and lived near the centre of the city, while the poor and relatively powerless lived on the margins. Money-making and economic activities were deemed to be alien to the religious-philosophical value system of the dominant group. Distinctive quarters reflected differences in trade activities and the presence of foreigners and minority religious groups. Repulsive environments on the urban periphery, narrow streets throughout the city which impeded movement, and the tightly knit structure of elite groups worked together to reinforce the contrast between the city's core and its periphery.

More recently, Vance (1971) has re-worked both the evidence and the terminology in his study of land assignment in what he described as 'pre-capitalist', 'capitalist' and 'post-capitalist' cities. He has placed particular attention on the importance of gilds and other social institutions in the creation of urban morphologies before inanimate forms of energy were adopted widely. Gild membership was open to professing Christians who were skilled men and had the right to own property in burgage plots. Membership permitted the chance of participation in civic life and might influence the spatial organization of urban life. For Vance the gilds were crucial instruments for explaining city form but for Sjoberg they were of minor importance. Both scholars emphasized that pre-industrial cities contained many foci, each with its own shops and workplaces and housing for a wide social spectrum, but Vance recognized that some high status groups might acquire wealth and would then occupy central locations in what he termed 'merchant cities'. Eventually the capitalist city would come into being as the communal organization of the gilds declined and as groups and individuals with differing degrees of access to capital competed to occupy central locations. Housing and workplaces became separated with the rich abandoning the city centre to the poor as pleasanter environments were sought in suburbia.

Langton (1975) has examined seventeenth-century Exeter, Dublin and especially Newcastle-upon-Tyne in the light of the hypotheses proposed by Sjoberg and Vance using hearth tax returns which reflect the size of houses in the town and the wealth of their occupants. In similar fashion, Glass (1966) used tax data to determine the distribution of 'substantial households' in London in 1695. The resulting patterns seem to corroborate Sjoberg's hypothesis, with marked peaks of affluence giving way to a rapid decline in wealth toward the walls or outskirts of the city (Fig. 3.3). Crafts and other occupational groupings were concentrated, indeed segregated, in differing degrees but these cities lacked single central business districts around which all economic activities were articulated. Quarters with large houses tended to accommodate the wealthiest trades and vice versa. Langton's analysis and discussion is intricate and his original paper is well worth studying for the light that it sheds on the importance of social and institutional structures in the modelling of towns and cities in times past. He shows clearly how burgage plots were occupied intensively by the households of traders and craftsmen, with penthouses overhanging narrow streets, and also horizontally, as outhouses and sheds were inserted behind the street lines. Many town houses were microcosms of much greater forms of social diversity, with ground floors accommodating retail and manufacturing activities, first and second floors housing masters and their families, and upper floors and attics accommodating apprentices and servants and also providing room for storage. In broad terms, social status was in inverse relationship to height above the ground. This kind of vertical differentiation was to continue in English town houses until much more recent times.

## London as a Pre-Industrial City

In London, before and indeed after the Great Fire of 1666, craft and victualling trades were strictly controlled within the area of the 'Liberties' of the City by the gild companies and the City Corporation. As a result London exemplified the characteristics of the pre-industrial city in a particularly dramatic way. Westcheap or Cheapside formed the main commercial street, with members of particular trades clustering along various sections of its length (Fig. 3.4). Printing activities were concentrated around St. Pauls, in Paternoster

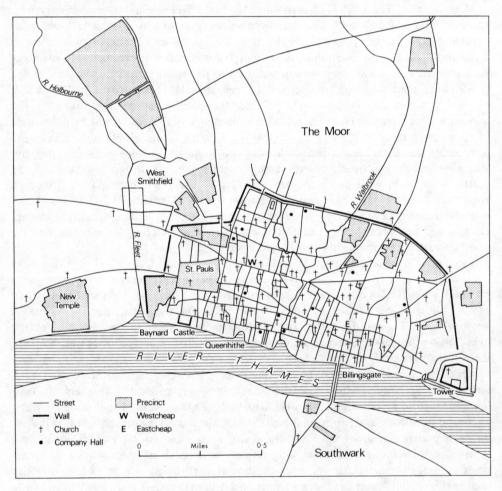

FIG. 3.4. *Medieval London (after Smailes, 1964).*

Row and in Fleet Street and the segregation of the capital's markets provided a fine example of a spatial response to social institutions. Until the Civil War the City resisted the establishment of markets beyond its Liberties. Meat was sold in Eastcheap and in the Shambles (modern Newgate Street), and the Poultry, at the eastern end of Cheapside, spoke for itself. Bucklebury sold groceries and the length of Cornhill was known as the Stocks, where fish, meat and ultimately fruit and vegetables and flowers were sold. New Fish Street and Queenhithe sold fish, with Billingsgate originally being a market for corn and waterborne coal. It only changed its function to the sale of fish during the late seventeenth century. Prior to their dissolution in the sixteenth century the religious houses of London gave rise to distinctive precincts inside the city walls. In addition, these religious houses occupied extensive areas outside the walls which were ripe for conversion to alternative uses at the Reformation. Certainly Henry VIII took advantage of confiscated church lands between and beyond the palaces of Whitehall and St. James for the creation of a deer park. This was the origin of the great royal parks of St. James, Green Park and Hyde Park which form such striking components in London's modern landscape. What is more these parks and their associated palaces served to reinforce social and economic differences between west and east London which are still very much in evidence today (Clark and Slack, 1976, Chapter 5).

Of course, London was much more than the City. Enforcement of rules and regulations inside the line of the walls encouraged certain people and certain activities to settle beyond them and contributed in a very real way to creating the complex character of inner London. Smithfield, for example, to the north of the walls, had supported a horse fair since the eleventh century and this area functioned as a slaughter house for the Shambles meat market between 1614 and 1869 when the Shambles market was closed and its function was assumed by Smithfield. Southwark, on the south bank of the Thames, escaped the regulations of the City (Fig. 3.5). London Bridge was closed at curfew until morning and late arrivals had to seek accommodation on the south bank which acquired a dubious reputation for its inns, theatres, brothels and pleasure grounds. Outcasts and vagrants lived in conditions of poverty under the less strict control of the Surrey magistrates. In 1550, Southwark became a ward of the City but control was never exercised so strictly as on the north bank and the City's powers were gradually eroded. Many noxious industries operated beyond the City walls, following the banishment of tanning from the lower Fleet river to Bermondsey in the fourteenth century. Such activities were particularly numerous on the north bank and in close proximity to the Thames in what was to become known as the East End.

Extra-mural areas also functioned as reception zones for migrants from all parts of England and also for European refugees who brought distinctive types of manufacturing with them which enhanced the economic base of the capital but caused disquiet among long-established craftsmen. The citizens of London resented the presence of the newcomers but it was of course much easier to start a business outside the walls since gild membership was not required. The gilds made efforts to extend their powers beyond the City but they met with only limited success and by the mid-sixteenth century their zone of influence had shrunk back to the line of the City walls. Unsuccessful attempts were also made to prohibit the construction of new buildings outside the City in order to contain the flow of migrants. New houses were technically prohibited and so old buildings were patched up and extended by digging cellars and tacking on extra rooms. When regulations were defied and new buildings were thrown together they were hidden behind existing facades. Poor building techniques became habitual in the East End and continued after restrictions had been lifted. Merchants abandoned their houses in areas such as Bethnal Green and moved to new housing

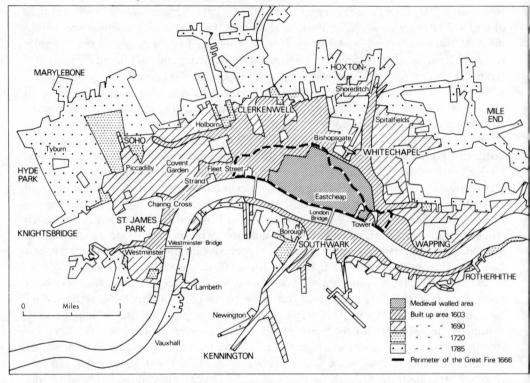

FIG. 3.5. *Growth of London from medieval times to 1785.*

schemes on the estates of west London. In their place came the poor, but to quote Clark's (1972) words "London was the graveyard of pauper England" (p. 36). J. W. Archenholz (1794) captured the contrast most clearly. "The East End, especially along the shores of the Thames, consists of old houses, the streets there are narrow, dark and ill-paved, inhabited by sailors and other workmen. . . . The contrast between this and the West End is astonishing; the houses here are mostly new and elegant; the squares are superb, and the streets straight and open." There was "truly a migration from the East End to West, thousands passing from that part of the City to this end where fertile fields and most agreeable gardens are daily metamorphosed into houses and streets." As the traders left the East End their place was taken by refugees. Huguenots settled in Shoreditch and Spitalfields after the Revocation of the Edict of Nantes (1685), bringing their silk weaving with them. Dutch printers moved into Clerkenwell and at the Restoration a colony of Sephardic Jews established itself in Whitechapel, to be followed by many other groups of Jewish immigrants in later centuries. In the second half of the twentieth century the migrant groups have changed with, for example, Jews and Huguenots being replaced by Pakistanis in Spitalfields, but the old-established reception function of the East End remains nonetheless.

   For all its great dimensions and weight of numbers London in the seventeenth and eighteenth century was still a hand-made city. Its population grew from 200,000 in 1600 to 575,000 in 1700 and 900,000 in 1800 when one Englishman in every ten lived there. Trades and crafts flourished by the thousand in the capital but they were carried on in homes and in small workshops and relied on human muscle rather than on power-driven machines (Glass, in Clark, 1976). Massive in-migration was required to provide so much human energy. After due consideration of mortality trends, Wrigley (1967) has hypothesized that roughly 12,000 migrants must have moved to London annually between 1650 and 1750 and Smith (1978) remarks that "it may have absorbed up to half the natural increase of the total population, recruiting its migrants from considerable distances" (p. 224). For example, an analysis of 104 working men living in Stepney and Whitechapel between 1580 and 1639 showed that well over two-thirds had originated from settlements more than 50 miles away and which were spread fairly evenly across the country. As today it was mainly young adults who arrived. However, London's real strength lay with its trade rather than with its crafts. Wealth derived from trade allowed the capital to grow rapidly, to develop as the centre of consumption and to dominate English society. As well as its diet of human flesh the monster that was London needed to consume humbler fare and the drive to satisfy these demands stimulated fundamental social and economic changes in many parts of the English countryside.

## The Demise of Pre-Industrial England

It is hard to characterize the demise of pre-industrial England, since different regions and sectors of economic and social life experienced the processes of modernization at different times and with differing degrees of intensity. As the decades passed, more and more people became exposed to national rather than local influence and their lives were gradually transformed. Pre-industrial communities had been small in size, local in orientation and relatively simple in economic terms, however the society they comprised was "a highly complex arrangement of persons" (Laslett, 1971, p. 159). Agriculture and industry had co-existed with a high degree of harmony and within the context of the family whose unity was not seriously jeopardized. In the eighteenth and especially the nineteenth century the operation of economic functions was removed from the biological family and was subject to new forms of organization associated with industrialization and the emergence of a mass society. At the same time the role of agriculture in English life declined substantially and more rapidly than in all other European countries. As a result, the differentiation between town and country and between manufacturing and farming became increasingly obvious as the nineteenth century progressed. England was rushing headlong into a precocious urban revolution which distinguished it from all other parts of the world.

Rural manufacturing activities were being transformed in the first half of the nineteenth century but not until after mid-century were craftsmen to lose the struggle with urban factories and agricultural mechanization permitted a release of farm labour on a massive scale. Villages lost most of their craftsmen, service workers and landless labourers. Their pre-industrial structure was transformed and they became 'agriculturalized' with the great majority of their remaining residents, whether they were landowners, tenants or workers, being associated with just one activity, namely agriculture. Landless labourers on farms and in workshops had always been more mobile than those with a stake in property. As a result rural depopulation drew farm labourers away in great quantities and village communities became pale shadows of what they had once been. Indeed it may even be inappropriate to speak of 'communities' at all in Victorian times since traditional forms of reciprocity and communal organization were disappearing. Individualism became the watchword as the social life of the countryside gradually acquired characteristics that were very different from those of pre-industrial times.

Traditional forms of social and economic organization were waning in Victorian times but were identifiable nonetheless in vestigial form in many parts of the English countryside. Economic forces were moulding the geography of England in more powerful ways than ever before, and structures that had been inherited from pre-industrial times had to be re-shaped or erased in this new industrial age. Social institutions old and new, small and great, rural and urban exercised their powers to generate fascinating exceptions to what might be expected from the operation of economic rules. New industrial towns were inserted into the framework of pre-urban landownership units and manifested the social ideals and attitudes of millowners, town councillors and others with access to social and economic power. Likewise the pattern of population change in the countryside was fashioned by the interaction of social as well as economic influences. To interpret such real life complexity, as well as appreciating idealized situations, is one of the major challenges facing the social geographer.

### References and Further Reading

The classic study of pre-industrial conditions is:
Laslett, P. (1971) *The World We Have Lost,* Methuen, London (2nd ed.).

A useful collection of essays in historical geography (including work by Smith on population) is:
Dodgshon, R. A. and Butlin, R. A. (eds.) (1978) *An Historical Geography of England and Wales,* Academic Press, London.

Medieval social conditions are reviewed in:
Brooke, C. (1971) *The Structure of Medieval Society,* Thames & Hudson, London.
Postan, M. M. (1972) *The Medieval Economy and Society*, Penguin, Harmondsworth.

The concept of the community is examined, together with more recent British examples, by:
Bell, C. and Newby, H. (1971) *Community Studies: an introduction to the sociology of the local community,* George Allen & Unwin, London.
Frankenberg, R. (1966) *Communities in Britain*, Penguin, Harmondsworth.

Communities in pre-industrial England are characterized in:
Chambers, J. D. (1972) *Population, Economy and Society in Pre-Industrial England*, Oxford University Press, Oxford.
Clapham, J. (1957) *A Concise Economic History of Britain from the Earliest Times to 1750*, Cambridge University Press, London.
Everitt, A. (1967) Farm labourers and The Marketing of agricultural produce, in J. Thirsk (ed.), *The Agrarian History of England and Wales, Vol. IV, 1500–1640.* Cambridge University Press, London.
Eversley, D. E. C. (1966) Population history and local history, in E. A. Wrigley (ed.), *An Introduction to English Historical Demography,* Weidenfeld & Nicolson, London.
Laslett, P. (ed.) (1972) *Household and Family in Past Time,* Cambridge University Press, London.
Patten, J. (1972) Village and town: an occupational study, *Agricultural History Review*, 20, 1–16.
Perry, P. J. (1969) Working-class isolation and mobility in rural Dorset, 1837–1936: a study of marriage distances, *Transactions, Institute of British Geographers*, 46, 121–41.
Thirsk, J. (1967) The farming regions of England, in J. Thirsk (ed.), *op.cit.*

Pre-industrial urbanism is analyzed by:
Clark, P. and Slack, P. (eds.) (1972) *Crisis and Order in English Towns 1500–1700*, Routledge & Kegan Paul, London.
Clark, P. and Slack, P. (1976) *English Towns in Transition 1500–1700*, Oxford University Press, Oxford.
Everitt, A. (ed.) (1973) *Perspectives in English Local History*, Macmillan, London.
Langton, J. (1975) Residential patterns in pre-industrial cities: some case studies from seventeenth-century Britain, *Transactions, Institute of British Geographers*, 65, 1–27.
Langton, J. (1977) Late medieval Gloucester: some data from a rental of 1455, *Transactions, Institute of British Geographers, New Series*, 2, 259–77.
Patten, J. (1978) *English Towns: 1500–1700*, Dawson, Folkestone.
Sjoberg, G. (1960) *The Preindustrial City,* Free Press, New York,

Vance, J.E. (1971) Land assignment in the precapitalist, capitalist and postcapitalist city, *Economic Geography,* 47, 101–20.

A valuable collection of essays by more than a dozen authors (including Everitt on market towns, Fisher on London as a demand centre, and Glass on the socio-economic status of London's residents) is:
Clark, P. (ed.) (1976) *The Early Modern Town: a reader,* Longman, London.

London as a pre-industrial city is depicted in:
Appleby, A. B. (1975) Nutrition and disease: the case of London, 1550–1750, *Journal of Interdisciplinary History,* 6, 1–22.
Biddle, M. (1973) *The Future of London's Past,* Rescue, Worcester.
Glass, D. V. (1966) London's inhabitants within the walls, *London Record Society Publications,* 2, xxxv–xxxvii.
Smailes, A. E. (1964) The site, growth and changing face of London, in R. Clayton (ed.), *The Geography of Greater London,* George Philip, London, pp. 1–52.
Wrigley, E. A. (1967) A simple model of London's importance in changing English society and economy 1650–1750, *Past and Present,* 37, 44–70.
Wrigley, E. A. (1972) The process of modernization and the industrial revolution in England, *Journal of Interdisciplinary History,* 3, 225–59.

A fascinating contemporary account of London in the late sixteenth century is offered in:
Stow, J. (1956) *The Survey of London,* Dent, London.

Several useful papers on pre-industrial England, including Langton (1975) and Wrigley (1967), are collected together in:
Patten, J. (ed.) (1979) *Pre-Industrial England,* Dawson, Folkestone.

# 4
# The Modernization of English Society

## Population Change

THE first census of England and Wales in 1801 enumerated 8,900,000 inhabitants. In the same year Scotland contained a further 1,600,000 and Ireland, 5,200,000. By the end of the nineteenth century the population of England and Wales had increased to over 32,000,000 and by 1971 had reached nearly 49,000,000. During the Victorian era the Scottish population grew less dramatically, to 4,500,000 in 1901, and achieving 5,200,000 by 1971. The Irish experience was radically different: a peak of 8,200,000 in 1841 followed by rapid decline associated with the potato famine of the 1840s. Mass emigration and death from hunger reduced the population of Ireland to 6,500,000 in 1851, from which it declined more slowly for the rest of the century. In terms of numbers, therefore, England and Wales have increased their dominance, accounting for only 56 per cent of the population of the British Isles in 1801, but 78 per cent by 1901. Restricting our attention to the United Kingdom, England and Wales included 85 per cent of the U.K. population at the beginning of this century, increasing this proportion to 88 per cent by 1971 (Table 4.1).

It is impossible to state precisely how many of the population could be classified as 'urban' and how many 'rural' at any date because there are so many different definitions of 'urban' and 'rural' that could be adopted. It seems likely that the first official estimates of 'urban population', dating from the census of 1851, are underestimates since they excluded the suburbs of many rapidly expanding industrial towns. Nevertheless, the census estimates that as early as 1851 over half the population of England and Wales (50.2 per cent) could be classified as 'urban'. Later in the nineteenth century a more realistic definition was adopted, as first newly created municipal boroughs, then urban sanitary districts and finally the administrative units of county and municipal boroughs and urban districts — units which

TABLE 4.1. *Population changes in the British Isles,*
*1801–1971*

| Date | England | Wales | Scotland | N. Ireland | S. Ireland/ Eire |
|------|---------|-------|----------|------------|------------------|
| | (figures in millions) | | | | |
| 1801 | 8.3 | 0.5 | 1.6 | 5.2 | |
| 1851 | 16.8 | 1.2 | 2.9 | 1.4 | 5.1 |
| 1901 | 30.5 | 2.0 | 4.5 | 1.2 | 3.2 |
| 1951 | 41.2 | 2.6 | 5.1 | 1.4 | 3.0 |
| 1971 | 45.9 | 2.7 | 5.2 | 1.5 | 3.0 |

TABLE 4.2. *Levels of Urbanization in
England and Wales, 1801—1971*

| Date | per cent urban (after Law, 1967) | per cent urban (census) |
|---|---|---|
| 1801 | 33.8 | – |
| 1821 | 40.0 | – |
| 1851 | 54.0 | 50.2 |
| 1871 | 65.2 | 61.8 |
| 1901 | 78.0 | 77.0 |
| 1911 | 78.9 | 78.1 |
| 1951 | – | 80.8 |
| 1971 | – | 78.3 |

Note:   Law (1967) defined 'urban' as administrative
areas with a minimum population of 2,500,
a minimum average density of 1 per acre, and
the majority of the population concentrated
in one nucleated settlement. The Census of
England and Wales defined 'urban' as everywhere not lying in administrative rural
districts.

survived until local government reorganization in 1973 — were counted as 'urban'. In 1911
the proportion 'urban' reached 78.1 per cent and continued to increase gradually to a peak
of 80.8 per cent in 1951 (Table 4.2).

By 1951 such a small proportion of the population lived in rural areas that it was difficult
for the urban *proportion* to increase any more, although in *absolute* numbers the urban
population has continued to grow. Since the Second World War it seems that the urbanization
process has gone into reverse. In 1971 the 'urban' share was back to 78.3 per cent of the total
population of England and Wales. However, this trend does not signify any process of
'de-urbanization', but the spreading out of the urban population into areas still admini-
stratively 'rural', as workers in the conurbations commute over longer distances from
dormitory villages, as young professional families are forced to become 'reluctant commuters'
to London from the Outer Metropolitan Area where houses are cheap enough for them to
afford, as employment decentralizes to modern industrial estates in 'expanded towns' and
'new towns', and as more city dwellers retire to the countryside. Few of these out-migrants
have abandoned the city because they want to escape urban ways of life, so that their
migration in fact represents a spreading of urbanism as a way of life and a reduction of the
differences between urban and rural societies.

Between 1801 and 1911 the total population of England and Wales quadrupled but, as
Law (1967) has pointed out, rural population barely increased (and actually decreased after
1861) while urban population increased nine and a half times (Fig. 4.1) (Table 4.3). A few
towns grew by less than the national average (4x), including some small market towns
unaffected by industrialization and by-passed by the railways, coastal ports which lost trade
to competing railway companies, a few early industrial centres based on water power in
remote locations and some large regional centres located far from the coalfields. The most
important of these places was Norwich. At the other extreme were those towns which grew
by more than the urban average (9x): seaside resorts which benefited from rising living
standards, the institution of annual holidays and the excursion activities of railway companies (e.g. Southend, Torquay, Blackpool); coal ports (e.g. Cardiff, Hartlepool) and

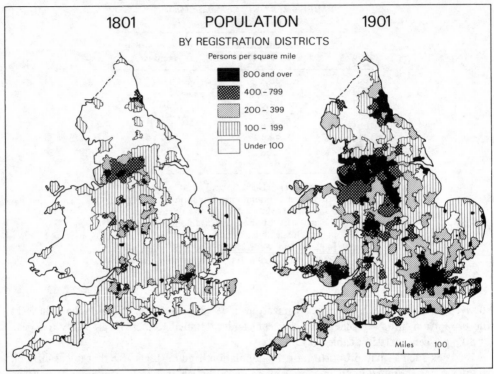

FIG. 4.1. *Population distributions in England and Wales (after Darby, 1973).*

associated mining settlements in Durham, South Yorkshire and South Wales; and industrial towns which grew from nothing (e.g. Crewe, Middlesbrough). The figures are somewhat misleading, for while these towns had the fastest *rates* of growth they started the century with such small base populations that *any* growth yielded a very high percentage growth rate. In terms of absolute population growth the largest increases were recorded in the major cities: Birmingham, Liverpool, Manchester, Leeds, Bradford, Sheffield, Newcastle and, of course, London.

Two other features of nineteenth-century urban growth have been illustrated by Robson (1973). Firstly, for any particular decade, the range of growth rates is much greater for small than for large towns. Calculating the mean growth rate and standard deviation for towns in

TABLE 4.3. *Urban and rural population growth in England and Wales, 1801–1911* (after Law, 1967)

Population figures in millions

| Date | Total | | Urban | | Rural | |
|------|-------|------|-------|------|-------|------|
| | Growth Index | Popn. | Growth Index | Popn. | Growth Index | Popn. |
| 1801 | 100 | 8.8 | 100 | 3.0 | 100 | 5.9 |
| 1851 | 202 | 17.9 | 322 | 9.7 | 140 | 8.2 |
| 1871 | 255 | 22.7 | 492 | 14.8 | 134 | 7.9 |
| 1891 | 326 | 29.0 | 718 | 21.6 | 126 | 7.4 |
| 1911 | 406 | 36.1 | 946 | 28.5 | 129 | 7.6 |

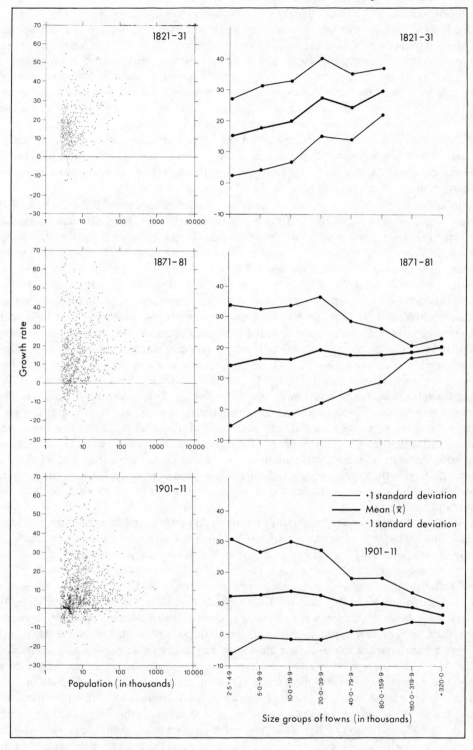

FIG. 4.2. *Growth rates and town size in England and Wales, 1801–1911 (after Robson, 1973).*

different size classes we find a pattern of decreasing variance with increasing city size (Fig. 4.2). Robson explains this by associating urban growth with the adoption of industrial and commercial innovations. He assumes that most innovations, such as new industrial processes, new systems of financing like banks and building societies, new forms of communication such as telephones and telex, and new forms of power supply for heating, lighting and industry, are adopted first in the largest cities and then diffuse down the urban hierarchy to successively smaller towns and outwards according to a distance-decay effect to more remote towns. Large towns will adopt every innovation that is offered so that the timing and extent of their growth will follow similar cycles. Smaller places will adopt more selectively and at different dates according to their location in the urban system, so that their patterns of population growth will appear haphazard. In fact, this aspect of variable growth is characteristic of most urban systems in the developed world (Bourne, 1975).

In contrast, the second feature is specific to nineteenth-century Britain. Until 1871 there was a weak but positive relationship between a city's existing size and its rate of growth: the larger a city, the faster it grew, so that the gap between large and small places widened. From 1871 until 1901 all sizes of town grew at similar rates. After 1901 smaller towns grew more rapidly than large towns (Fig. 4.2) and this trend has also been apparent in recent years. For example, between 1961 and 1966 four of the six largest English cities (defined as Standard Metropolitan Labour Market Areas, whereby the population of administrative districts that are adjacent to major centres and have significant links with them is counted with that of the central cities) lost population, while the fastest growing towns were smaller places, either free-standing and diversified cities like Leicester and Southampton, or independent towns within reasonable commuting distance of — but clearly separate from — London: Oxford, Luton, Reading and Southend (Table 4.4). We might explain the latter in terms of the broadening influence of the metropolis. The longer-term trends may be attributed to diseconomies of scale, as the largest cities faced problems of violent crime, mental illness, pollution and traffic congestion, or to elaborations of the diffusion theory already outlined. It is argued that there were few radical innovations in British industry in the early twentieth century which could have initiated new phases of population growth in the major cities. Meanwhile, some of the earlier innovations were gradually being adopted in smaller towns which were thus enabled to catch up with the stagnating cities.

Whatever the reasons for these trends in population growth and redistribution they have important consequences for the validity of models such as Wirth's theory of urbanism or Burgess' zonal model of residential segregation within cities. Both models emphasize the social consequences of increasing size and density and the reaction of residents to life in unfamiliar surroundings with large numbers of people unlike themselves. Our cursory review of population growth in England and Wales suggests that such models may be applicable to nineteenth-century towns which were growing at unprecedented rates to unprecedented sizes. But they may be less appropriate in the twentieth century when the largest cities have played a less dominant role and most cities have experienced a decrease in average density. The figures that have been cited on the levels of urbanization at successive censuses show that a large proportion of city dwellers in Victorian England must have originated in rural areas: urban growth was the result of migration from a variety of different origins. By contrast, in contemporary England most urban growth results from natural increase within cities. With the exception of New Commonwealth immigrants, urbanites have been born in the city in which they are currently resident or have migrated from another, probably very

TABLE 4.4. *Urban population changes, 1951–1971*

(a) Metropolitan labour market areas with populations greater than 250,000 with (1) rapidly increasing, (2) rapidly decreasing populations, 1961–6 (after Hall, 1973).

| Area | Popn. (thousands) 1961 | 1966 | % Change |
|---|---|---|---|
| (1) Luton | 267 | 299 | 12.2 |
| Reading | 242 | 279 | 11.4 |
| Leicester | 457 | 504 | 10.3 |
| Southend | 247 | 271 | 9.8 |
| Oxford | 287 | 311 | 8.3 |
| Southampton | 402 | 433 | 7.7 |
| Coventry | 644 | 688 | 6.8 |
| (2) Newcastle | 1062 | 1057 | −0.5 |
| Manchester | 2042 | 2013 | −1.4 |
| Liverpool | 1481 | 1450 | −2.1 |
| London | 9157 | 8891 | −3.0 |

(b) County boroughs with populations greater than 125,000 (approximately equivalent to the inner rings of metropolitan labour market areas) with (1) rapidly increasing, (2) rapidly decreasing populations, 1951–71.

| County Borough | Popn. (thousands) 1951 | 1961 | 1971 | % Change per annum 1951–61 | 1961–71 |
|---|---|---|---|---|---|
| (1) Basildon | 43 | 89 | 129 | 7.36 | 3.84 |
| Luton | 114 | 140 | 161 | 2.11 | 1.41 |
| Dudley | 150 | 162 | 186 | 0.75 | 1.37 |
| Reading | 114 | 120 | 132 | 0.49 | 0.96 |
| Northampton | 111 | 118 | 127 | 0.62 | 0.69 |
| Coventry | 266 | 317 | 335 | 1.76 | 0.56 |
| Teesside | 336 | 374 | 395 | 1.10 | 0.55 |
| Southampton | 190 | 205 | 215 | 0.76 | 0.47 |
| (2) Greater London | 8197 | 7992 | 7379 | −0.25 | −0.79 |
| Portsmouth | 234 | 215 | 197 | −0.82 | −0.87 |
| Birmingham | 1114 | 1111 | 1013 | −0.03 | −0.91 |
| Salford | 178 | 155 | 130 | −1.37 | −1.70 |
| Newcastle | 292 | 270 | 222 | −0.78 | −1.92 |
| Manchester | 703 | 662 | 541 | −0.60 | −1.99 |
| Liverpool | 791 | 746 | 607 | −0.58 | −2.04 |

similar, city: they are not unfamiliar with the urban environment. Such was not the case for most migrants to Victorian cities.

## Rural Life in Victorian England

As we examine rural conditions during the nineteenth century we must not give the impression that labour in pre-industrial England was immobile. Temporary migration operated in many parts of the country and towns and cities relied on regular arrivals of newcomers for their very survival. Wrigley (1967) has demonstrated that the rate of population increase in London in the seventeenth and eighteenth centuries, when mortality exceeded fertility in the capital, necessitated the net in-migration of 8,000 persons each year. He inferred that at some time in their lives one-sixth of adult males in England must have experienced life in their capital city. Rural—urban migration was certainly not a novel phenomenon in the nine-teenth century but the scale at which it operated was new. At the beginning and even mid-way through the century the greater share of the British population was far more aware of the local influences than the national forces that affected their lives. Changes in com-munication gradually eroded that spatial and social isolation as the railway opened up new possibilities of travel, as primary education raised literacy rates, and as the penny post and newspapers enabled information to be transmitted into every settlement in the land in a hitherto unknown way. Knowledge of an alternative, urban way of life invited comparison with conditions on England's farms and in her villages. Countryfolk by the million voted with their feet and transferred their allegiance from their home community to the attractive and often idealized urban environment of which they had come to learn.

Each rural settlement needed to support a range of economic activities and services in order to be relatively self-supporting prior to the construction of the railway network which enabled goods to be hauled speedily over great distances. As well as landowners, tenant farmers and agricultural labourers most villages contained a host of craftsmen and service workers whose livelihoods were summarized by Augustus Petermann's maps accompanying the 1851 census but whose very existence would hardly be imagined now. As Samuel (1975) explains: "occupational boundaries in the nineteenth-century countryside were fairly fluid. They had to be, where so much employment was by the job rather than by the regular working week, and where work was difficult to get. . . . There was a great deal of movement from one class of work to another" (p. 5). By-employments, for example combining farming with another activity, were widespread in rural England and in some parts of the country survived until the early years of the present century.

The distribution of water power and workable mineral deposits, including coal, helped explain the spatial arrangement of many rural industries but others could not be accounted for in that way. They owed their existence to the availability of labour that was surplus to the needs of agriculture or of other activities that simply served the local community and its neighbours. Lace making, framework knitting, boot and shoe making, straw plait and hat manufacturing in various parts of the English Midlands represent classic examples of nine-teenth-century industrial locations which may not be explained satisfactorily in terms of raw materials and fuel supplies (Mills, 1973; Mingay, 1979). Rural activities such as these, whether they produced for local consumption or to meet wider needs, were highly vulnerable to contraction as the nineteenth century wore on. Some decayed because raw materials were exhausted or changes in taste rendered them redundant. Some failed to adapt to new technological opportunities and many collapsed in the face of overwhelming competition from factory producers. Saville (1957) described how some crafts lingered on, with for example bootmakers becoming shoe repairers, but others were snuffed out. Corn milling in the countryside came into the latter category as the industry moved first to market towns and then to ports as greater quantities of bread grains were imported. Some rural industries were transformed radically, with the chairmakers of villages in the Chilterns being supplanted by furniture factories in High Wycombe and the rural papermakers of Devon concentrating only on very high-quality paper. All were vulnerable and their contraction or disappearance contributed to the 'agriculturalization' of Victorian villages.

The spatial diversity of rural crafts in the early nineteenth century was paralleled by great complexity in the agricultural realm. England's farming systems on the eve of the railway age most certainly reflected the country's agricultural resource base but also formed a subtle expression of economic and social factors. Some regions were more attuned to the market requirements of commercial farming than others which were more orientated to satisfying the producers' own needs. Regions with large landed estates, employing many landless labourers, contrasted with other areas in which tenant farmers or smallholders predominated. Farm workers were housed in many different ways and the survival of such distinctive regional traditions has had important expression both in the pattern of rural settlement and in the vexed issue of the agricultural tied cottage (Orwin and Whetham, 1971). In Scotland married labourers were boarded in farm cottages and groups of unmarried men lived in bothies, whilst in northern England stockmen and other skilled workers were accommodated in farmhouses or in cottages but day-labourers often had to walk several miles from their cottages to work each day. Wales was predominantly a land of small farms with far less of a social gap between farmers and workers than in many other parts of Britain. Midland and southern England contained some of the richest agricultural areas but also very poor housing and working conditions as Thomas Hardy's novels show so clearly. Unlike upland Britain there were relatively few local alternatives to agricultural employment and the harshness of rural life was reflected by labourers' revolts in the 1830s, the Tolpuddle Martyrs and outbreaks of rick-burning in the name of 'Captain Swing'. The large estates of the eastern counties witnessed the early success of the 'agricultural revolution' but they supported remarkably harsh systems of labour management and displayed striking social contrasts in community organization. Gangs of agricultural labourers, many of whom endured brutal conditions, were moved from farm to farm for harvesting and other essential tasks. They were particularly vital in areas where 'close' villages predominated.

Contrasts in landownership, in other words in local access to social control, lay at the heart of the distinction between 'close' and 'open' villages. Each close settlement and the farmland that surrounded it was the property of an individual landlord or of a small group of owners who worked in co-operation. All the housing was in their hands and they could effectively determine the growth or stagnation of the village in question. By contrast, numerous landowners held property in open villages and hence tight social control was impossible. The underlying *raison d'être* for close villages was the operation of the poor law system which until 1860 required each parish or township to maintain its own poor from the parish poor rate. If the arrival of newcomers who might include some folk in need of relief could be controlled the local poor rate could be kept to a minimum. Although the system of support changed soon after mid-century, the underlying prejudice remained.

Close villages experienced very limited population growth and even population loss. In some cases cottages were demolished by landlords to keep out undesirables. Estate workers predominated in close villages and craftsmen, service workers and shopkeepers were few and far between. Perhaps 20 per cent of English villages were close settlements in the early nineteenth century, with the proportion rising to 40 per cent in northern parts of the Midlands, in the South-West and the Cotswolds, but falling to 15 per cent or less across southern England (Holderness, 1972). Open villages were just the opposite, being overcrowded, insanitary and ill-regulated. Many small landowners leased out tumbledown cottages to newcomers at extortionate rents. Open villages supported craftsmen, traders and beer retailers and such settlements grew as their 'close' neighbours stagnated or declined. Labourers travelled round distances of up to 8 or 9 miles each day as they walked or rode donkeys from their home cottage to their place of employment on a 'close' estate. Victorian observers drew attention to such hardships as well as to the drunkenness and immorality of the poor in open villages. Trollope provided a perfect illustration of both types of settlement in *Framley Parsonage,* with the neat and tidy village of Framley, its

Hall, park and landscaped gardens standing in contrast with the rough and straggling parish of Hogglestock which contained brickfields as well as farms. The detailed landscapes, economies and societies of the Victorian countryside were very much the manifestation of which particular stratum of local society controlled the power structure.

In the mid-nineteenth century rural Britain was still predominantly a nation of manual workers, ranging in status from comfortable family farmers to the completely landless who would be on relief for part of their lives and would end their days in the workhouse. Official reports, social histories and novels captured the harshness of life of many of our forefathers. In a report on agriculture in Devon, submitted as late as 1919, A. D. Cochrane could write of bad housing, long hours of work, successive days of labour without intermission, low wages, indifferent food, the lack of good boots and stout clothing, and a loss of hope among farm labourers that better conditions would come (Saville, 1957). Of course there had been some improvements in social conditions in the countryside in Victoria's reign. Poaching and game laws had been repealed in the 1830s to outlaw mantraps and halt the transportation of convicted poachers, who could still however be imprisoned for up to seven years. The Gangs' Act of 1869 tried to overcome the worst abuses inherent in the agricultural gangs' system which was condemned so soundly by Victorian observers for its brutality and immorality. Following the Act no child under eight years was to be employed in a gang and measures were taken to make the gangs more humane but not to abolish them. The Agricultural Children's Act (1873) withdrew all children under eight from any kind of agricultural employment and the Education Act (1876) made schooling compulsory for children up to fourteen years. Nevertheless, young arms were still needed for the harvest home as in times past and for certain weeks of the year many rural schoolrooms were virtually empty. Social improvements were slow indeed and problems of poor rural housing remained widespread throughout the century. Successive royal commissions examined the conditions of the rural working classes and farm workers began to organize themselves into agricultural trades unions in an attempt to improve their material lot. Agricultural depression in the final quarter of the nineteenth century added to the many social and economic problems of the English countryside (Perry, 1973). Commodity prices fell substantially and a run of bad seasons and animal diseases reduced output and raised costs. Arable farming, in particular, received a sharp shock and farmers tried to reduce costs by simplifying systems of production, converting to other forms of husbandry (especially livestock), experimenting with mechanization and cutting labour costs by dismissing workers. Out-migration from countryside to town and emigration from Britain to the opening vistas of the Empire were the result. More and more countryfolk put into practice the information that they had received about alternatives to their local world. Their decisions contributed to the 'agriculturalization' of the countryside and to the vicious downward spiral of rural depopulation.

The lives of many members of the rural working class in Victorian times were unquestionably hard as seen through our eyes. Ambrose (1974) has shown that the average agricultural labourer living in Ringmer (Sussex) in the 1870s worked for 12–14 hours per day, 6 days a week, with no paid holidays except for 4 bank holidays a year. He had little or no formal education but stood an even chance of being able to read. His family lived in a tied cottage and managed to satisfy most of their basic needs in the parish. They walked occasionally the three miles to Lewes, the nearby market town, but had never seen the sea just a few miles along the Ouse valley. Material life was poor but there was also "a poverty of the spirit . . . which reflected a lack of access to education, travel and information . . . a lack of incentive and motivation to rise above the inherited circumstances" (Ambrose, 1974, p. 23). The inhabitants of Ringmer were not exceptions: they were the rule. However, as time passed greater numbers of rural people acquired the means to change their lot with the hope of improving it. Gradual betterment of living and working conditions, better diets, shorter working hours and acquisition of some savings by members of the rural working class were manifestations of social improvement in the final quarter of the nineteenth century, but rising rates of literacy, the penny post, and the opportunity of travelling by train and receiving goods carried by rail brought rational attitudes into the far backwoods (Perry, 1969). The countryside was less of a world apart than ever before.

## Migration in Victorian England

By the 1840s almost every registration district in England and Wales, including the most unhealthy towns investigated by Chadwick in his report on sanitary conditions, was gaining population by natural increase. However, in each decade only a minority of districts showed net gains from migration, and even fewer districts gained in every decade during the century: most places recorded net losses from migration, in a few cases sufficiently great to cancel out the gains by natural increase and produce an overall population loss. The regions to gain by migration included the industrial and coalfield areas of Lancashire and Yorkshire, the North-East, South Wales and London and the Home Counties, but within these areas there were wide variations from one decade to the next, reflecting cycles of immigration, especially from Ireland, and emigration, as migrants from rural areas opted for America in preference to English industrial cities during periods of economic stagnation at home. The relative timing of prosperity and depression within each industrial sector was equally important. Thus Lancashire attracted large numbers of migrants as the cotton industry boomed early in the century. Later, the lead passed to the Yorkshire woollen and worsted industries, and later still to coalfield towns in South Yorkshire, the North-East and South Wales. In general, however, colliery districts owed more of their growth to natural increase than migration (Fig. 4.3). As a result their populations were less heterogeneous and as they also engaged in a narrower range of occupations than elsewhere they were less likely to conform to Wirth's model. Even where migration was important natural increase must not be discounted. Since most migrants were young adults they swelled the proportion of the population of child-bearing age and so stimulated natural increase in the next generation (Lawton, 1978).

Following research by Saville (1957), Lawton (1968) has provided a generalized account of rural—urban migration in nineteenth-century England in terms of 'push' and 'pull' factors. 'Pushes' included the decline in agricultural employment, especially farm labourers (with the total agricultural population falling from 1,900,000 in 1861 to 988,000 in 1901), the loss of domestic and craft industries to urban factories and the increasing accessibility of big towns, primarily as a result of railway construction from the 1840s onwards. 'Pulls' included the higher wages and more varied job opportunities available in towns. However, Cairncross (1949) was emphatic that the prime cause of rural depopulation was the development of railways, both as a source of employment in their construction and operation, and as a means of access to industrial centres. He noted that the peaks in rural—urban migration occurred during decades when farming was at its *most prosperous.* Moreover, the principal sources of migrants to industrial cities were adjacent counties, where agriculture was at its most profitable and labour intensive, for example in areas of market gardening and intensive

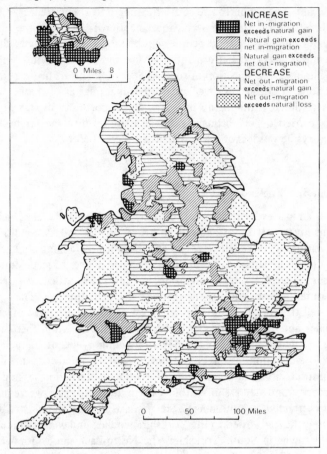

FIG. 4.3. *Population trends in England and Wales, 1851–1911 (after Lawton, in Dodgshon and Butlin, 1978).*

dairying around London. Peripheral parts of the country, where agriculture was more depressed, despatched emigrants to the United States, for example from Devon and Cornwall through Plymouth, rather than migrants to British cities. It was the perception of relative prosperity and the accessibility of urban opportunities that mattered more than any real differences between town and country. Home Counties labourers could see and hear about, at times inaccurately, the opportunities on offer in the metropolis. Agricultural labourers in remote counties received less information, accurate or inaccurate, about conditions elsewhere. Rural–urban migration reflected a wider range of social and economic processes than push/pull explanations would suggest. Millions of individual decision-makers were involved as they received, evaluated and acted on information and compared their home community with the imperfectly-known attractions of city life.

The characteristics of Victorian migration were well summarized by a contemporary statistician, E. G. Ravenstein (1885), who propounded seven laws of migration. Ravenstein observed that most migrants moved only short distances – to their nearest urban centre; that migrants from peri-urban areas were replaced by immigrants from further afield; that long-distance migrants generally went by preference to the largest cities; that every main migratory current had a counter-current, albeit much smaller in volume; that females were more migratory than males within Britain, while males more frequently moved abroad; that most migrants were young single adults rather than families; and that the process of dispersion was the inverse of absorption but exhibited similar features (Grigg, 1977).

Some of these laws may be illustrated by reference to recent research. Anderson (1971) found that less than half the population of Preston in 1851 had been born in the town. Of the 52 per cent born outside, seven in every ten came from less than 30 miles away, one in seven had been born in Ireland, and so less than one in six had been born in Great Britain, but more than a day's tramp from Preston. Small towns attracted fewer long-distance migrants than large cities; only 10 per cent of the residents of Huddersfield in 1871 had been born outside their county of residence (Yorkshire) whereas 17 per cent of the population of the neighbouring but much larger town of Leeds originated outside Yorkshire. Long-distance migrants usually took up higher status jobs at their destination than short-distance migrants: in Liverpool, Welsh migrants were employed as skilled artisans (often sufficiently well-off to afford a servant to help in the house) while those from townships adjoining the city were more likely to be unskilled labourers. Skilled coachbuilders at the Saltley Coachworks in Birmingham were attracted from a wide area; skilled ironworkers at Coatbridge, near Glasgow, were recruited from Staffordshire (Ashworth, 1954; Lawton, 1978; Pooley, 1977). The major exceptions to this rule were Irish immigrants, who arrived in force in all the principal industrial towns of Great Britain from the 1820s onwards, but especially in the 1840s (Fig. 4.4). The Irish invariably took low-status jobs as building labourers, navvies and porters, or were self-employed as hawkers, dealers and costermongers. They occupied much the same role in nineteenth-century society that New Commonwealth immigrants have fulfilled in more recent times.

Given that most migrants travelled only short distances, they were unlikely to form a very mixed bunch with respect to their beliefs, values and previous experience. They may have acquired some familiarity with their destination from having visited it when it functioned as market rather than place of manufacture. For example, textile manufacturing towns in Yorkshire had long functioned as markets for the distribution of raw materials and sale of finished cloth from the rural domestic textile industry, as evidenced by their eighteenth-century inns and cloth halls. Migrants may have suffered the effects of urban size and density, but the more obviously disruptive effect of heterogeneity was important only in relationships with Irish, who were also often Catholic, and Jews, and in the case of some special groups of long-distance migrants, whose distinctiveness was often exaggerated by their residential segregation: in Merthyr Tydfil immigrant workmen "lived together clannishly, the Pembrokeshire men in one quarter, the Carmarthenshire men in another" (Ashworth, 1954, p. 29). The phenomenon of stepped migration meant that low-status migrants who had been born far from their ultimate destination usually arrived in large cities with previous experience of urban life in smaller towns. Only a minority moved direct from remote rural areas to unfamiliar big cities.

All this evidence casts doubt on the validity of Wirthian sociology in a British context, even in the nineteenth century. But our doubts must not be exaggerated: Victorian writers referred to their time as 'the age of great cities'. They were increasingly conscious of segregation within their cities, the irreligion of the urban proletariat, the problems associated with overcrowding, and the difficulties of integrating Irish, Jewish and host populations (Coleman, 1973). The Victorian age saw the proliferation of special-interest and sectarian

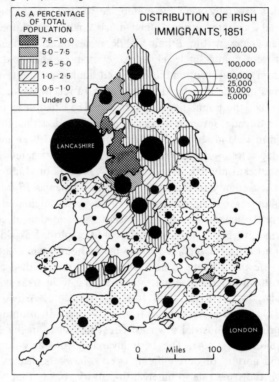

FIG. 4.4. *Distribution of Irish immigrants in England and Wales, 1851 (after Darby, 1973).*

groups, and the development of class consciousness as workers and employers confronted one another as interest groups rather than as known individuals.

### Industrialization

Whereas Wirth's theory focuses on the effects of urbanization, Shevky and Bell's social area theory and McElrath's concept of modernization emphasize urbanization and industrialization equally. We are accustomed to think of the two processes together: for example, some underdeveloped countries with relatively high proportions of their populations living in cities but few people engaged in manufacturing industry have sometimes been criticized as 'over-urbanized'. Yet the origins of the Industrial Revolution were frequently in rural areas, as at Abraham Darby's ironworks at Coalbrookdale on the Severn or Arkwright's mills at Cromford in Derbyshire. Many industrialists feared that if the labouring classes lived together in large towns they would unite in working-class revolution as 'respectable' skilled workers were corrupted by the influence of the 'undeserving poor'. The identification of an 'undeserving poor' was reflected in Mayhew's division of the London poor into 'those who will not work' and 'those who cannot work'.

In fact the pauper classes were usually apolitical. They had enough to do finding a bed for the night and food for the day without bothering about radical politics. Most working-class radicals were self-educated, skilled workers, often men who had gained experience of leadership as Methodist 'class-leaders' or lay preachers. One way of preventing working-class combination was by legislation, as in the Combination Laws of 1799 which outlawed trade unions until 1825. Other approaches had more obvious geographical consequences: many writers campaigned for the extension of the parochial system to urban areas and in 1821 Thomas Chalmers advocated his 'principle of locality' as a means of ensuring that every working-class district contained a leavening of clergy, doctors and teachers. Later in the century the settlement movement had a similar objective: young gentlemen — often Oxbridge graduates — would live in settlement houses in working-class areas where they could set an example of morality and respectability for the poor to follow. Young ladies were not exempt from such schemes. They found employment as charity visitors or as rent collectors in early 'self-help' housing organizations, such as that organized by Octavia Hill in London in the 1870s, in which they both collected the rent and kept a watchful eye on the maintenance and cleanliness of dwellings, proffering advice to working-class wives and mothers on the fundamentals of household economics.

Nevertheless, in the early years of the Industrial Revolution the most satisfactory way to maintain surveillance of the labouring classes and prevent their undesirable combination was to isolate them in small groups in separate industrial villages where their employer was free to impose his own conditions of work, housing, education and religious observance. Pollard (1964) has noted Richard Arkwright's reflection that "in a large town he could not have the control over his workers which he had in Cromford" and also Lee's observation that "those who live in manufacturing towns are in some degree commanded by the customs of the population" (pp. 526–7). However, industrial villages were rarely exclusive in the sense that all their inhabitants worked for the same employer. For example, in the Lancashire mill community of Low Moor, a mile to the west of Clitheroe, the population in 1851 totalled 1,272, of whom 627 were employed in textile occupations, presumably at Low Moor Mill, but 136 — mostly males — worked in occupations unconnected with the mill. Since the total number employed at the mill was 842, at least a quarter of the workforce — mostly female — must have travelled in daily from outside the community (Ashmore, 1963).

Most industrialists desired isolation for the sake of expediency but a few were imbued with more humanitarian, philanthropic or idealist consciences, and for them too the best way of establishing their heaven on earth was to get as far as they could from the rest of the earth. Robert Owen ran the factory village of New Lanark following the principles laid down in his *New View of Society* published in 1813, while in the 1850s Titus Salt moved his alpaca mills from Bradford to Saltaire where he established a model community complete with school, sanatorium, various denominations of religious building and a public park (Fig. 4.5). Other utopian schemes never got beyond the drawing board: J. S. Buckingham's plan for 'New Victoria' (1849) may be regarded as a forerunner of the garden cities of the early twentieth century and the new towns established since the Second World War.

An obvious environmental reason for the rural location of many factories was their dependence on water power. The best sites were often in remote locations, for example high up in the Pennine valleys. Only after about 1820 did steam become more important than water as a source of power for cotton spinning, stimulating a shift of industry to coalfield locations. As late as 1850, water provided 23 per cent of horsepower in woollen mills and 11 per cent in worsted mills in the West Riding. As for weaving, power looms had been developed after 1785 but were widely used in the worsted industry only after the 1830s and in the woollen industry after 1850. Handloom weaving was carried out by groups

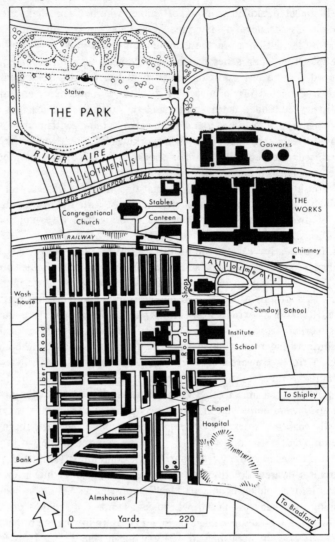

FIG. 4.5. *Titus Salt's model town of Saltaire, founded in 1851 (after Stewart, 1952).*

of families living in small hamlets and dependent on an adjacent spinning mill or a master clothier for supplies of yarn.

In all these situations industry was limited in scale. Primary relationships were as frequent as in agricultural villages of similar size and, in domestic industry as in agriculture, the family continued as the unit of production. Marriages continued to be contracted locally and jobs were handed down from father to son.

Working contrary to the forces for rural industrialization were the advantages to be gained from agglomeration. For an employer unconcerned for the morals or politics of his workforce, it was clearly cheaper to locate in cities where there was no need to provide housing, schooling or religion. Housing could be left to speculative builders, education to

National or British schools, religion to the provisions of the Ecclesiastical Commissioners or nonconformist missionary zeal. Dependence on coal necessitated the concentration of industry in locations accessible to railways, which also provided an efficient means of distributing finished goods. Location near to other industries permitted the benefits expounded by urban economists: easier exchange of information and ideas, and of product where separate firms were responsible for different stages in its manufacture, expansion of demand through multiplier effects, and the provision of a financial infrastructure to support future investment.

Pollard (1964) noted that "few works outside the factory villages had large housing programmes" (p. 518). Housing might be provided for a few key workers, but of 881 large firms who made returns to the Factory Commissioners in 1833, 299 gave no details, 414 made no housing provision and 168 provided some houses, in most cases only a few. However, the lack of cheap public transport, coupled with the long hours of work, meant that most workers lived close to their place of employment despite the failure of their employers to provide any housing themselves. Often the better-paid workers, clerical staff, managers and even the owner lived in the same area as the unskilled workers. In Huddersfield in 1851, most workers at Edward Fisher's Silk Mills lived within half a mile of their workplace. In several cases more than one member of a family was employed at the mills, and Edward Fisher himself lived in a villa adjacent to the factory. On the edges of several Lancashire towns, 'industrial colonies' grew up around particular cotton mills: Freetown on the outskirts of Bury, Brookhouse on the fringe of Blackburn (Marshall, 1968) (Fig. 4.6). In her novel *North and South* (1855), Mrs. Gaskell described a Lancashire millowner, Mr. Thornton, living in a house adjoining his mill. The heroine of the book, Margaret, fresh from rural life in the south of England "wondered why people who could afford to live in so good a house, and keep it in such perfect order, did not prefer a much smaller dwelling in the country, or even some suburb; not in the continual whirl and din of the factory" (Volume I, Chapter 15).

The situation in the early nineteenth century has been summarized by Vance (1966) as "an industrial landscape of small cellular units with short and modest daily journeys by workmen but a constant almost vascular flow of the product to and from other cells" (p. 307). Cities grew by 'cellular reproduction': *not* by a wave-like expansion of the urban fringe in all directions, but by the addition of new factories on greenfield sites, each of which was soon surrounded by the housing necessary to accommodate its labour force, or by the absorption of previously free-standing factory villages into the urban area. It is evident, therefore, that even where industrialization went hand in hand with urbanization the scale of community life was little different from that experienced in more remote factory villages. This form of urbanization generated few situations of large size or heterogeneity, as encountered by individual inhabitants. Urbanites lived in communities or 'urban villages' *within* the city and these units, and not the city as a whole, were their frames of reference. If a working-class family moved beyond its home neighbourhood it was as likely to leave the city altogether as to move to another neighbourhood in the same city.

Yet, despite these forces for social stability, forces for change were also at work. Pahl (1970) has attributed "the crystallization of a class society" to the process of industrial urbanism in the nineteenth century, and Thompson (1968) has discussed *The Making of the English Working Class* in the late eighteenth and early nineteenth centuries. In the Lancashire cotton industry in particular, industrialization soon achieved a scale at which relationships between worker and management became impersonal; second-generation millowners *did*

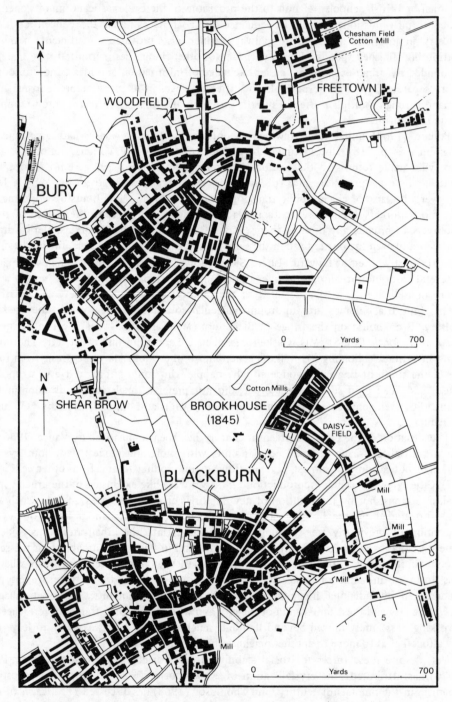

FIG. 4.6. *Industrial colonies in Lancashire: Freetown, Bury and Brookhouse, Blackburn in 1845 (after Marshall, in Dyos, 1968).*

follow Margaret Hale's expectations and move out to country villas or exclusive middle-class suburbs; the family became a less significant source of social interaction than the factory. We argued earlier that industrialization was associated with specialization, the breakdown of the family as the unit of work and the employment of women outside the home. Under the factory system different operations on the same product, which had previously been carried out by different members of the same household under the same roof, were separated in space. It became possible to distinguish between the residence—workplace link of the household head (in Vance's terminology, the 'determinative tie') and that of other members of his family ('contingent ties'). The father's position as sole breadwinner for his family was undermined, the separation of parents and children during long hours of work loosened bonds of kinship and reduced the control that parents could exercise over their offspring. It was argued that unmarried factory girls could not develop housewifely skills and worked in situations that devalued chastity and the sanctity of family life. On the other hand, the factory system offered opportunities for educational and social improvement, through attendance at mechanics' institutes or evening classes and mutual improvement associations attached to factories. The worker's potential range of social contacts was enlarged and there was the prospect of upward social mobility to an improved standard of living as a consequence of conformity, education and hard work: the Victorian ethic of self-help.

Laslett (1965) has described pre-industrial England as a 'one-class society'. He observes that if by 'class' we mean 'social status' pre-industrial society was a multi-class society, but a more useful definition of 'class' relates to wealth and power, access to the means of production and a mutual consciousness of sharing the same access and the same power. On this basis, only the 5 per cent of the population of pre-industrial England who were nobility or gentry, who owned wealth and made decisions that affected others, constituted a class. In similar vein, Thompson (1968) has written: "Class is a social and cultural formation which cannot be defined abstractedly, or in isolation, but only in terms of relationship with other classes. . . . When we speak of *a* class we are thinking of a very loosely defined body of people who share the same congeries of interest, social experiences, traditions and value system, who have a *disposition* to *behave* as a class . . . class itself is not a thing, it is a happening" (quoted in Thompson, 1968, p. 939). Following this definition, the late eighteenth and early nineteenth centuries witnessed the emergence of a class structure in England. For example, Foster (1968) has contrasted a number of early industrial towns in terms of the consciousness of their working class as reflected in social and political behaviour. Foster analyzed patterns of marriage on the assumption that marriages are contracted between individuals from families that they perceive to be from the same class, and patterns of residence on the assumption that most people live next door to others whom they perceive as belonging to the same class. He found that in Northampton in the 1840s occupational status was the basis for interaction: shoemakers' sons married shoemakers' daughters more often than the daughters of other labourers or tradesmen. This was a pattern of interaction typical of Sjoberg's pre-industrial or Vance's pre-capitalist city in which the gild was an important unit of social and economic organization. But in Oldham, Foster found a broader working-class consciousness reflected in patterns of marriage, in which the offspring of skilled craftsmen frequently married into the families of unskilled workers. This class structure was confirmed by the success of radical candidates in elections, the working-class dominance of local government and a tradition of industrial unrest dating from the years of suppression of trade unions under the Combination Laws.

The consequence of this broad class consciousness was a low degree of residential segregation of skilled artisans and unskilled labourers. However, an alternative explanation of this pattern is in terms of the lack of public transport and the small-scale provision of working-class housing. A standard form of development was the court, infilling between terraced housing fronting the main streets (Fig. 4.7). The front houses let at relatively high rents to skilled workers, the houses inside the courts, which were often airless and insanitary, let at lower rents to poorer families, while beneath the houses cellar dwellings were occupied by the poorest members of society.

It is not yet clear how typical Oldham was of early industrial society, and even in Oldham the dominance of the working class was short-lived. Tradesmen and millowners regained political control from mid-century onwards, and the labouring classes became more conscious of minor variations in status, skill and income. The 'working class' fragmented into a hierarchy of status groups, the result predicted by social area theory. Whether or not this status hierarchy was paralleled by the development of a more complex pattern of residential segregation depended on the practicability of segregation as well as the preference for it, a question to which we shall return in the next chapter.

There is a further consequence of this debate on the definition of 'class' that social geographers have too often ignored. If 'class', defined in terms of relationships rather than simply occupation or income, changes its meaning through time, we should not use the same sets of social indicators to map the human geography of different periods. A map of areas defined by the socio-economic status of their inhabitants may be an appropriate way of depicting the social geography of a Western city in the late twentieth century, but it may be quite inappropriate as an indication of the social geography of pre-industrial or even nineteenth-century cities. We need to study the social geography of past periods, or of cultures

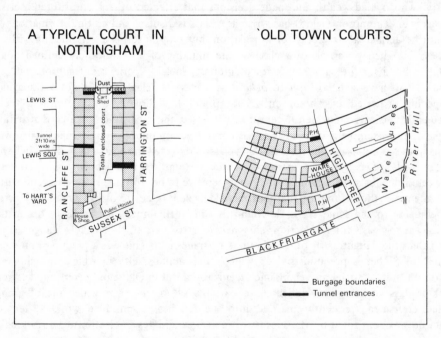

FIG. 4.7. *The layout of courts in Nottingham (1845) and Hull (1850) (after Hoskins, 1955; Forster, 1972).*

different from our own, in terms of the social organization that mattered to the inhabitants of those times or areas, rather than in terms of our contemporary social system.

In this chapter we have hypothesized that in England the nineteenth century exhibits closer parallels than the twentieth to Wirth's preconditions, but more detailed examination of patterns of population growth, migration and industrial expansion has suggested that the theories are not totally applicable ·even in nineteenth-century situations. As the following chapters will show, English cities may have exhibited the consequences predicted by North American sociologists and economists, but the explanation of those consequences often lies in features unique to English society.

## References and Further Reading

England immediately before the 'Industrial Revolution' is described by:
Hoskins, W. G. (1955) *The Making of the English Landscape,* Hodder & Stoughton, London.
Laslett, P. (1965) *The World We Have Lost,* Methuen, London.
Wrigley, E. A. (1967) A simple model of London's importance in changing English society and economy, 1650–1750, *Past and Present,* 37, 44–70.

Patterns of population change and migration are discussed in:
Cairncross, A. K. (1949) Internal migration in Victorian England, *Manchester School of Economic and Social Studies,* 17, 67–81.
Grigg, D. B. (1977) E. G. Ravenstein and the 'laws of migration', *Journal of Historical Geography,* 3, 41–54.
Lawton, R. (1968) Population changes in England and Wales in the later nineteenth century: an analysis of trends by registration districts, *Transactions Institute of British Geographers,* 44, 55–74.
Lawton, R. (1978) Population and society 1730–1900, in R. A. Dodgshon & R. A. Butlin (eds.), *An Historical Geography of England and Wales,* Academic Press, London, pp. 313–66.
Pooley, C. G. (1977) The residential segregation of migrant communities in mid-Victorian Liverpool, *Transactions Institute of British Geographers,* New Series, 2, 364–82.
Ravenstein, E. G. (1885) The laws of migration, *Journal of the Statistical Society,* 48, 167–227.
Redford, A. (1926) *Labour Migration in England, 1800–1850,* Manchester University Press, Manchester.
White, P. and Woods, R. (eds.) (1980) *The Geographical Impact of Migration,* Longman, London.

Studies of nineteenth-century urban growth include:
Ashworth, W. (1954) *The Genesis of Modern British Town Planning,* Routledge & Kegan Paul, London.
Carter, H. (1978) Towns and urban systems 1730–1900, in R. A. Dodgshon & R. A. Butlin (eds.), *op.cit.,* pp. 367–400.
Law, C. M. (1967) The growth of urban population in England and Wales 1801–1911, *Transactions Institute of British Geographers,* 41, 125–43.
Robson, B. T. (1973) *Urban Growth: An Approach,* Methuen, London.
Stewart, C. (1952) A Prospect of Cities, *Longman, London.*

while current trends in the growth of the English urban system are reviewed in:
Bourne, L. S. (1975) *Urban Systems,* Oxford University Press, Oxford.
Hall, P. *et al.* (1973) *The Containment of Urban England,* Allen & Unwin, London.

Aspects of rural life in Victorian Britain are examined in:
Ambrose, P. (1974) *The Quiet Revolution: social change in a Sussex Village 1871–1971,* Chatto & Windus, London.
Collins, E. J. T. (1976) Migrant labour in British agriculture in the nineteenth century, *Economic History Review,* 29, 38–59.
Hobsbawm, E. J. and Rudé, G. (1973) *Captain Swing,* Penguin, Harmondsworth.
Holderness, B. A. (1972) 'Open' and 'close' parishes in England in the eighteenth and nineteenth centuries, *Agricultural History Review,* 20, 126–39.
Mills, D. R. (ed.) (1973) *English Rural Communities,* Macmillan, London.
Mingay, G. E. (1979) *Rural Life in Victorian England,* Futura, London.

Orwin, C. S. and Whetham, E. H. (1971) *History of British Agriculture 1846–1914,* David & Charles, Newton Abbot.

Perry, P. J. (1969) Working-class isolation and mobility in rural Dorset, 1837–1936: a study of marriage distances, *Transactions Institute of British Geographers,* 46, 121–41.

Perry, P. J. (1973) *British Agriculture, 1875–1914,* Methuen, London.

Saville, J. (1957) *Rural Depopulation in England and Wales, 1851–1951,* Routledge & Kegan Paul, London.

Samuel, R. (ed.) (1975) *Village Life and Labour,* Routledge & Kegan Paul, London.

Williams, W. M. (1963) *A West Country Village, Ashworthy: family, kinship and land,* Routledge & Kegan Paul, London.

The impact of industrialization on social and spatial structure is considered by:

Anderson, M. (1971) *Family Structure in Nineteenth Century Lancashire,* Cambridge University Press, Cambridge.

Ashmore, O. (1963) Low Moor, Clitheroe: a nineteenth-century factory community, *Transactions of the Lancashire and Cheshire Antiquarian Society,* 73, 124–52.

Forster, C. A. (1972) *Court Housing in Kingston upon Hull,* Univ. of Hull Occasional Papers in Geography 19.

Foster, J. (1968) Nineteenth-century towns – a class dimension, in H. J. Dyos (ed.), *The Study of Urban History,* Arnold, London, pp. 281–99.

Marshall, J. D. (1968) Colonisation as a factor in the planting of towns in north-west England, in H. J. Dyos (ed.), *op.cit,* pp. 215–30.

Pahl, R. E. (1970) *Patterns of Urban Life,* Longmans, London.

Pollard, S. (1964) The factory village in the Industrial Revolution, *English Historical Review,* 79, 513–31.

Thompson, E. P. (1968) *The Making of the English Working Class,* Penguin, Harmondsworth.

Vance, J. E. (1966) Housing the worker: the employment linkage as a force in urban structure, *Economic Geography,* 42, 294–325.

Vance, J. E. (1967) Housing the worker: determinative and contingent ties in nineteenth-century Birmingham, *Economic Geography,* 43, 95–127.

A selection of contemporary views on the process of urbanization is included in:

Coleman, B. I. (ed.) (1973) *The Idea of the City in Nineteenth-Century Britain,* Routledge & Kegan Paul, London.

An interesting continental view of social change in England is provided by:

Bédarida, F. (1979) *A Social History of England 1851–1975,* Methuen, London.

Nineteenth-century society is placed in the wider context of historical geography in:

Darby, H. C. (ed.) (1973) *A New Historical Geography of England,* Cambridge University Press, Cambridge.

# 5

# Social Patterns in Nineteenth-Century Cities

### Contemporary Observations

"IT was a town of red brick, or of brick that would have been red if the smoke and ashes had allowed it; but, as matters stood it was a town of unnatural red and black like the painted face of a savage. It was a town of machinery and tall chimneys, out of which interminable serpents of smoke trailed themselves for ever and ever, and never got uncoiled. It had a black canal in it, and a river than ran purple with ill-smelling dye, and vast piles of building full of windows where there was a rattling and a trembling all day long, and where the piston of the steam-engine worked monotonously up and down, like the head of an elephant in a state of melancholy madness. It contained several large streets all very like one another, and many small streets still more like one another, inhabited by people equally like one another, who all went in and out at the same hours, with the same sound upon the same pavements, to do the same work, and to whom every day was the same as yesterday and tomorrow, and every year the counterpart of the last and the next" (Dickens, 1854, Chapter 5).

Dickens' description of 'Coketown', derived from his experience as a reporter in Preston in 1854, seems to confirm the arrival of a new way of life, industrial urbanism, by the middle of the nineteenth century. The city is impersonal and monotonous in its architecture and physical layout, and the implication is that city life is also monotonous and wearisome. Nothing changes, everything is the same day after day.

Elsewhere, for example in *Oliver Twist* (1839), Dickens portrayed the squalid and insanitary conditions typical of inner-city slums. Of Saffron Hill he wrote: "A dirtier or more wretched place [Oliver] had never seen. The street was very narrow and muddy, and the air was impregnated with filthy odours" (Chapter 8) while Jacob's Island in south-east London contained "tottering house-fronts projecting over the pavement, dismantled walls that seem to totter as [the visitor] passes, chimneys half crushed half hesitating to fall, windows guarded by rusty iron bars that time and dirt have almost eaten away, every imaginable sign of desolation and neglect" (Chapter 50). In a new preface written twenty-eight years after the first publication of *Oliver Twist*, Dickens was at pains to confirm the authenticity of his description.

This contrast between the new, but monotonous, and the old and squalid recurs in Engels' description of Manchester in 1844. At one extreme were families of poor Irish immigrants living in overcrowded and unhealthy cellar dwellings beside the river Irk, at the other, the "unmixed working-people's quarters, stretching like a girdle, averaging a mile and a half in breadth, around the commercial district" and beyond them, "the upper and middle bourgeoisie, the middle bourgeoisie in regularly laid out streets in the vicinity of the working

61

quarters . . . the upper bourgeoisie in remoter villas with gardens in Chorlton and Ardwick, or on the breezy heights of Cheetham Hill, Broughton and Pendleton, in free, wholesome country air, in fine comfortable houses, passed once every half or quarter hour by omnibuses going into the city" (Engels, 1969 edn., p. 79). In fact, Engels' account closely parallels the concentric zone model devised by Burgess in Chicago eighty years later. Burgess identified successive zones of land use in Western industrial cities: central business district, zone-in-transition (including slum housing for recent arrivals to the city), followed by zones of successively higher social status farther out from the centre (see Chapter 6).

It is frequently argued that the nineteenth century witnessed a transition from the form of pre-industrial city described by Sjoberg to the ecological city of Burgess. Burgess' model, like Sjoberg's, has been much criticized, and alternative models of residential segregation have been developed as outlined in the following chapter. For the moment, the important point is that almost all urban theorists agree that the modern city is characterized by residential segregation according to socio-economic, family or ethnic status (although the locations of different status groups may vary between cities), whereas these different status dimensions were interrelated in pre-industrial cities. This is the argument of social area theory that we considered earlier.

Of course, cities had been organized according to capitalist principles of land allocation long before the Industrial Revolution, and the gilds that were so influential in pre-industrial cities had long since declined into insignificance, but elements of the spatial structure proposed by Sjoberg and Vance still existed at the beginning of the nineteenth century. At least some of the elite — merchants, solicitors and surgeons, for example — continued to live in fashionable town-houses in the centres of cities, often combining their residence with their place of work. For most people segregation existed only at the scale of the individual dwelling; in fact, vertical segregation within each dwelling, whereby social status decreased as you ascended from the master's rooms on the first floor to the servants in the attic, or descended from the ground floor shop to the apprentices in the basement, was often more important than horizontal segregation between adjacent houses or streets. It was rare to observe whole districts of uniform social status, except for the segregation of the elite at one end of the spectrum, and immigrant groups — usually Irish or Jewish — at the other.

One reason for elite residence close to their places of work in the inner city was the lack of good communications. The same factor was responsible for the cellular structure of suburban areas. Not everybody worked where they lived, as most had done in the pre-industrial city, but it was still essential for everybody to live within easy walking distance of work, whether manager, clerk, foreman, operative or machine-minder. Hence the pattern of craft workshop quarters and factory villages described in Chapter 4.

In the course of the nineteenth century the old urban fabric was either cleared to make way for purpose-built shops, offices and philanthropic dwellings for the working classes, or modified to accommodate new uses, by conversion to commercial premises or subdivision into rented rooms for the urban poor. The new suburbs, built to house the massive increase in urban population, followed the pattern of Dickens' Coketown or Engels' Manchester.

Both Dickens and Engels were middle-class observers fitting their descriptions of the cities they visited to their preconceived models of society. In applying a model that depicts the Victorian city as 'transitional' between the 'pre-industrial' and the 'modern' there is a danger that we may be equally guilty of imposing a structure that was alien to the people who actually lived in Victorian cities. Thus, a contrary, although equally partisan view of Manchester in the 1840s was provided by Parkinson:

"In most places ... there is such a thing as neighbourhood, for the poor as well as the rich; that is there is an acquaintance with each other arising from having been born or brought up in the same street; having worked for the same master; attended the same place of worship; or even from having seen the same face, now grown 'old and familiar', though the name and even the occupation of the individual might be unknown altogether, passing one's door at wonted hours, from work to meal, from meal to work, with a punctuality which implied regular and steady habits, and was of itself a sufficient testimony of character" (Parkinson, 1841, cited in Anderson, 1968, p. 245). Parkinson was describing the same city that Engels perceived as "unmixed working people's quarters", and emphasized the same regular and predictable routines that Dickens described for Coketown. But whereas Dickens found them monotonous and boring, Parkinson associated them with security, familiarity and the continuity of community life despite the impersonality of the built environment. The moral is that we must consider not only the patterns of segregation that conform to our twentieth-century expectations, but also the community structure as reflected in the behaviour and social interaction of contemporary residents.

## Segregation in Victorian Cities

An initial problem in discussing Victorian cities lies in the diversity of the subject matter. Briggs (1968) warned that "the first effect of early industrialization was to differentiate English communities rather than to standardize them" (p. 33) and Harrison (1971) has noted that:

"One of the more unfortunate impressions left by an older generation of historians and sociologists is that all large towns in the nineteenth century were more or less the same — that is, equally smoky, soulless and horrible to live in. ... Too often our impressions of urban growth have been derived from an over-concentration on the northern textile towns, though even among them their problems were by no means identical" (pp. 15–16).

Another problem concerns the scale at which cities are studied. For the four censuses from 1841 to 1871 detailed information is available from the original census enumerators' books — transcriptions made by the census officials of the schedules completed by or on behalf of individual households. The enumerators' books include data on occupation, birthplace, age, sex, marital status and household structure. Had the information on the addresses of households always been recorded, it would have been possible to plot the exact location of every dwelling and its occupants and measure the extent of segregation at any desired scale. Unfortunately enumerators rarely recorded street numbers, so that it is often impossible to locate households *within* streets. Thus Warnes (1973) in his study of the "emerging industrial town" of Chorley, Lancashire, classified his data by streets, "the smallest possible units which could be precisely located", while researchers working on larger cities have frequently used sample data accumulated at the scale of enumeration districts (an enumeration district usually contained about 200 households). Given that a principal form of housing in the early Victorian period was the enclosed court (Fig. 4.7), with different qualities of housing in close proximity, it is scarcely surprising that few areas as large as entire enumeration districts were internally homogeneous with respect to economic or family status. All 'working-class' districts were likely to contain a range of inhabitants from skilled artisans to casual labourers.

At the time of writing the 1871 census is the most recent for which the enumerators' books are available, as more recent censuses are protected by a 100-year confidentiality rule. Until subsequent censuses are released for inspection we will know more about the mid-nineteenth century than about more recent periods, for which a much more haphazard collection of data is available. Entries in ratebooks indicate the rateable value of each property and may show whether it was tenanted or owner-occupied, entries in the 'court' section of local directories may be used to illustrate the distribution of 'principal inhabitants' (i.e. the better-off) or of particular middle-class occupational groups (e.g. doctors, solicitors), and entries in electoral rolls show the distribution of electors — again an indication of status and property rights prior to the 1884 Reform Act. But the information that these and other occasional sources yield is poor by comparison with the wealth of material in the census books for the earlier period.

Nevertheless, the information that *is* available indicates a modernization of the spatial structure of Victorian cities, in line with the predictions of social area theory. It also appears that, at any particular date, the larger the city the more 'modern' its structure, where modernity is denoted by the separation of socio-economic and family status dimensions in factor analyses of census data, and by the development of segregation *within* the labouring classes, for example the segregation of skilled from unskilled workers.

Even in quite small places the extremes of society were segregated. The rich lived in central squares and terraces, often above the offices where they practised as surveyors, solicitors or accountants or, increasingly, in suburban villas, usually on rising ground upwind of industrial areas. These villas were often situated on estates developed by cautious land-owners who offered 99-year building leases, hedged about with restrictive covenants to ensure that only expensive houses were built and non-residential land uses were excluded. In contrast the poorest families lived in low-lying areas with poor drainage and non-existent sanitation. Sometimes they occupied houses that had been the homes of middle-class families before their exodus to the suburbs, and which were then subdivided to accommodate several poor families. More often they lived in houses that had been slums ever since they were built: houses built back-to-back with no through ventilation, or houses built in enclosed courts or yards approached from narrow entrances between or under the properties that lined the main street. Such courts were dark and airless, with a single privy and water tap shared between all the inhabitants of each court. Over 25 per cent of the population of Liverpool lived in courts in 1841, at an average of 5.13 persons per two-roomed house. Another 9 per cent lived in one-roomed cellar dwellings, at a density of 3.29 persons per dwelling. Cellars averaged 10—12 feet square, lacked ventilation, were constantly damp — especially if they lacked a stone floor — and were filled with polluted air. Privies were cleansed infrequently, and emptied only when there was a profit to be made from the sale of 'night-soil' as manure. In 1844 only 56 out of 243 working-class streets in Liverpool had any drains or sewers and courts were never visited by the municipal scavengers. Water might be available only on alternate days, and then only for 1—2½ hours (Chapman, 1971; Sutcliffe, 1974).

One area of 10 acres in central Liverpool included 7,938 persons, a density of more than 500,000 per square mile. In Nottingham, in 1832, 883 houses containing 4,283 inhabitants were packed on to 9 acres and it was estimated that of 11,000 houses in the city, 7—8,000 were back-to-back, often in courts that were closed at both ends and entered by tunnels 3 feet wide, 8 feet high and 25—30 feet long. So hidden away were these courts behind the facades of the main streets that it must have been true of Liverpool and Nottingham, as Engels (1969 edn.) wrote of Manchester, that:

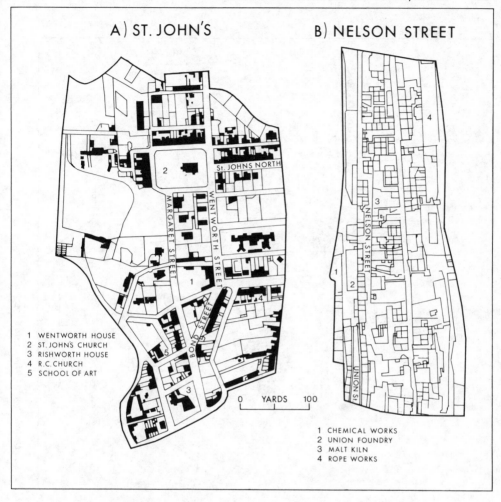

FIG. 5.1. *Social (class) areas in Wakefield, 1893 (after Cowlard, 1979).*

"A person may live in it for years, and go in and out daily without coming into contact with a working people's quarter" (p. 79).

In Wakefield, the Nelson Street area, occupied by the Irish and the unskilled, was a warren of narrow passages lined by shared dwellings, small workshops and obnoxious industries. It lay close to the centre of the town, but hidden behind the main streets so that there was no through traffic and passers-by on the major thoroughfares need never visit it or even know of its existence. By contrast, St. John's was the home of Wakefield's elite, a suburb created by the imposition of restrictive covenants which guaranteed high-quality development, centred on a new Anglican church and supplied with such desirable amenities as private schools and botanical gardens (Fig. 5.1). Many of the town's councillors lived in St. John's and used their influence to ensure that the area retained its character. For example, they refused permission for industrial development in the vicinity of St. John's but permitted it in Nelson Street. The town gas works, supplying light and heat to the

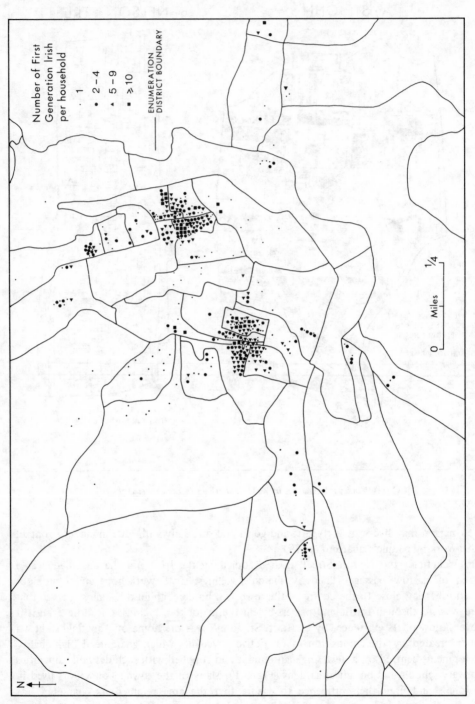

FIG. 5.2. *Distribution of Irish in Huddersfield, 1851.*

residents of St. John's, was located adjacent to Nelson Street, whose residents suffered its pollution but were too poor to make use of its gas (Cowlard, 1979).

Despite the increasing suburbanization of the middle classes some wealthy families continued to live in the traditional pre-industrial location of the elite, the city centre. In Huddersfield they occupied a central core of town-houses separating the two major concentrations of poor Irish households. Most of the Huddersfield Irish lived in two main groups of courts immediately east and west of the town centre, but there were also isolated courts, some distance from the centre, that were almost entirely Irish, for example Kirkmoor Place, mentioned in the enquiry to the town's 1848 improvement bill as one of the least desirable parts of the town (Fig. 5.2).

The same pattern was apparent in the Welsh iron-making centre of Merthyr Tydfil. A central enumeration district with high proportions of professional people and dealers was sandwiched between two poor areas where labourers formed the dominant occupational group (Fig. 5.3). The prosperous central district attracted long-distance migrants from England and Wales, while the poorer areas accommodated large numbers of Irish immigrants. Ironworks and mines, distributed through the outlying districts of the town, employed the majority of locally-born men, who lived near their places of work in a series of industrial villages (Carter and Wheatley, 1978). Indeed, the history of the growth of Merthyr is really the story of the fusion of these separate centres into one large industrial town. The occurrence of such patterns makes it difficult to reach any firm conclusion about the spatial structure of small Victorian cities. There were incipient elements of the zonal and sectoral patterns that were to become dominant in the early twentieth century, but there were also cellular structures, each cell containing a mixture of land uses and status groups.

Certainly, the great majority of the labouring classes, neither so poor to be confined to cellars or the worst courts, nor so rich to afford the rent of an elegant town-house or suburban villa, displayed no obvious pattern of segregation. Engels (1969 edn.) referred to Lancashire industrial towns as "almost wholly working-people's districts, interspersed only with factories, a few thoroughfares lined with shops, and a few lanes along which the gardens and houses of the manufacturers are scattered like villas" (p. 76). In Chorley, near Preston, marked variations in status or family structure were "extremely local — at the scale of the street or part of a street, and there was in 1851 little sign of distinctive status, demographic or immigrant areas having been created" (Warnes, 1973, p. 182).

It has been argued that segregation had been carried farthest in the largest cities. From evidence on the zoning policy employed on Lord Calthorpe's estate in Edgbaston, Birmingham, where the largest elite residences were sited at the centre of the estate and streets of lower middle-class housing were confined to the periphery, Cannadine (1977) has suggested that segregation in British cities developed earlier than in North America. However, Edgbaston was only a small part of Birmingham and interesting as this example of segregation within the middle classes is, it still does not confirm the existence of residential differentiation among the labouring classes. Nor, apart from his remarks on the Irish, which relate to ethnic rather than purely socio-economic segregation, does Engels' account of Manchester. Instead his emphasis is on the undifferentiated nature of working-class areas, although this may merely reflect his ideology, in which the only social division that mattered was between those with command over the means of production and those without.

In Liverpool too, the principal dichotomy as late as 1871 was between high-status, servant-keeping areas and central decayed, overcrowded areas, occupied by the Irish and avoided by migrants from England. However, differences were also identified between the

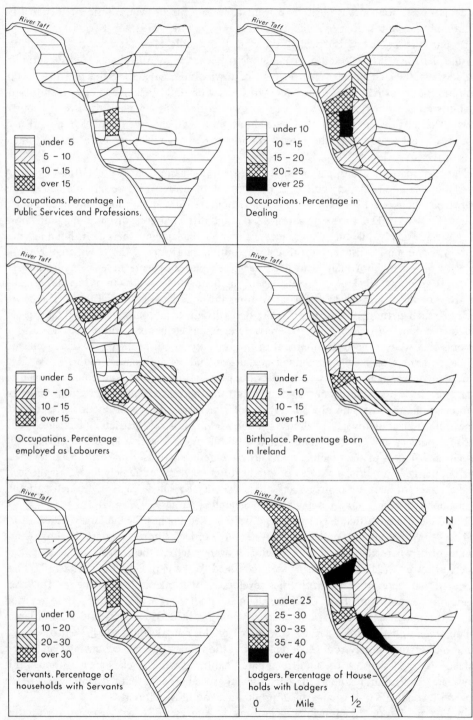

FIG. 5.3. *Distribution of selected occupational and social groups in central Merthyr, 1851 (after Carter and Wheatley, 1978).*

unskilled, but non-Irish, and the skilled working classes, while within the latter group migrants from Scotland and Wales occupied distinct areas. Lawton and Pooley (1975) attributed this pattern to the operations of the housing market which in turn depended on patterns of land ownership and estate development, local topography and the location of industry and lines of communication. So they were not surprised that clearly defined zonal or sectoral social areas did not exist. Nevertheless, the identification of separate dimensions of socio-economic and family status led them to conclude that "there would thus appear little reason to consider the large city of the mid-Victorian period as anything other than essentially modern as regards industrial and social structure. The basic aggregate dimensions of social stratification, variations in family structure, housing and ethnicity — shown to exist. in almost all modern towns — had emerged and can be measured" (Lawton and Pooley, 1975, p. 37).

In contrast, Ward (1975) concluded that exclusively residential suburbs for the lower middle class and securely employed working class seldom developed before the last quarter of the nineteenth century. He suggested that, apart from districts accommodating the extremes of wealth and poverty, "most new sections of early and mid nineteenth-century industrial cities housed people of diverse occupations which recorded limited but significant differences in remuneration and status" (p. 145).

However slow Victorian cities were to adopt a modern spatial structure, their social ecology was changing in the direction predicted by social area theory. For example, Pritchard (1976) has concluded that until about 1820 the structure of Leicester was 'pre-industrial'. From 1820 until 1865 he designates the city as 'early industrial' and from 1865 until the First World War as 'ecological', conforming to the classical models devised by Burgess and his associates. With the rapid growth of population during the early-industrial period, social segregation developed quickly but "it was still unsophisticated.... The city was extra-ordinarily fluid but formless and chaotic" (p. 187). Only in the latter decades of the century did the introduction of public transport, the free-market provision of housing and the 'maturing industrial economy' yield concentric and sectoral patterns typical of twentieth-century cities.

## Migrant Populations

The most conspicuous segregated groups in Victorian cities were the members of religious or ethnic minorities. In Liverpool in 1851, 22.3 per cent of the population had been born in Ireland and another 9.1 per cent in Scotland or Wales. In Bradford the Irish-born comprised over 8 per cent of the population in 1851, almost all concentrated in areas of poor sanitation, overcrowding, multiple occupancy and high rates of poverty and disease (Richardson, 1968). Similar concentrations were found in almost every industrial or commercial city. After 1851 the proportion (but not necessarily the absolute number) of Irish-born declined — to 9.1 per cent in Liverpool and 2.5 per cent in Bradford by 1891. But a decline in numbers of Irish-born inhabitants did not signify a decline in the 'Irishness' of the area since it ignored the children born in England to Irish parents, and brought up within the dominant culture of an Irish, usually Catholic, community.

The majority of Irish immigrants took unskilled, poorly paid jobs often with no security of employment. Table 5.1 illustrates their predominance in labouring and street-selling.

The implication is that the residential segregation of the Irish can be explained in socio-

TABLE 5.1. *Proportion of Irish-born*
*in specified occupations, 1851*
*(after Richardson, 1968;*
*Lawton, 1959)*

| Bradford | |
|---|---|
| % total population born in Ireland | 8 |
| % railway labourers born in Ireland | 43 |
| % other labourers born in Ireland | 62 |
| % hawkers & pedlars born in Ireland | 81 |
| *Liverpool (sample area)* | |
| % total population born in Ireland | 26 |
| % unskilled workers born in Ireland | 38 |
| % all labourers born in Ireland | 65 |
| % dock labourers born in Ireland | 77 |

economic terms. Poor pay and irregular employment necessitated residence in cheap housing located close to employers of unskilled labour. From the 1840s onwards legislation to improve the quality of working-class housing created a shortage of new low-rent dwellings and actually exacerbated the overcrowding and multiple occupancy of houses designed as single-family dwellings. Irish immigrants were concentrated in this type of housing: average household size in Bradford in 1851 was 5.5, but Irish households contained an average of 7.96 persons and approximately one-third of Irish were lodgers, often in the houses of other Irish.

There was little change in the degree of segregation of the Irish as the century progressed: the larger the number of migrants the more segregated they became. Thus, in Oldham in 1841, 37 Irish families had Irish neighbours but 152 did not. By 1861, 576 Irish families lived next door to other Irish and only 372 had English neighbours (Foster, 1974). Nor was there any appreciable improvement in the status of first-generation immigrants. Sufficiently modern figures are not yet available for England and Wales because of the 100-year confidentiality rule, but in Scotland the enumerators' books may be examined after only 70 years, and for one town, Greenock, comparable in its Irish population with many towns in north-west England, Lobban (1971) has calculated that in 1891, 29 per cent of the total population and 62 per cent of the Irish-born population were labourers, unskilled workers or shop assistants. These figures show almost no change from the situation in 1851, when 27 per cent of the total population and 61 per cent of the Irish were so employed.

The children of Irish immigrants had few opportunities for upward social mobility. Upward mobility by marriage into a higher status group was especially rare for Catholic Irish who generally married other Catholic Irish. However, in Liverpool, the port of entry and final destination of many migrants, it was possible to identify a group of skilled working-class Irish, possibly of pre-Famine origin, who by 1871 had taken advantage of their superior financial status to move into outer suburbs such as Everton (Pooley, 1977).

If the segregation of the Irish was entirely due to their limited rent-paying ability we should expect to find little segregation between them and the minority of English or Scottish-born unskilled workers. In fact the two groups were clearly separate in most cities, indicating that we must consider other factors to account fully for the segregation of the Irish. Certainly the indigenous population showed some hostility towards the newcomers and the parallels with current extremist attitudes towards coloured immigrants are striking. The Irish were regarded as carriers of disease: in Huddersfield typhus was popularly termed 'Irish fever'.

Some Irish, like many Asians today, were distrusted for their inability to speak English and their adherence to a different form of religious belief. It was also argued that cheap Irish labour was used in strike-breaking and that its constant availability depressed working-class wages. In the same way that West Indian landlords today accommodate fellow West Indians as tenants or lodgers, so most Irish landlords housed Irish lodgers, and few Irish lodgers had non-Irish landlords. This pattern was partly the result of discrimination but it also reflected the flow of information in Victorian society and the supportive nature of the Irish community. New arrivals naturally drifted to areas of established immigrant residence where they could expect a friendly welcome, a bed and advice on job opportunities. Prospective migrants depended for information on letters or visits from friends and relatives who had already set up home in England. Similar channels of information produced segregated communities among migrants moving much shorter distances than the Irish. For example, the majority of migrants from Kendal, a declining area of handloom weaving, to Huddersfield, a flourishing modern centre of the textile industry, took up residence in the same two suburbs in the south-east of the town. In Preston, too, clusters of families from the same Lancashire villages could be identified living in the same streets (Anderson, 1971).

The same pattern existed in late Victorian Jewish communities. The Jews, of course, had even more powerful cultural reasons for seeking segregation than the Irish. They demanded a home close to their synagogue, depended on specialist food shops and worked mainly in small workshops, particularly in the clothing industry. In the Leylands area of Leeds, 80–90 per cent of householders in some streets were Jewish by the 1890s and certain streets were associated with particular towns or *shtetls* of origin in eastern Europe (Connell, 1970). On its eastern side the community was cut off from the rest of the city by a low wall, reviving memories of Sjoberg's (1960) description of pre-industrial cities in which "various sections of the city are sealed off from one another by walls, leaving little cells, or sub-communities, as worlds unto themselves" (p. 91). However, there is little evidence from British cities that would warrant the use of the term 'ghetto'. Exclusion was on the basis of income, association on the basis of shared culture, but there were few premeditated attempts to confine minority groups to particular districts.

Migrant communities were distinctive features of Victorian cities but no more than they were of pre-industrial cities or are of twentieth-century cities. Indeed, much of their interest lies in the characteristics that they share with contemporary patterns of ethnic and religious segregation. But they are not, therefore, relevant to hypotheses about the transitional nature of nineteenth-century cities. In fact they are the one unchanging feature in the evolution of urban structure.

The changes which occurred in the scale and form of residential segregation of rich and poor in Victorian cities may be related to three sets of processes:

(1) the unstable balance between a broad class consciousness and the perception of a finely ordered status hierarchy;
(2) the improvement of public transport; and
(3) the development of urban land.

## Class and Status

The development of a class society and some of its consequences for residential segregation have already been noted in the preceding chapters. But it is worth returning to the issue here, if only because past generations of geographers (and some historians) have been strangely insensitive to the distinction between class and status. Many writers have arbitrarily defined five 'socio-economic classes' on the basis of occupation (perhaps seasoned with additional information on the presence of servants or lodgers), often importing a twentieth-century classification of occupations into the mid-nineteenth century. This definition of class disregards patterns of interaction and common interest within and between occupational groups and is, more accurately, a measure of socio-economic *status*. Some occupations are valued and rewarded more highly than others, but in a class-conscious society these differences in valuation may be transcended by social interaction between members of groups whose status is different but who share the same relationship to the means of production.

In pre-industrial cities there was, in Laslett's (1971) terminology, a 'one-class society' with no class consciousness among the labouring population whose interests were confined to the particular industry in which they were employed. Society was small in scale, social mobility was limited, there was no need to use residential area as a status symbol. In any case, there was little segregation in the quality of the housing stock: in many towns the largest homogeneous unit of housing was the court or street. Apart from new and exclusive suburbs for a very rich minority there was little residential differentiation, but social interaction was confined to people of the same occupational status.

In some areas, such as Foster's (1974) example of Oldham, the emergence of industrial urbanism was associated with the development of working-class consciousness. Interaction now extended to families of different status provided that they shared the same class, but it was still confined to cellular communities within cities because transport had not improved, nor had hours of work declined sufficiently to permit much separation of residence and workplace for any but the elite. Housing allocation continued on the basis of rent-paying ability and, since most housing areas were mixed in character, segregation on the basis of either class or status remained limited. This leads to some ambiguity in the interpretation of quantitative evidence on class structure in the early nineteenth century. The social heterogeneity of residential areas might indicate the existence of a broadly defined working class, the survival of a pre-industrial pattern or the frustration of a preference for segregation by socio-economic status. The use of interaction data (e.g. on visiting friends or intermarriage) may help to resolve this ambiguity by showing whether friends were selected on the basis of class, status, proximity or some other variable. For example, Foster found that in 1851 fewer labourers lived next door to craftsmen in Oldham than in Northampton. We might assume that this indicated a broader working-class consciousness in Northampton, but in terms of interaction there were more marriages between the families of craftsmen and labourers in Oldham. Foster eventually concluded that Oldham labourers and craftsmen were class-conscious, while Northampton remained in the pre-industrial era in terms of its social and spatial structure.

The long-term effect of large factories and an increasing division of labour was a hierarchy in which social mobility was commonplace and status jealously guarded. But however desirable segregation by status might be, it was still impracticable for most people to live more than a few minutes' walk from their workplace. And despite the possibility of modifying some existing housing to satisfy new forms of demand, perhaps by subdividing large villas in areas of predominantly small houses to accommodate several poor families instead of one rich family, there was inevitably a phase in which the supply of housing failed to match the demand for residential areas of uniform status. In Huddersfield one indication of this mismatch was an increase in marriage distance (the distance separating the premarital addresses of bride and groom). Single adults had to search wide areas of the town to find suitable marriage partners of their own status. In previous decades the acceptability of partners of the same class but different status had meant that there were sufficient eligible members of the opposite sex living locally for marriage distances to remain short (Dennis, 1977).

Eventually a situation emerged where segregation was considered both desirable and feasible. Interestingly, the consequence for interaction patterns was a slight reduction in marriage distance for unions between people of the same status, not because transport had deteriorated forcing them to interact locally, but because transport had improved, facilitating longer journeys to work and more complete segregation by socio-economic status. As a result it was possible, but no longer necessary, to travel long distances in search of a marriage partner of the same status. So close-knit 'urban villages' in late-Victorian and Edwardian England should not be regarded as survivals from pre-industrial times. 'Urban villages' comprised people of similar, usually low, status and were a product of the changes in transport and housing provision that characterized the second half of the nineteenth century.

## Transport

Improvements in public transport have often been regarded as a major cause of urban growth and suburbanization in the nineteenth century. Historians refer to the 'Railway Age' (e.g. Perkin, 1970) while in North America, Warner (1962) christened suburban housing schemes as 'streetcar suburbs'. Although the effect of railway construction and the associated electric telegraph cannot be denied at a national scale, breaking down rural isolation, facilitating agricultural specialization, accelerating rural–urban migration and imposing standardization on products and ideas, the impact of new transport facilities within cities was often less immediate.

The earliest forms of intra-urban public transport – horse buses – were too expensive and ill-timed to cater for the labouring classes. They permitted the decentralization of the wealthy to such "breezy heights" as Engels recorded in Manchester, but it is doubtful whether they generated completely new residential areas. In most instances they catered for an existing demand. The same was generally true of trams. For example, steam trams made their first appearance in the streets of Huddersfield in 1883, but although the trams ran more frequently, began earlier in the morning and ended later at night, carried more passengers and charged lower fares than horse buses, they operated over the same routes. The trams accelerated the drift of better-off artisans and clerks to lower middle-class estates, designed as infill in and around existing middle-class suburbs.

In North America tramways were laid down in association with the building booms of the late nineteenth century. Tramway operators in league with property companies were perfectly placed to dictate the course of urban development. But in England the tram became popular only after the period of most rapid urban growth and there are few examples of tramway companies owning or associating with building firms. Where routes were extended beyond the limits of the built-up area it was usually because adjacent local authorities had each laid tracks to their administrative boundaries in the hope of creating an inter-urban network that would rival local railway services. This type of extension was common in Lancashire and Yorkshire where it was the boast of tramway advertising that you could ride all the way from Leeds to Liverpool by tram! Tracks were also extended into rural areas in the hope of attracting Sunday afternoon excursion traffic. In time, the picnic sites of city dwellers became their permanent homes. The frequency of tram stops produced a pattern of ribbon development following the roads where the trams operated. By contrast railway suburbs resembled 'beads on a string', each 'bead' associated with its local station.

Because most tram services were operated by local authorities they proved instrumental in the location of the first suburban council housing estates in the years prior to World War I. For example, the London County Council (LCC) started the construction of suburban estates south of London at Tooting in 1903 and Norbury in 1906 (Fig. 5.4). Land cost £29 per dwelling at Tooting, compared with £454 in central London and the rent for a 5-roomed house could be as low as 10/6d. per week compared with 14/- for roughly equivalent accommodation in the centre. Nevertheless, artisans could only be attracted to Tooting if the cost of travel to work in inner London was reduced. This the LCC was able to do, offering special workmen's fares of 2d. return on its tram services from Tooting to Westminster and the City (Jackson, 1973).

Rail travel too was limited to the better-off until regular cheap trains were introduced. The construction of city termini such as King's Cross and the extension of railways through inner-city areas resulted in the demolition of large areas of slum property and the displacement of thousands of slum residents. Railway companies argued that their activities cleansed cities of insanitary slums and provided slum dwellers with the opportunity to

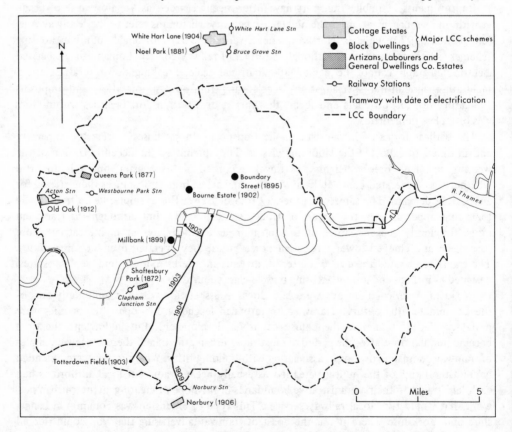

FIG. 5.4. *Housing and transport for the working classes in London, 1870–1914.*

start new lives in healthy suburban estates from which they could commute to work in the city centre. In practice, even small new houses on cheap suburban land were beyond the resources of the poor, so the displaced families simply moved into other inner areas, over-crowding and converting them into new slums. During the 1850s and 1860s, therefore, the principal effect of railway construction on the working classes was to crowd them into a diminishing stock of cheap housing (Kellett, 1969).

With the passing of the Cheap Trains Act in 1883, by which railway companies were obliged to offer special workmen's fares as required by the Board of Trade, the better-off working classes were able to move to the suburbs in large numbers. By 1913, more than 820,000 London workers were making daily journeys to work by train or tram. One company, the Great Eastern, operating out of Liverpool Street, had encouraged working-class commuters by offering cheap fares at 2d. return for distances of up to 10 miles on its services to Edmonton, Tottenham, Walthamstow and Leyton, beginning in 1864. Middle-class suburbs on the same routes rapidly declined in status and the managing director of the company claimed that they were "utterly destroyed for ordinary passenger traffic" (cited in Kellett, 1969, p. 377). We can see, therefore, that differences between the fares policies of public transport operators played an important role in determining patterns of segregation in large cities.

Most urban centres, however, were too small for railways to be used for commuting purposes. In fact, the majority were sufficiently compact to be traversed on foot in little more than an hour. We may doubt, then, whether the provision of public transport had more than a psychological impact outside the largest cities and even there, a pattern of large-scale residential segregation could only develop with the co-operation of those who provided housing.

## Housing

Of the different ways in which a plot of land could be made to yield a crop of houses, the leasehold system was more widely employed in the nineteenth century than it is today. Under this system the landowner would grant a building lease either to a developer acting as middleman or to a builder for a fixed term of years. Short leases, not exceeding 99 years, were preferred, although their precise length varied. The builder/developer would usually have to submit plans for both the layout of the estate (roads, drains, etc.) and the design of individual houses, so that the landowner could guarantee the quality of development on his estate. When he had completed the houses the builder might retain the leasehold him-self, continuing to pay the landowner an annual ground rent and collecting house rents from tenants occupying the dwellings on short-term agreements. But given the limited capital resources of most builders, and their dependence on a credit cycle whereby they began their next venture on the security of their last, it was more likely that the builder would sell the leasehold to a third party, although still not necessarily the occupiers of the houses. Whoever owned the houses continued to pay a ground rent to the landowner until the lease expired (e.g. after 99 years) when all rights reverted to the landowner, who might decide to demolish the buildings and begin the process over again, or to renew the leases for a further term. Ground rents would be increased in the new lease, reflecting the rate of inflation and changes in the desirability of the area over the period of the previous lease. The insecurity of this system for the leaseholder explains why properties with only short leases now fetch far less than equivalent properties with long leases and are often unable to attract building-society mortgages. We will return to this issue in Chapter 8: here it is sufficient to note that the 1967 Leasehold Reform Act granted some but not all leaseholders the right to buy the freehold of their property, but in the nineteenth century it was a complicated process to acquire the freehold. Some builders who had leased large estates bought the freehold prior to selling off the individual houses to owner-occupiers, but many large freeholders preferred to retain their land.

The leasehold system offered the landowner all the benefits and none of the risks of property development. He was assured the steady income of ground rents and the enhanced value of his estate when the leases expired. He need have none of the responsibility of finding tenants for the houses, a responsibility that proved the downfall of many builders during periods when the supply of upper middle-class town houses far exceeded the demand. In practice many landowners (or their agents) did take a healthy interest in the selection of tenants, since the quality and reliability of the tenants determined whether the value of the estate would increase through time, and by how much ground rents could be increased at each redrafting of the leases.

The usual result of the short-lease system was a glut of high-status housing. For example, on the Duke of Bedford's estate in Bloomsbury, Thomas Cubitt contracted in 1824 to build 167 houses, all suitable for the upper middle classes, but it took over 30 years to complete the work and even in 1860 tenants had not been found for all the houses. Cubitt's problem was that his houses were too large and expensive for all but the very wealthy, and his development came at a time when people who could afford to live in Bloomsbury no longer wanted to — the centre of London society was moving west to Kensington and Belgravia. The agent to the Bedford estate would not permit subdivision of large houses for occupation by two or more families, and Cubitt was reluctant to curtail the high-class development and finish the estate with slightly cheaper houses, since this would have made it even more difficult to find tenants for the outstanding expensive properties (Jenkins, 1975; Olsen 1976). In Cardiff, most nineteenth-century suburban development lay on the Bute, Tredegar or Windsor estates, all developed with strict controls (on minimum plot size, minimum rental or sale price, regular redecoration and maintenance, and the exclusion of nonconforming land uses) on 99-year leases. The refusal of landowners to allow small, cheap houses in a city with relatively few middle-class residents inevitably led to multiple occupancy. In 1911, 36 per cent of families in Cardiff shared houses. However, because the houses were large and well-built, shared occupancy did not signify overcrowding or slum conditions as it did in many cities where even small, poorly built dwellings accommodated several families (Daunton, 1977).

Whereas the granting of short leases indicated a landowner's desire for a steady return over a long period, the selling of freehold reflected his preference for a quick profit. Some contemporaries claimed that the leasehold system favoured small builders who could not raise the large capital outlay required to purchase a plot outright, but a more usual argument was that builders could afford to buy small plots freehold, using the proceeds they obtained from the sale of completed houses, and were then free to erect what they liked: often high density, poor-quality housing, effectively purpose-built slums. The preference for freehold made it difficult for landowners to find developers willing to accept short-lease arrangements unless they had a local monopoly of available land. As the century progressed the 99-year lease was increasingly restricted to very large estates or to situations, as in Cardiff, where several neighbouring landowners together held a monopoly and agreed on a common policy of short leases. Elsewhere, a compromise of granting 999-year leases was offered, sufficiently long to compare with freehold from the buyer's viewpoint, but still giving the ground landlord some control over development. Where landownership was divided among large numbers of smallholders it was almost certain that somebody would sell for a quick profit, and once one low-quality land use had been introduced, it was difficult for neighbouring owners to attract higher-class development. As a crude generalization, therefore, we can conclude that where landholdings were small, development was freehold or on long leases, and frequently low-status; where holdings were large, development was carefully controlled on short leases, and generally high-status.

This contrast has been explored in detail in several Yorkshire industrial towns. In Leeds, smallholdings to the south of the pre-industrial town gave way to working-class terraces, the peculiarities in street layout reflecting the awkward shape of some plots (Fig. 5.5). Larger farms to the north were replaced by low-density middle-class housing and the largest estates had to await the greater purchasing power of local authorities in the twentieth century before producing a crop of council houses (Ward, 1962).

In many towns plots near the centre were smaller than plots in out-townships. The result was that inner-city development included a jumble of different land uses and frequent discordances where the developers of adjacent plots failed to co-ordinate their plans. Typical features were culs-de-sac, and 'blind-back' or 'half-back' housing. Later suburban development was more regular, partly because the imposition of local building acts raised standards of design and layout, partly because the size of building firms increased and with it the scale of development they could undertake, and partly because more consolidated landholdings were available in the suburbs. Beresford (in Chapman, 1971) has accounted for the origins of 'back-to-back' housing in terms of inner-city patterns of landholding. Some of the earliest working-class housing in towns such as Nottingham and Leeds was built 'blind-back' against the walls of back gardens and innyards, running at right angles away from the

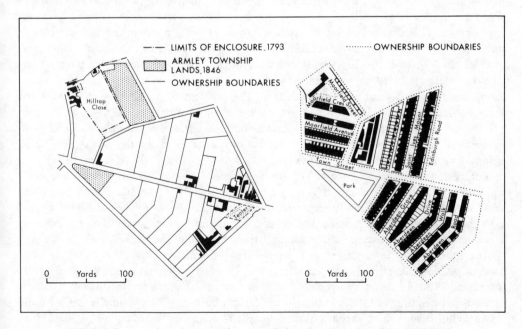

FIG. 5.5. *Property boundaries and housing development in Leeds (after Ward, 1973).*

main street and approached by narrow passages between or tunnels under the inns and shops that fronted the streets. It was a short step from building houses blind-back against the boundary walls of plots to building pairs and rows of houses back-to-back. Finally, their acceptance in inner areas where high land values necessitated high-density development paved the way for their construction in suburban areas, where lower land values and more readily available land made them economically unnecessary, although of course they yielded higher profits to their developers: a cautionary tale against purely economic or purely cultural explanations of urban land-use patterns. Back-to-back housing, deficient in through ventilation and light, was a principal source of accommodation for the working classes in northern industrial towns throughout the century. Manchester banned them in 1844, but was reported to have 10,000 back-to-backs in the 1890s, Liverpool outlawed them in 1861; incredibly, the last back-to-back house in Leeds was built as recently as 1937 and in 1920 78,000 out of 108,000 houses in Leeds (71 per cent) were back-to-back.

Most new housing was speculative in the sense that the builder did not have a particular client in mind, and most was designed for renting by the middle and lower-middle classes, regardless of the more urgent need to improve the living conditions of the poor. Thus in Cardiff the need of the working classes was for 3–4-roomed dwellings let at about 5/- per week. But the cheapest houses that landowners sanctioned were 6-roomed, costing 9/- per week. Elsewhere, the immediate causes of mismatch between need and supply were local bye-laws. In Liverpool the casually employed Irish could not afford more than 3/- per week in rent. Until 1846 this demand was met by the construction of admittedly low-quality cellar dwellings let at about 2/- per week and a substantial number of houses valued at less than £12 p.a. (approximately 4/6d. per week). But after 1846 the supply of cheap housing dried up, despite the growth in demand from an increasing population of Irish immigrants. Building regulations, introduced in 1842 and strengthened in 1846, outlawed the construction of slums, diverted the attention of builders to higher-status development, and effectively worsened the housing conditions of the poor, by increasing levels of overcrowding in the cheap property that remained. Of course, the root cause of the problem was poverty. It was impossible for builders to provide sufficiently spacious, well ventilated and sanitary dwellings at rents that the working classes could afford, a situation little different from the modern situation that is resolved by such devices as subsidized council housing and artificially cheap mortgages. The two most direct solutions to the problem of housing the poor were to increase their wages or subsidize their housing, but both were rejected on the grounds that the former would increase the cost of manufactured goods and make British exports less competitive, while the latter smacked too much of charity in an age that worshipped self-help and when even philanthropy was expected to show a modest profit (Gauldie, 1974).

For better-off artisans two solutions were possible. One was the process of 'levelling-up' whereby the working classes moved into houses vacated by the middle classes for whom most new housing was intended. Unfortunately, 'levelling-up' rarely benefited the really poor, because high rates of immigration of poor families and programmes of slum clearance created a constant shortage of accommodation at the bottom of the market.

The other solution was a self-help one offered by building clubs, the forerunners of modern building societies. In the earliest societies a piece of building land was bought or leased and divided into as many plots as the society had members. Each member paid a monthly subscription and when sufficient capital had been raised to build a house, a ballot was held to decide which member should benefit. When everybody had been housed, the society was wound up: hence the name 'terminating building societies' by which they were known in the first half of the nineteenth century. One problem of terminating societies was that it was difficult for new members to join once a society had started; another was that the member who received his house last waited almost as long as if he had invested his savings independently. So, from the 1840s onwards, 'permanent building societies' became more important: the Leeds Permanent was founded in 1848, the Woolwich Equitable in 1847, the Halifax in 1853. A distinction could now be drawn between borrowers and investors and societies were subject to the regular accusation that continues today that they were more interested in accumulating investors' savings than in helping people to buy houses. In fact, most borrowers were not owner-occupiers but private landlords who owned a few houses with the aid of a mortgage, and repaid the mortgage from the rents they collected. The administration of a permanent society demanded accounting skills not required in a terminating society. Not surprisingly, the societies soon became middle-class and lost their role of helping the working classes to help themselves (Gauldie, 1974).

They did, however, continue to build houses or to promote house-building quite directly, unlike present-day societies. One of the earliest clubs, the Crackenthorpe Garden Building Club (1787), constructed back-to-back cottages in a suburb of Leeds, a form of development that would have been frowned upon by more recent societies! Later on, in the mid-nineteenth century, the Leeds society co-operated with local housing reformers in the provision of 'model cottages' and 'improved dwellings', while the Halifax society built four-storey blocks of flats for rent at only 1/3d. per room.

Flats were one way of accommodating the poor cheaply, cleanly and centrally, and they proved invaluable in Scottish cities and on the Continent, but they were disliked by the English working classes. Private builders constructed very few flats in England, partly because of the difficulty of finding tenants but also because small firms could not afford the capital outlay or the long period of building before any return was received. Interestingly, the same objection — the slow return on capital — is put forward by major building firms today as one reason why they dislike building large blocks of flats.

The construction of working-class flats was left to a variety of philanthropic agencies, such as the Society for Improving the Condition of the Labouring Classes, which was founded in 1844 and promoted a series of model housing schemes in London (Tarn, 1973; Wohl, 1977). The society aimed to be exemplary: to demonstrate that private enterprise could house the poor *and* make a modest profit. It was followed by a succession of companies that were philanthropic to the extent that their investors accepted a much lower dividend than could have been obtained elsewhere: hence the term 'five per cent philanthropy'. Two London companies with dwellings still inhabited today (although now administered by local councils) were the Improved Industrial Dwellings Co. founded in 1863 and the East End Dwellings Co. established in 1884. Several philanthropic *trusts* were also created, the best known being the Peabody Trust, founded in 1862 following a gift of £150,000 from George Peabody, an American banker, to "ameliorate the condition and augment the comforts of the poor" in London (Tarn, 1973).

The philanthropic agencies were more significant for the ideas they embodied and the example they set to later housing reformers than for the number of people they housed. In 1875 all the London agencies between them housed less than 33,000 people and by 1914 there were still under 100,000 rooms in philanthropic dwellings, only enough to accommodate two years' population increase in London. Only in a few inner areas such as East Finsbury did the philanthropists house even 20 per cent of the population. Outside London land values were lower and the casual poor less conspicuous, but philanthropic agencies undertook a few housing projects, in Hull, Leeds, Salford and especially in Birkenhead and Liverpool (Sutcliffe, 1974).

None of these schemes was an outstanding success. Rents were invariably too high for casual labourers to afford, nor were many working-class families prepared to accept rules and regulations that imposed middle-class standards of cleanliness and temperance. It was also difficult to attract investors prepared to accept only a 5 per cent return. In practice, the companies derived much of their funds from the Public Works Loan Commissioners, a government agency which from 1866 onwards made loans for the erection of working-class dwellings, at an interest rate of only 4 per cent. On the one hand this eased the financial problems of the philanthropists; on the other it reduced the flexibility with which they could act, since they were bound to make a 4 per cent profit year in, year out, to repay their debt to the government. There is a parallel here with present-day housing associations which frequently have to adopt more cautious policies than they would prefer, in order to satisfy local or central government upon whose continued financial support they depend.

Yet another problem concerned the supply of scarce and expensive inner-city land. After 1875 philanthropists took advantage of the provisions of the Cross Act, which authorized local authorities to buy and demolish whole areas of unfit housing. Clearance was to be followed by the erection of as many dwellings as had previously existed and as private developers were not interested in this kind of work, it was usually possible for philanthropic agencies to acquire very cheaply sites for which the local authority had paid the full market value. In effect, therefore, indirect subsidization of working-class housing dates from 1875, although direct subsidies from central government were introduced only in 1919.

It has been argued that philanthropic building on slum-clearance sites had the same effect as railway and road construction. The slum dwellers themselves rarely benefited, they could not afford to live in model dwellings and so they moved into adjacent areas of poor housing, increasing the level of overcrowding in these areas. Another charge is that the philanthropists delayed the introduction of council housing by leading people to believe that the housing problem could be solved by private enterprise (Gauldie, 1974). It seems more likely that political and public opinion was simply not prepared to accept the idea of direct state intervention until the end of the century and that if the philanthropists had not existed the plight of the working classes would have been even worse. In fact, Liverpool Corporation, the first local authority to build council housing to rent — completed in 1869 — directly copied the 5 per cent companies in financing the scheme with a loan from the Public Works Loan Commissioners. Liverpool remained in the forefront of local authority housing provision until the First World War, but even by 1914 less than 3,000 corporation dwellings had been erected in the city.

As with philanthropic dwellings so with council flats, it was claimed that they were too expensive for the people they displaced, who were forced to crowd into neighbouring slums. This occurred in the LCC's pioneer scheme in the 1890s at Boundary Street, Bethnal Green (Fig. 5.6). In addition, many of the slum dwellers had carried on businesses (e.g. matchbox making) in their homes. This was forbidden on the new estate, whose tenants included clerks, policemen, skilled artisans and even schoolteachers! Up to World War I most council housing was in high-density, inner-city tenement blocks. A few suburban estates were built by the LCC but the major expansion of suburban council housing did not occur until the inter-war period.

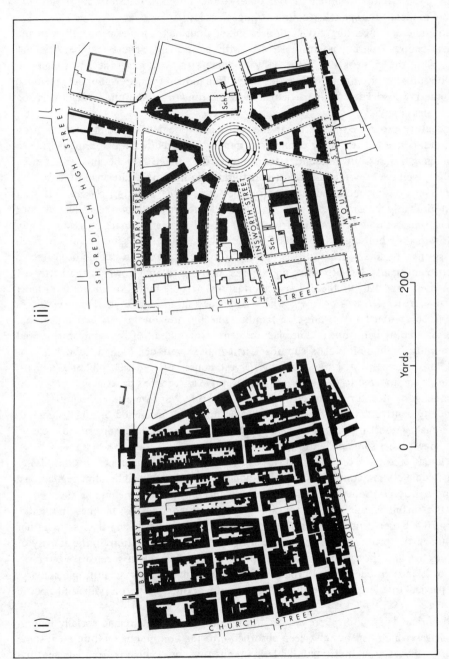

FIG. 5.6. *The Boundary Street scheme (after Tarn, 1973) (i) before slum clearance; (ii) after rebuilding.*

**Spatial Structure**

We must now attempt to integrate our observations on class, transport and housing in an improved model of the spatial structure of English cities.

The early nineteenth-century city comprised mixed housing for tradesmen, craftsmen and professional people fronting its main streets, with poor-quality court and back-to-back housing infilling the gardens and yards between these streets. Bourgeoisie and proletariat lived in close proximity, although the latter were often hidden from view. Suburbs included company housing associated with particular mills or ironworks, and middle-class villas on exclusive estates (Fig. 5.7).

As the century progressed properties in the centre might be demolished in town improvement schemes, converted to purely commercial uses or filtered down the housing market to become lodging houses. In residential terms, therefore, the centre became either non-residential or exclusively poor. The oldest court housing might be demolished to make way for roads, railways, or model dwellings for the respectable working classes, but if it survived it probably became even more squalid and overcrowded, as the displaced poor sought similar accommodation to that from which they had been evicted, or as the supply of new, low-quality housing was curtailed by local by-laws. In the suburbs, well-planned middle-class areas retained their status, especially if houses were sold leasehold or protected by restrictive covenants; less attractive middle-class housing filtered down to the better-off working classes, especially if there was a shortage of purpose-built artisan housing, most common in short-lease towns or towns where land was sold in large units. Factory villages continued to be occupied by working-class families, selected now on the basis of status rather than place of employment, but middle-class residents (the salariat of the company) moved out into purpose-built middle-class suburbs. Their houses were demolished, subdivided, or converted into offices. The grounds of the largest houses offered rich building land or, occasionally, were donated to the local authority to serve as 'people's parks'.

Summarizing the structure of the city at the eve of World War I we can distinguish:

(1) In the city centre, some pre-Victorian housing, now multi-occupied or non-residential; some poor-quality court housing, occupied by casual labourers and new arrivals to the city; and in the largest cities some philanthropic or council flats.

(2) In different sectors of the suburbs (a) speculative housing for the upper working classes and lower middle classes, controlled in density and layout only by local building regulations; or (b) more tightly controlled speculative development, occupied by the middle classes or — if there was a surfeit of this type of housing — by pairs of working-class families. In middle-class areas 10—20 per cent of houses were owner-occupied, in working-class areas rather fewer, although the proportion varied between towns, reflecting variations in the activity of building societies and the cost of housing. Within the suburban sea of speculative building, a number of islands stood out: the product of building-club or semi-philanthropic activity, the latter particularly dependent on the availability of workmen's fares on trains and electric trams.

(3) On the urban fringe, some pre-industrial, previously free-standing and socially hetero-geneous villages which had by now been absorbed into the continuous built-up area; some early factory villages, now indistinguishable in architecture or occupants from adjacent by-law terraces; and a few estates of local authority cottage dwellings or privately developed co-operative housing experiments.

The theme of this chapter has been the modernization of urban structure and interaction

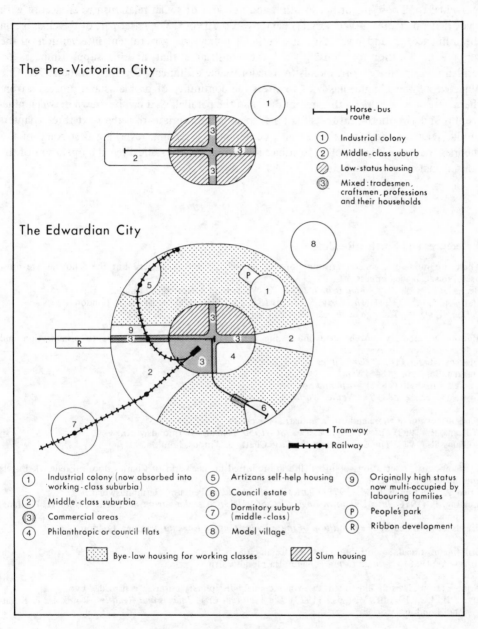

The Pre-Victorian City

Horse-bus route

1 Industrial colony
2 Middle-class suburb
Low-status housing
3 Mixed : tradesmen, craftsmen, professions and their households

The Edwardian City

1 Industrial colony (now absorbed into working-class suburbia)
2 Middle-class suburbia
3 Commercial areas
4 Philanthropic or council flats
5 Artizans self-help housing
6 Council estate
7 Dormitory suburb (middle-class)
8 Model village
9 Originally high status now multi-occupied by labouring families
P People's park
R Ribbon development

Bye-law housing for working classes    Slum housing

Tramway
Railway

FIG. 5.7. *A model of evolving urban structures: the Pre-Victorian city and the Edwardian city.*

patterns in industrializing England. The description of segregation, discussion of minority groups, and explanation of segregation in terms of class or status, and the freedom of the individual to choose his or her location and network of social relationships all accord with ideas that dominated urban social geography in the 1960s. The latter part of the chapter, on the influence of land ownership, institutional policy and government intervention on the supply and location of housing, and the constraints that housing supply imposes on residential segregation corresponds to a major theme of human geography in the 1970s. One objective of this chapter has been to stress the continuity of problems and processes from the nineteenth century to the present day, and the parallels that can be drawn between nineteenth- and twentieth-century situations, so it is appropriate that the next three chapters should take up the same themes in a contemporary setting, reviewing first some of the theories that have been applied to urban residential patterns and then the operation of the housing market in modern cities.

### References and Further Reading

There are numerous general introductions to nineteenth-century society but the following are most useful to social geographers:
Best, G. (1971) *Mid-Victorian Britain 1851–75,* Weidenfeld & Nicolson, London.
Harrison, J. F. C. (1971) *The Early Victorians 1832–51,* Weidenfeld & Nicolson, London.
Perkin, H. (1970) *The Age of the Railway,* Panther, London.

Many contemporary novels shed interesting light on (middle-class) attitudes to urbanization and industrialization, for example:
Dickens, Charles (1854) *Hard Times.*
Disraeli, Benjamin (1845) *Sybil.*
Gaskell, Elizabeth (1855) *North and South.*
Gissing, George (1889) *The Nether World.*

For a discussion of these and other 'industrial novels' see:
Williams, R. (1963) *Culture and Society 1780–1950,* Penguin, Harmondsworth.
Williams, R. (1973) *The Country and the City,* Chatto & Windus, London.

Contemporary observations of urban life are reported in the works of Charles Booth, Frederick Engels and the 'social explorers':
Fried, A. and Elman, R. M. (1971) *Charles Booth's London,* Penguin, Harmondsworth.
Keating, P. (1976) *Into Unknown England 1866–1913: Selections from the Social Explorers,* Fontana, London.
Engels, F. (1969 edn.) *The Condition of the Working Class in England,* Panther, London.

Still the most readable introduction to Victorian cities is:
Briggs, A. (1968) *Victorian Cities,* Penguin, Harmondsworth.

A more recent, lavishly illustrated, two-volume, multi-disciplinary coverage is provided by:
Dyos, H. J. and Wolff, M. (eds.) (1973) *The Victorian City: Images and Realities,* Routledge & Kegan Paul, London.

Geographical perspectives on Victorian urbanism include:
Carter, H. (1978) Towns and urban systems 1730–1900, in R. A. Dodgshon & R. A. Butlin (eds.), *An Historical Geography of England and Wales,* Academic Press, London, pp. 367–400.
Institute of British Geographers (1979) *The Victorian City* (Transactions, New Series, Volume 4, No. 2).
Lawton, R. (1972) An age of great cities, *Town Planning Review,* 43, 199–224.
Ward, D. (1973) Living in Victorian towns, in A.R.H. Baker & J. B. Harley (eds.), *Man Made The Land,* David & Charles, Newton Abbot, pp. 193–205.

Detailed studies by historical geographers and social historians include:

Anderson, M. (1968) Family structure in nineteenth-century Lancashire, unpublished Ph.D. thesis, University of Cambridge.

Anderson, M. (1971) *Family Structure in Nineteenth-Century Lancashire,* Cambridge University Press, Cambridge.

Cannadine, D. (1977) Victorian cities: how different?, *Social History,* 4, 457–82.

Carter, H. and Wheatley, S. (1978) Some aspects of the spatial structure of two Glamorgan towns in the nineteenth century, *Welsh History Review,* 9, 32–56.

Connell, J. (1970) The gilded ghetto: Jewish suburbanization in Leeds, *Bloomsbury Geographer,* 3, 50–59.

Cowlard, K. (1979) The identification of social (class) areas and their place in nineteenth-century urban development, *Transactions Institute of British Geographers,* New Series, 4, 239–57.

Daunton, M. J. (1977) *Coal Metropolis, Cardiff 1870–1914,* Leicester University Press, Leicester.

Dennis, R. J. (1977) Distance and social interaction in a Victorian city, *Journal of Historical Geography,* 3, 237–50.

Foster, J. (1974) *Class Struggle and the Industrial Revolution,* Weidenfeld & Nicolson, London.

Lawton, R. (1959) Irish immigration to England and Wales in the mid-nineteenth century, *Irish Geography,* 4, 35–54.

Lawton, R. (1979) Mobility in nineteenth-century British cities, *Geographical Journal,* 145, 206–24.

Lawton, R. and Pooley, C. G. (1975) The urban dimensions of nineteenth-century Liverpool, *Social Geography of Nineteenth-Century Merseyside Projects: Working Paper,* 4.

Lobban, R. D. (1971) The Irish community in Greenock in the nineteenth century, *Irish Geography,* 6, 270–81.

Pooley, C. G. (1977) The residential segregation of migrant communities in mid-Victorian Liverpool, *Transactions Institute of British Geographers,* New Series, 2, 364–82.

Pritchard, R. M. (1976) *Housing and the Spatial Structure of the City,* Cambridge University Press, Cambridge.

Richardson, C. (1968) Irish settlement in mid-nineteenth century Bradford, *Yorkshire Bulletin of Economic and Social Research,* 20, 40–57.

Ward, D. (1962) The pre-urban cadaster and the urban pattern of Leeds, *Annals of the Association of American Geographers,* 52, 150–66.

Ward, D. (1975) Victorian cities: how modern?, *Journal of Historical Geography,* I, 135–51.

Warnes, A. M. (1973) Residential patterns in an emerging industrial town, *Institute of British Geographers Special Publication 5* (Social Patterns in Cities), 169–89.


The role of transportation is discussed in an American context by:

Warner, S. B. (1962) *Streetcar Suburbs,* Harvard University Press, Cambridge, Mass.

and in Britain by:

Kellett, J. R. (1969) *The Impact of Railways on Victorian Cities,* Routledge & Kegan Paul, London.

Jackson, A. A. (1973) *Semi-Detached London,* Allen & Unwin, London.


The history of housing has recently attracted considerable attention:

Burnett, J. (1978) *A Social History of Housing 1815–1970,* David & Charles, Newton Abbot (in paperback, 1980, Methuen, London).

Chapman, S. D. (ed.) (1971) *The History of Working-Class Housing,* David & Charles, Newton Abbot.

Gauldie, E. (1974) *Cruel Habitations,* Allen & Unwin, London.

Jenkins, S. (1975) *Landlords to London,* Constable, London.

Olsen, D. J. (1976) *The Growth of Victorian London,* Batsford, London.

Sutcliffe, A. (ed.) (1974) *Multi-Storey Living,* Croom Helm, London.

Tarn, J. N. (1973) *Five per cent Philanthropy: An Account of Housing in Urban Areas between 1840 and 1914,* Cambridge University Press, Cambridge.

Wohl, A. S. (1977) *The Eternal Slum: Housing and Social Policy in Victorian London,* Arnold, London.


Finally, to compare Victorian society with what went before, see:

Laslett, P. (1971) *The World We Have Lost,* Methuen, London.

Sjoberg, G. (1960) *The Preindustrial City,* Free Press, Glencoe, Illinois.

# 6
# Structural Models of English Cities

## Introduction

UNTIL the 1960s most geographers interested in the internal structure of cities restricted their concern to physical morphology. Studies of the distribution and behaviour of different population groups within cities remained the preserve of urban sociologists, including the Chicago school of human ecologists — notably Park, Burgess and Wirth, their critics such as Firey, and the social area theorists like Shevky and Bell, whose ideas were outlined in Chapter 2. It was only in the 1960s that the ideas of these writers were absorbed into human geography. Since then British researchers have undertaken numerous tests of ecological and social area theories, but often these tests have involved little more than a comparison of the spatial pattern predicted by the theories with the spatial patterns present in actual British cities. It was assumed without questioning that models developed in North America were applicable in Britain, and few attempts were made to construct indigenous urban theories or understand the processes influencing population distributions and movements in English cities.

Another weakness of many pattern-testing exercises was that they stopped at the point at which they became interesting. For example, the application of factor analysis to small area data for British cities frequently resulted in the identification of factors labelled 'life cycle' or 'housing tenure', demonstrating the effects on residential location of a household's stage in the life cycle or its position in the housing market, whether renting privately, renting from the council or owning its dwelling. Logically, the identification of a life cycle factor should have stimulated more detailed studies of *why* people live in different areas at different stages in their life cycle, and how and why they move house when their family circumstances change. Likewise, the fact that 'housing tenure' or 'housing conditions' often emerged as an important factor in English cities but not in American studies should have generated research on the distinctive characteristics of the English housing market.

In fact, studies asking 'how?' and 'why?' became more common during the 1970s but they were carried out less often by factor analysts and quantitative geographers than by their critics. The late 1960s and early 1970s witnessed the adoption of a behavioural approach, linked to an increasing interest in perception studies and concerned with understanding processes of individual decision-making. For example, studies were made of the conditions likely to stimulate a family to move house, of the requirements (including location) that movers demanded of their new dwellings, and of the ways in which they acquired information on potential dwellings and finally selected their new home. This approach acknowledged the constraints on individual behaviour imposed by income and incomplete information but primarily emphasized the individual's freedom of choice. Again it was an approach that originated in the free-market experience of the North American private housing market; but almost a third of British households live in dwellings provided by local authorities and another quarter own their homes only with the assistance of a building society mortgage.

Consequently, an even more recent trend than behaviouralism has been a reaction against studies that focused on the preferences of the consumer or householder, emphasizing instead the roles of 'gatekeepers' and 'urban managers' in constraining the freedom of individuals to decide their own location in the city (Robson, 1975). 'Gatekeepers' include local authority housing officials, building society managers, solicitors, surveyors and estate agents, all of whom possess the keys necessary to unlock various 'gates' providing access to different types, ages, tenures and locations of housing. Central government decisions also complicate individual decision-making, for example by changing the legislation that determines the relationship between private landlords and their tenants, or by changing the levels of subsidy that accrue through tax relief to owner-occupiers or through Exchequer Grants to local authorities and their tenants. Landowners, speculators and builders all play a part in regulating the supply of dwellings and their decisions, too, will depend on central government policy. All these agencies, it is argued, play more important roles than do individual families in shaping the social geography of British cities. This approach has become so important in recent years that the geography of housing merits an entire chapter to itself in this book, while the present chapter and the next are devoted to the sociological models that lie behind the growth of urban social geography, geographical applications of these models and the behavioural reaction.

## Ecological Theory

The origins of human ecology lie with Robert Park who began life as a Chicago journalist and derived his ideas from walking round cities, reporting life in the raw. In 1916, Park published a paper entitled *The City: Suggestions for the Investigation of Human Behaviour in the Urban Environment,* in which he posed a series of questions about urban life which he considered merited further research. Some of these questions are just as topical over sixty years later: questions about race, class consciousness, the source of urban political power and the problems of an inner-city floating population. Park pursued his own research by developing analogies between human communities and plant and animal communities, hence the label 'human ecology'. Plant and animal communities function entirely at a *biotic* level, at which the fundamental process is one of *competition*: different species vie for the most desirable locations. Similarly, different land uses or population groups compete quite impersonally for the most desirable locations within cities. But plants and animals also form communities within which they are mutually interdependent, as in the concept of an 'ecosystem' in which the modification of one element may have repercussions for all the others. Likewise, Park viewed the city as an organism, its various land uses and population groups all interlinked, their behaviour represented by a number of ecological processes, of which the most important were 'invasion' and 'succession'. Invasion denoted the displacement of one group or land use by another, which then succeeded to a position of dominance in that part of the city. Invasions in modern cities include the expansion of business districts into adjacent residential areas and the movement of immigrant groups into previously indigenous areas.

The human ecologists were primarily concerned with cities that were growing rapidly, like Chicago, and growing as a result of in-migration more than natural increase. New arrivals lived first of all in the oldest and most overcrowded housing in inner-city areas where they were engaged in low-status, economically marginal occupations. Subsequently, they moved up the social hierarchy and outwards geographically, invading the areas previously inhabited by higher-status or American-born populations. An even more recent wave of migrants succeeded to their low-status jobs and inner-city location. Members of the highest status group, living in the outermost zone of the city, were assumed to move out to new houses built especially for them on the expanding urban fringe (Park *et al.*, 1925).

It is the process of growth by in-migration, coupled with invasion and succession, and a wave-like pattern of urban expansion and residential mobility, that forms the core of Burgess' famous model of the concentric structure of cities. Burgess' model, and particularly his diagram of five concentric zones, has been frequently described — and almost as frequently misapplied. Burgess produced his model in 1925 in a paper entitled *The Growth of the City*. Indeed, the famous diagram is accorded the same title, immediately warning against its application in many modern cities that are not growing. Burgess described a city made up of five concentric zones, which he exemplified by reference to Chicago: one half of the diagram labels the zones as they appear in any city of the Chicago type, the other half provides references to particular areas of Chicago: Deutschland, Chinatown, the Roomers' Underworld and so on (Fig. 6.1). Zone I, the Central Business District, or in Chicago parlance the Loop, was the centre for high-order retailing, offices and entertainment. At its periphery was a Wholesale Business District of markets and warehouses close to major transport routes out of the city. Beyond the business districts was Zone II, the Zone-in-Transition, although in reality, every zone was constantly in transition in response to invasion

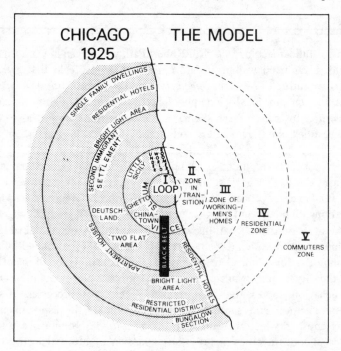

FIG. 6.1. *Burgess' model of the growth of the city (after Park* et al., *1925).*

and succession. However, in Zone II the transition was most obvious, involving a change in land use from residential to commercial, while other areas experienced only a change in the quality and density of residential occupation. The zone-in-transition was the original residential area of the city. Through time, its buildings deteriorated and were handed over to lower-status residents, especially recent in-migrants. The original residents moved out to a new urban fringe. Furthermore, an increased population necessitated an enlarged business district which also expanded into the zone-in-transition. Consequently the zone was characterized by mixed uses: some businesses unable to pay the high rents demanded at the core of the Central Business District, some light industry where residential buildings had been modified or demolished, and some lodging houses or large old houses occupied by several families. Burgess also described the zone-in-transition as the haunt of criminals and prostitutes. Zone III comprised independent workingmen's homes occupied by stable working-class families, often second-generation migrants who had succeeded in escaping from the zone-in-transition, but who still needed to minimize their journey to work which, it was assumed, lay in the city centre. Zone IV was a zone of better residences, high-status apartments or detached houses occupied by white-collar workers and their families, invariably native-born Americans. Finally Zone V, the commuters' zone, comprised physically separate but functionally linked dormitory towns.

In checking the empirical validity of Burgess' model we should not expect to find clear-cut boundaries between successive zones. Indeed, many other studies undertaken by human ecologists interested in patterns of crime or mental illness assumed the existence of continuous gradients from high values in the city centre to low values in the suburbs (Theodorson, 1961). Clearly, therefore, Burgess used the zonal concept as a convenient simplification of reality.

Nor should we expect too close a fit with the concentric geometry of Burgess' model. Even Chicago did not fit precisely: "It hardly needs to be added that neither Chicago nor any other city fits perfectly into this ideal scheme. Complications are introduced by the lake front, the Chicago river, railroad lines, historical factors in the location of industry, the relative degree of the resistance of communities to invasion, etc." (Burgess, 1925, pp. 51–52). Yet it is for ignoring these types of factors that Burgess has often been criticized.

An interesting feature of the model is that it assumes a correlation between migrant status, family status and economic status. The inner areas of Burgess' city are characterized by single people, unmarried mothers, divorcees; the suburbs by stable nuclear families. The inner areas are also inhabited by low-status, blue-collar workers; the suburbs by wealthier, white-collar workers. The inner areas are the home of immigrants; the suburbs the homes of native-born white Americans. So we should not apply Burgess' model uncritically to modern cities in which these different dimensions of urban structure clearly exhibit different spatial patterns. Nor are concentric zones, if they exist at all, the *only* significant form of ecological structure. The ecologists also referred to 'natural areas', defined by Burgess (1964, cited in Timms, 1971) as territorial units "whose distinctive characteristics – physical, economic, and cultural – are the result of the unplanned operation of ecological and social processes" (p. 458); by Zorbaugh (1926) in terms of distinct physical boundaries – roads, railways, rivers – which restricted inhabitants to particular areas; and by McKenzie (1925) with respect to the characteristics of their populations. For McKenzie a natural area must be homogeneous with respect to the class, occupation, income or race of its inhabitants. Many of the natural areas to which Burgess referred on his diagram, for example Little Sicily or Chinatown, formed only a small part of one zone. Others, most notably the Black Belt, overlapped several zones and reproduced the entire structure of the city within one sector. Again, this evidence warns us against elevating the zonal model to a status it does not deserve.

Another important criticism of ecological theory was made by Firey (1945). We have already stressed the origins of human ecology in biological analogy and its emphasis on impersonal, biotic processes. But Park, Burgess and their colleagues were not so determinist in their thinking that they failed to recognize an additional dimension to human society provided by culture and tradition. What Park did assert was that the two levels – biotic and cultural – could be studied separately, and that the cumulative effect of a large number of individual decisions, as in an urban environment, was a pattern predictable at the biotic level. Firey disagreed. He argued that cultural factors like sentiment and symbolism could counteract ecological or economic forces. In Boston, Massachusetts, the original high-status area, Beacon Hill, maintained its status for more than half a century. According to ecological theory, Beacon Hill should have been abandoned by the upper classes, but because of their attachment to the area, its literary and historical associations and their determination to resist invasion, it maintained its high status. Equally deviant behaviour was displayed by Italian immigrants to Boston who began urban life in the North End, in the inner city, but remained there despite their ascent of the social hierarchy. The North End held some sort of sentimental attachment for them (Gans, 1962).

While we may accept that cultural factors modify biotic forces, it is impossible by their very nature to generalize about them or to predict their operation, hence a theory of 'cultural ecology' is unattainable. Moreover, many cultural factors can be reduced to economic variables. The ecologists recognized that different groups had different abilities to resist invasion: the upper classes were able to resist a working-class invasion more easily than the working classes could resist a commercial invasion, because the upper classes were economically and politically more powerful than the working classes. Consider two English examples which, at first sight, appear to confirm Firey's thesis of sentiment and symbolism as ecological variables. Cannadine (1977) suggested that the survival of Edgbaston as an upper-class enclave of Birmingham was an English example of Firey's argument. Certainly it is true that the Birmingham elite wanted to remain in Edgbaston, and to that extent they were sentimentally attached to the area, but their preference could only be maintained because of their political control of Birmingham Council, on which 11 out of 16 aldermen and 22 out of 48 councillors in the 1880s lived in Edgbaston, and because of the restrictive covenants imposed by the landowner, Lord Calthorpe. A second example from the present day, the survival of Dulwich Village, as an elite enclave in inner South London, again illustrates the critical role of the landowner, in this case the Estate Governors of Dulwich College. Certainly the Georgian and Victorian houses, the extensive park, common, art gallery and public school all have symbolic value, but equally significant factors have been the college's maintenance of a private toll road at one end of the village, which acts as a deterrent to through traffic, careful estate management and the continued sale of properties leasehold rather than freehold.

Our discussion of Firey's ideas in an English context leads us to a more general evaluation of ecological theory in English cities. If we examine the spatial structure of London we can identify elements of a concentric pattern (Shepherd, Westaway and Lee, 1974). Inner London suburbs are predominantly low-status and have higher population densities, more overcrowding and more unfit housing than outer London suburbs which are predominantly high-status (Fig. 6.2). But there are major exceptions to this rule: local authority housing, which caters mainly for manual workers, is not confined to inner London but exists in every

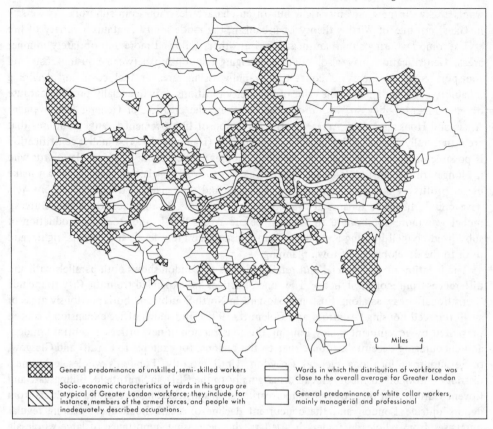

FIG. 6.2. *The distribution of socio-economic groups in Greater London, 1971 (after Wilcox, 1977).*

London borough with particularly large estates in outer areas such as Becontree, St. Helier and Watling, all constructed between the wars by the London County Council as a suburban solution to the inner London housing problem. More recently, the Greater London Council has moved even farther afield, with estates in such places at Thetford, Basingstoke and Andover. The ring of London new towns, such as Crawley and Harlow, and more recently, Milton Keynes and Peterborough, may also be regarded as a displacement of the skilled working class from Burgess' Zone III to the Outer Metropolitan Area. So government intervention, and particularly local authority housing policy, may distort a simple concentric pattern.

At the other extremity of the class spectrum are inner suburbs like Dulwich, Hampstead and Blackheath that have retained their exclusiveness; central residential areas like Mayfair and South Kensington where only the very rich, or those whose housing is provided by their business, can afford to live; and areas that began as middle-class suburbs in the nineteenth century, experienced invasion, succession and a decline into overcrowded or substandard conditions in the first few decades of the twentieth century, but are now regaining a professional, middle-class population, for example Islington, Chelsea and parts of Stockwell and Camden Town (Hamnett, 1976). The regeneration of these areas, popularly termed 'gentrification', indicates a set of values alien to Burgess' model. Not everybody wants to live in new, amenity-rich, but often characterless houses in suburbia. As we saw in Gans' critique of Wirth's theory of urbanism, the modern city contains a variety of life styles, some favouring suburban locations, but others followed more appropriately in inner areas. Gentrification may also reflect a changing relationship between housing costs and transport costs, as increased congestion, rapidly rising fares or fuel costs and declining reliability of service enhance the value of inner-city locations. It is financially possible because of government policy in favour of rehabilitation: the creation of General Improvement Areas and Housing Action Areas and the allocation of Improvement Grants to houses that are structurally sound but lacking in basic amenities (Hamnett, 1973). Finally, gentrification is possible because increasing numbers of old houses are being sold by private landlords who no longer find it profitable to let their properties to working-class tenants: they can make bigger profits by investing their money elsewhere and they claim that successive Rent Acts have unduly favoured tenants at the expense of landlords. The implication is that Burgess' model was more appropriate to London before World War I, prior to the introduction of subsidized council housing and government legislation on rent levels and tenants' rights, and prior to the development of town planning.

The location of commercial and retail activities in London shows both parallels with and differences from ecological theory. The zone of offices has expanded from the City to include 'transitional' areas, as along Euston Road and in North Southwark, both previously areas of small terraced housing (Ambrose and Colenutt, 1975). But much office expansion has been prevented by government policy limiting the construction of new offices in central London, and encouraging decentralization either to the regions, for example to Cardiff and Glasgow, or to suburban locations such as Croydon. Until recently, London's wholesale business district conformed to theory, located marginally to the CBD, in Smithfield, Billingsgate and Covent Garden. But the growth of supermarket chains distributing own-brand products from depots outside London and the concurrent decline of small shopkeepers making regular purchases from wholesale traders has led to the decreasing importance of large wholesale markets. Those that remain have decentralized, as with the movement of fruit and vegetable wholesalers from Covent Garden to Nine Elms.

Changes in the location of demand for unskilled or casual labour, such as market porters, are reproduced in other industries too (e.g. the downstream shift of the functioning port and its associated warehouses) and mean that the inner city is no longer the optimum residential location for the unskilled, particularly recent migrants. But as the inner city still contains the worst housing, and often the only housing to which the poor and rootless have access, they continue to live in London's equivalent of Burgess' Zone II and invasion and succession continue to typify these areas. All but one of the districts defined as 'Housing Stress Areas' by the GLC in the wake of the Milner-Holland Report on Housing (1965) lay in the inner residential area, including Deptford, Camberwell, Newington, Clapham, Notting Hill, Willesden, Holloway, Shoreditch and Wapping (Fig. 6.3). The only outer London stress area — Southall — was associated with large-scale Asian immigration. Many of these districts contain housing that started life in the late nineteenth century as middle-class town houses, terraced and multi-storied. With age and technological change they became unsuitable for the middle classes, with a decline in family size and the employment of domestic servants they became too large for single-family occupation: hence their rapid deterioration and decline into multi-occupation, by 'problem families' (e.g. unmarried mothers and their children), or by immigrants (often renting from an immigrant landlord), or by students in bedsitters sharing unimproved facilities (Mellor, 1973).

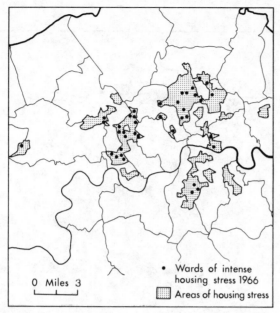

FIG. 6.3. *Housing stress areas in Greater London, 1966.*

Robson (1969) demonstrated the operation of invasion and succession in Sunderland, by carrying out a regression analysis of rateable values in the town in 1892 and 1963. The average rateable value of dwellings in each district of the town in 1892 was plotted against the value associated with the same area seventy years later, and a best-fit regression line was drawn from which 1892 values could be predicted given 1963 data. Districts plotted above the best-fit line had declined relative to the town as a whole. Spatially, they were clustered just south of the town centre at the apex of a middle-class sector, a classic zone-in-transition that had been among the most desirable residential areas in the nineteenth century but subsequently declined in status as new high-status accommodation was provided in more distant suburbs (Fig. 6.4).

Robson's study revealed a concentric pattern of social areas in North Sunderland, north of the River Wear, but a sectoral pattern south of the river and adjacent to the Central Business District, a pattern also found by Jones (1960) in his study of Belfast. Robson concluded that there were two principal forces shaping the social geography of Sunderland: the location of industry and the location of the rich. The Sunderland elite desired easy access to the CBD, which was situated just south of the river, but they were averse to locating anywhere near to heavy industry, which was concentrated along the banks of the river. In the south of the town, the elite could achieve both objectives by locating adjacent to the CBD but on the opposite side from the river. Hence, an elite sector developed south of the town centre. To the north, the elite could live near the centre only if they also lived adjacent to the industrial zone. This was unacceptable and a more remote location was preferred, interposing a zone of lower-status housing between elite and industry, and so producing a concentric pattern of CBD, industry, low-status housing and finally high-status housing. But it is a concentric pattern that owes little to the ecological

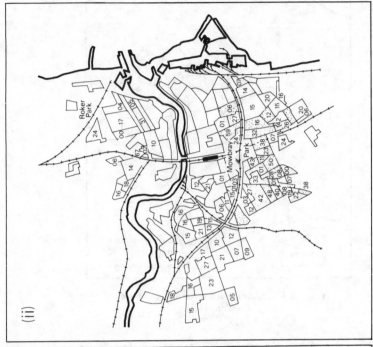

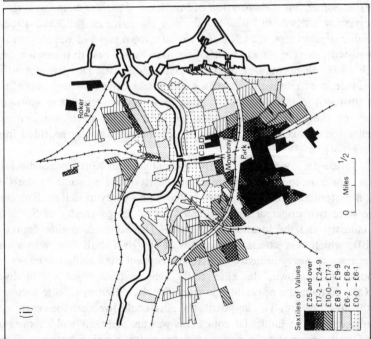

Sextiles of Values

£25 and over
£17·2 – £24·9
£10·0 – £17·1
£8·3 – £9·9
£6·2 – £8·2
£0·0 – £6·1

0    Miles    ½

FIG. 6.4. (i) Rating values in Sunderland, 1892; (ii) Changes in rating values, 1892–1963. All the 1892 residential areas are shown in outline. Positive or negative change in rating between 1892 and 1963 is indicated by decimal fractions in those areas which were residential at both dates. Areas showing negative change (i.e. relative decline) are stippled (after Robson, 1969).

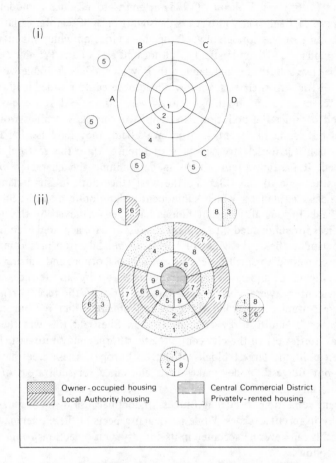

FIG. 6.5. *Models of urban structure: (i) Mann, 1965.*
*1 = The City Centre. 2 = Transitional Zone. 3 = Zone of*
*Small Terrace Houses in Sectors C and D; Larger By-*
*Law Houses in Sector B; Old Houses in Sector A. 4 =*
*Post-1918 Residential Areas, with post-1945 Develop-*
*ment mainly on periphery. 5 = Commuting 'villages'.*
*A = The Middle-Class sector. B = The Lower Middle-Class*
*sector. C = The Working-Class sector (including l.a.*
*housing). D = Industry and Lowest Working-Class areas.*
*(ii) Robson, 1975. 1 = inter-war owner-occupied. 2 =*
*high-status owner-occupied. 3 = post-war semi-detached*
*owner-occupied. 4 = post-war detached owner-occupied.*
*5 = student bedsitters. 6 = inter-war council estates/inner*
*city council flats. 7 = post-war council estates/inner-city*
*high rise. 8 = privately rented low status. 9 = rooming*
*houses.*

forces envisaged by Park and Burgess, and Robson goes on to note that even this crude concentricity exists only if the location of council housing is ignored.

Both Mann's (1965) and Robson's (1975) attempts to produce a model of the social geography of a typical English city also stress the significance of sectoral variations (Fig. 6.5). Mann takes account of the topography of the three cities on which his model is based — Sheffield, Nottingham and Huddersfield — all located east of the Pennines and containing desirable middle-class suburbs on high land to their west, and less desirable working-class and manufacturing districts to their east, on low-lying, more easily flooded land. The east—west dichotomy is accentuated by prevailing westerly winds: middle-class home-owners prefer a location upwind of industrial pollution. No doubt working-class families would also prefer to live upwind but, as in nineteenth-century Wakefield, they have neither the purchasing power nor the political muscle to gain their preference. Once this sectoral distinction has been established, it has important effects in determining the character of the zone-in-transition on either side of the CBD. To the west (the south in Sunderland) will be the original middle-class residences, which subsequently deteriorate much as Burgess hypothesized. In Sheffield, Broomhall's elegant houses have been annexed by the university, converted into offices, or subdivided into student houses, or have acquired even more notorious inhabitants. In Huddersfield, the villas of Highfield and Edgerton passed into Asian occupation or were converted to small hotels, private schools, offices and nursing homes. To the east, even the original occupiers of monotonous rows of 'by-law' terraces, erected at the end of the last century, were working-class families. Prior to the recent trend for rehabilitation, such areas were considerd ripe for redevelopment, either for purpose-built office accommodation or as multi-storey council flats. In Sheffield this was the fate of inner residential areas north-west of the city centre (Netherthorpe) and south-east (Hyde Park and Park Hill, when built the largest blocks of flats in Europe). These areas have always been working-class; but Burgess' model makes little allowance for such areas of *purpose-built* working-class housing.

We have spent some time discussing Burgess' model because of its dominant position in urban geography in recent decades. While particular aspects of the model may be applicable to English cities, it can never be accepted in its entirety. Our objections to the model may be summarized as follows:

(i) Burgess assumed a succession of ethnically, linguistically or culturally distinctive immigrant groups, each initially occupying the transition zone and subsequently decentralizing in a wave-like fashion. English cities have grown by natural increase more than by immigration, and the largest immigrant groups in English society — Jews, Irish, West Indians, Asians — have played different roles in the urban economy and have not assimilated into the host society as much as Poles, Finns, Ukranians and others have into American society. The Irish are still predominantly employed in low-status occupations and live in distinctive, often inner suburban areas 130 years after the Famine migration; West Indians are socially and geographically less mobile than Asian immigrants, but their culture and religion is more akin to that of the indigenous population.

(ii) Burgess assumed a city in which working-class housing was invariably old middle-class housing, and new housing was provided by private enterprise on the urban fringe. There was little allowance for inner-city redevelopment for residential purposes, or for state intervention in the housing market.

(iii) Burgess assumed a city dependent on public transport for journeys to work or shops. This restricted people's ability to live far from their place of work, and especially to make cross-town as opposed to periphery-centre journeys. Conversely, it limited the freedom of shops and workplaces to move out of the central area. In an automobile-dependent city, more diverse journey patterns become feasible and centres of business, production and entertainment are freer to locate on cheaper sites away from the city centre. This process has gone furthest in North America, where Berry (1970) has predicted that by the year 2000 many distance-decay patterns will have reversed: population densities, land values, retail expenditure will increase away from city centres that have been stifled by congestion, excessive rents and rates, street violence and obsolescence. But the problem is also recognizable in England, particularly in inner areas with high rates of out-migration of skilled workers and their places of employment, leaving a residue of unskilled and unemployed (see Chapter 9).

(iv) Finally, and most fundamentally, Burgess — like Wirth — assumed a city that was growing, yet many urban areas are now losing population.

However, it remains true that there *are* many elements of concentric zonal structure in the social geography of English cities. Either we explain these as 'relict features' that date from a time when Burgess' model did operate, or we seek an alternative explanation. Burgess' ecological forces are in many respects purely economic in character, but a more explicit economic theory of concentric urban structure has been provided by a succession of land economists, including Alonso (1960) and Evans (1973).

## Micro-Economic Theory

Alonso's (1960) theory of the urban land market is based, like Von Thünen's theory of location, on the concept of economic rent. Each land use or population group is associated with a unique bid-rent curve which defines the level of rent it is prepared to pay to occupy a given location. Like Von Thünen, Alonso assumes a city set on an isotropic plain in which transport is equally easy in all directions and transport costs rise as distance from the city centre increases. At the same distance from work, rich and poor will pay the same amount in transport costs (ignoring relatively minor details such as the higher petrol consumption of the rich man's larger car, or the supplement he pays for first-class travel). But the poorer man will be paying a much larger *proportion* of his income in transport costs. He will have less left over to spend on land (or housing) and consequently, at an equivalent location, the poor will occupy less land and live at higher densities than the rich. Furthermore, the poor will be sensitive to quite minor changes in the cost of transport, which will go relatively unnoticed by their rich neighbours. If fares rise, the poor will require a substantial reduction in the unit cost of land if they are to remain as well off as before. For the rich, the fare increase need be compensated by a much smaller reduction in the cost of each unit of land: since they own or rent more units of land than the poor, the total saving will be the same. In other words, poor households will have steeper bid-rent curves than rich households. They cannot afford the transport costs associated with suburban living, however cheap land may be on the urban fringe, The rich can make quite low bids for suburban land in the knowledge that their only competition is from agriculture. In consequence, we get the apparent paradox of the rich living on cheap land in the suburbs, and at low densities, while the poor live on expensive land, in the inner city, and at high densities (Fig. 6.6).

If Alonso's model, as outlined above, operates in reality, then:

(i)   Economic status should increase away from the city centre.

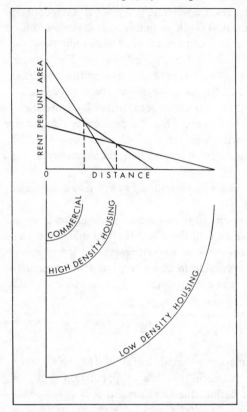

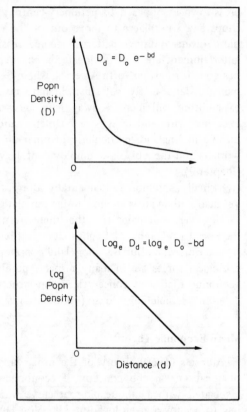

FIG. 6.6. *Rent–distance relationships and the
pattern of urban land use.*

FIG. 6.7. *Relationship between population
density and distance from the city centre.*

(ii) Land values should follow a distance-decay pattern, with high values at the centre and low values at the urban fringe.

(iii) Population densities should follow the same pattern as residential land values. The first effect has already been discussed in considering the utility of Burgess' model. Here we shall focus on patterns of population density.

Empirical studies point to a decreasing difference between central and peripheral densities the more recent the period to which data refer. Most researchers have hypothesized a negative exponential pattern which converts to a straight line relationship between population density and distance when density is expressed logarithmically (Clark, 1951) (Fig. 6.7). Through time the slope of this straight line decreases (i.e. suburban densities increase more quickly than central densities which may actually decrease) and the goodness of fit of the straight line, measured by calculating the correlation between log. density and distance, may also deteriorate (Berry, Simmons & Tennant, 1963). The scatter of values for different districts around the best-fit line increases, perhaps with the demolition of inner-city slums and their replacement by non-residential or lower-density residential development, and with the construction of more small town houses or blocks of luxury flats at relatively high densities in the suburbs. The implication is that transport costs to the city centre are a decreasingly significant determinant of density (or land value), either because transport costs play a minor role in most families' budgets today (which seems unlikely) or — more likely — because the city centre is no longer the location around which the population is organized. Instead, access to suburban employment or shopping centres has grown more important. Furthermore, the more advanced the transport technology, the more selective its application, and the less appropriate the assumption of equal ease of movement in all directions. In a 'walking city' transport costs and journey times increase at the same rate regardless of the direction of travel. In a city dependent on public transport certain routes receive more favoured treatment than others but most metropolitan transport systems at their peak, for example London Transport immediately before and after World War II, were still remarkably comprehensive in their coverage of possible routes. However, advanced transport facilities, especially urban motorways, are more expensive to build and more disruptive of existing land uses: only a few are constructed, where resistance to demolition and redevelopment is least, or where the financial basis is most secure, and so the accessibility surface of the city is distorted. The correlation between time, cost and distance breaks down.

One location in which the distance-decay model never fitted reality was the city centre, where there was invariably a 'density crater' (Fig. 6.8). The reason for this was quite in

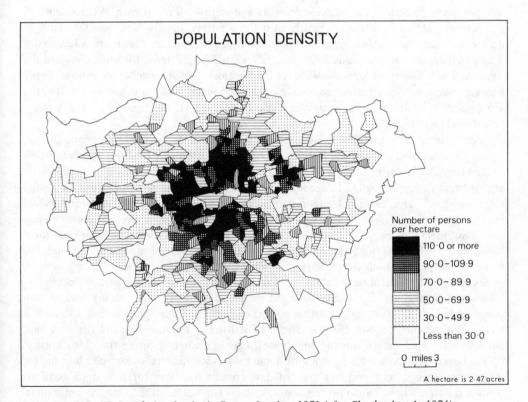

FIG. 6.8. *Population density in Greater London, 1971 (after Shepherd et al., 1974).*

accordance with Alonso's model: densities were low in city centres not because residents lived in large houses in large gardens, but because there were few residents in any kind of accommodation, given the superior rent-paying ability of retailing and commercial activities. In response to this complication, some researchers have worked in terms of Net Residential Density (i.e. population/residential land — including gardens and access roads but excluding land used for industry, shops, offices, parks, transport services, etc.). This eliminates the central crater, maintains a simple correlation between density and distance and emphasizes the continuing relationship between density and land value. Other writers have continued to use Gross Density but fitted more complex quadratic or polynomial functions which take into account the central crater and sometimes also the distorting effects of suburban business centres (Newling, 1969). This type of curve-fitting may be appropriate if the purpose is merely to describe population patterns using mathematical equations as a convenient short-hand, but it has little explanatory value unless correlations are identified between densities and other distributions. For example, Warnes (1975) has examined the parallels between urban population gradients — summarizing the distribution of population — and employment gradients — summarizing the distribution of workplaces. The disparities between the two gradients represent net commuting flows where there may be most pressure on transport facilities.

Where population densities *do* follow a simple distance-decay pattern, we still should not assume that Alonso's theory is thereby proven. The critical element in Alonso's model is the process of competitive bidding for urban land, and Harvey (1973) has argued that a distance-decay pattern of land values, densities and status will result even in the absence of competitive bidding in a free market. Even if the total demand for land near the centre is no greater than the demand for land on the urban fringe, the fact that there is less centre than periphery means that demand *per unit of land* will be greater in the inner city than the suburbs. The intensity of land use will increase the closer one approaches the centre, simply because central land is a scarcer commodity than peripheral land. In other words, it is the assumption of centricity that generates distance-decay patterns, regardless of any competitive bidding process.

Several other criticisms have been levelled against conventional micro-economic theory. Firstly, it is accused of ignoring history, laying down patterns of land use and population distribution at a moment in time (Alonso, 1964). The constraints imposed on land use by a varied morphology designed to accommodate a different urban structure during a period when economic and technical circumstances were also different are disregarded. Some modifications to built form are relatively easy to achieve: if economic circumstances demand it an Edwardian villa may be converted into offices or a private school, or a Georgian town house into small flats. But it is more expensive to reverse such processes: for example, to convert small purpose-built flats into large dwellings, or offices into homes.

Secondly, the model assumes a free market in which decision-makers have perfect knowledge and behave optimally. But government intervention in land and housing markets may prohibit the optimal (i.e. most profitable) use of land. For example, the imposition of a Green Belt around London has the effect of artificially inflating demand for land and, consequently, land values, on the suburban fringe, immediately inside the girdle created by the Green Belt. As a result, it is unprofitable for private builders to construct housing for low-income groups here, and this type of development has been forced out to locations beyond the Green Belt. Young professionals and their families become 'reluctant commuters' living in housing estates in deepest Kent, Sussex or Hertfordshire, not because of a preference for country life but because these are the only places where they can afford a house with a garden. A second example concerns the provision of council housing for low-income groups in locations other than those predicted by micro-economic theory. It is true that, within the public sector, most inner-city housing schemes are for high-density flats, most suburban developments are estates of low-density, semi-detached or terraced houses, but it is also true that many local authority developments are in locations too expensive for the unsubsidized private sector to consider.

Thirdly, the model is usually specified in terms of the renting or purchase of *land*, but most individual decisions involve land that is already in use. Most families buy or rent *houses* rather than land (Kirby, 1976). According to this line of reasoning, we should be less interested in land values than house prices. The relationship between cost of housing and distance from city centre has attracted considerable attention from urban economists in recent years but their evidence is inconclusive. Evans (1973) has argued that the property-value gradient parallels the land-value gradient. Considering the prices of post-1960 two-bedroom flats in a middle-class sector in north London, stretching from Regent's Park to Barnet, he found that distance 'explained' three-quarters of the variation in asking prices. But flats are only one segment of the private housing market, the one type of housing likely to occur in both central and suburban locations. In most cases it is impossible to define a meaningful house-price gradient because inner-city housing is so different in age, size and condition from suburban housing. In a detailed survey of house sales in Edinburgh, Richardson (1975) found a strong *positive* relationship between house price and distance from the CBD (i.e. prices increased as distance increased). But when allowance was made for social class, the relationship between distance and price was reversed: for a given class of housing selling price did decline as distance from the centre increased. However, that is a rather impractical conclusion since houses of the same class rarely exist at different distances from the centre.

In a review of house-price studies, mostly regression analyses in which house price was the dependent variable and factors such as distance, social class and environmental quality were the independent variables, Ball (1973) found that high correlation coefficients invariably resulted, although different studies included different sets of variables. Some analyses excluded distance yet obtained levels of 'explanation' equally as high as those that included distance, a finding that reinforces the oft-repeated caveat that correlation does not signify causality.

If, as seems likely, the overall house-price gradient is positive, prices increasing as distance increases at least to the edge of the continuous built-up area, then we cannot envisage a trade-off between costs of property and costs of travel. Families do not *opt* for low-density housing in the suburbs or high-density living in the inner city. Instead, they choose (or are constrained to join) a particular tenure group — owner-occupation, council housing or private renting — and that decision strongly dictates their area of residence, the price they pay and the density at which they live.

A final criticism of Alonso's model concerns the definition of 'value' and the relationship between 'use' and 'value'. Value only has meaning at the moment it is realized, when land actually changes hands. For most of the time, there is no such thing as a 'land-value surface'. You cannot choose to locate on land that is not available. Alonso's arguments also assume that when a piece of property enters the market its value reflects its potential use, as the site for factory, office or home, what we can term its 'use value' to the potential occupier. In practice, a ground landlord, property speculator, estate agent, solicitor or building society manager may also play important roles in setting the value of property. All these professionals earn their living through the exchange of property. For example, estate agents whose commission is usually a fixed percentage (2–3 per cent) of the purchase price of any house they sell have a vested interest in increasing the cost of housing and the frequency with which properties change hands. Speculators, whose profit depends on their command of scarce resources, may withhold some property from the market so that they can benefit from the artificial scarcity of the property they are prepared to release. But even the potential owner-occupier is not concerned only with the use of his purchase as a residence. We may select a sub-optimal location in the city if we think that the property market is likely to favour that area more than others in the future, so that the profit we make when we resell the property more than compensates for the additional transport or running costs that we incur in living there.

The list of criticisms of Alonso's theory may appear so extensive that the reader may be wondering why it was introduced into the discussion at all. Is it any more than a convenient Aunt Sally, useful only as a method of introducing such diverse topics into the discussion as population densities and house prices? At least three points may be made in the theory's favour. Firstly, it is appropriate to past periods, when there were fewer controls on the use and transfer of land and when much of the present land-use pattern of our cities was determined. Secondly, the model has proved remarkably, perhaps uncomfortably, successful in predicting patterns of land use and population distribution. Government and planners may have the right to veto the location of profitable, but socially undesirable, forms of business, but they are rarely sufficiently powerful to dictate unviable uses of land. Only the most doctrinaire of socialist local authorities plan in complete defiance of classical urban economics. Thirdly, while the model may not explain the behaviour of individual households deciding where to live in an already built environment it does help us to understand the decisions made by the institutions that create the built environment. If land is relatively cheap on the periphery that is because it has little potential for non-residential development. If land is expensive in the inner city, it is likely to be developed intensively, preferably as high-rise office accommodation, alternatively as luxury flats for foreign businessmen, or – with a subsidy – as high-density housing for lower-income groups who must live somewhere and cannot afford the time or the cost of a long journey to work. Finally, we should note that whether a classical economic approach or one based on political economy is adopted, the argument is the same: social patterns are determined by economic relationships.

## Alternative Geometries

So far this chapter has focused on alternative explanations of concentric or distance-decay patterns in the social geography of cities, yet the spatial structure of most English cities is far too complex to be described solely in these terms. Both Robson in Sunderland and Mann in Sheffield, Nottingham and Huddersfield noted the existence of sectoral variations. Sectoral differences were also apparent in the nineteenth-century cities discussed in Chapter 5. Willmott and Young (1973) have described the social geography of London as a working-class 'cross' separating middle-class 'quarters' (Fig. 6.2). The cross follows the Lea and Wandle valleys north and south of London, the Thames estuary to the east and the A4/M4 arterial roads linking central London to Heathrow Airport. All these sectors are associated with industrial areas: traditional, small-scale craft industries in the East End; industrial estates on extensive areas of flat, ill-drained land in the Lea and Wandle valleys;

large Thames-side factories like Ford's of Dagenham; industries associated with the docks east of London and the airport to the west; and inter-war industrial estates lining major roads out of London, as at Park Royal. One 'quarter' of middle-class housing follows the Thames upstream from historically upper-class suburbs in Westminster, Chelsea and Fulham to contemporary 'stockbroker' settlements such as Weybridge, Sunningdale and Virginia Water. Other middle-class sectors extend from elevated ground near the centre to even higher ground on the present urban fringe. In Victorian London middle-class suburbia included Primrose Hill, Hampstead and Highgate to the north, and elevated ground around Wimbledon, Clapham and Blackheath commons in the south. Some of these areas have maintained their elite status into the late twentieth century, while newer middle-class suburbs have been built farther out, but in the same sectors of the metropolis: on the slopes of the Chilterns (e.g. Chorley Wood) and the North Downs (e.g. Banstead and Chipstead Valley).

As well as topography, the transport network and the policy of independent railway companies prior to their nationalization in 1948 have exerted important influences on the character of sectoral development. From the 1870s onwards the Great Eastern Railway vigorously solicited the custom of the working classes by offering cheap fares on special workmen's trains. Thousands of artisans moved out from the East End to Tottenham, Walthamstow and Edmonton, but their invasion ended any hope that the Great Eastern Railway may have cherished of attracting a middle-class clientele. In contrast, the extension of suburbia into the Chilterns was facilitated by the construction and eventual electrification of the Metropolitan Railway running north-west from Baker Street. In its advertisements the Metropolitan Railway invited the middle classes to live in 'Metroland'. Builders offered free season tickets as an incentive to prospective housebuyers and the railway established its own property company to develop private housing estates adjacent to its stations (Jackson, 1973).

All these factors — the attraction of high ground for the better-off, the provision of purpose-built working-class housing close to industry and the role of communications — are included in Hoyt's sector theory, outlined in 1939 in his book on *The Structure and Growth of Residential Neighbourhoods in American Cities*. Like Burgess' model, Hoyt's theory was derived inductively: it was based on his observations of the cost of housing in 142 American cities. Again like Burgess, Hoyt was concerned with processes of urban growth and change, yet his model has frequently suffered the same fate as Burgess', its 'validity' being assessed by comparing the actual pattern at a moment in time with an expected sectoral pattern. Unlike Burgess, Hoyt focused his attention on the distribution of one particular variable: the average rental of housing in each city block.

Hoyt found that the highest rent areas were invariably located in one or more sectors, wedges that extended from city centre to periphery (Fig. 6.9). Low-cost areas rarely adjoined those of high rent; usually a buffer zone of intermediate rent was interposed. Once established a sector expanded in response to the factors already mentioned. Low-rent sectors were associated with industrial areas. High-rent sectors were attracted to high, well-drained ground with fine views and fresh air, to waterfront locations where these were neither unhealthy nor pre-empted by industry, and to areas convenient for commuter railways. Hoyt also recognized some of the institutional factors that we mentioned in the critique of Alonso's theory. He suggested that estate agents and property developers might bend the direction of new development to their own advantage, and that the independent and often irrational decisions to move made by 'leaders of the community' might set the fashion for elite migration in a new direction. However, the most significant aspect of sector theory is the recognition that low-income and high-income households belong to separate

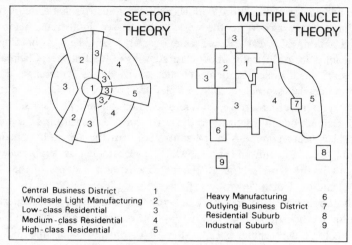

FIG. 6.9. *The sector and multiple nuclei models of urban structure (after Harris and Ullman, 1945).*

housing markets, each supplied with dwellings purposely designed for their own class. The only low-status dwellings to abut those of high status were at the apex of the high-status sector, where Hoyt identified a process of invasion and subdivision of old and unfashionable middle-class housing, much as Robson observed in Sunderland. But this low-status accommodation for one-person households, students, temporary residents, new arrivals, the chronic unemployed or problem families constituted a quite separate branch of the housing system from purpose-built working-class housing occupied by skilled or semi-skilled manual workers and their families. In England the former comprises mainly furnished rooms rented from private landlords, the latter unfurnished dwellings rented from either a local authority or a decreasing number of private landlords.

Harris and Ullman's (1945) multiple-nuclei model (Fig. 6.9) is frequently cited in the same breath as Burgess' and Hoyt's theories, but unlike them it offers no particular geometry of urban structure. The authors merely stated guidelines for understanding land-use patterns: unlike activities repel, complementary activities attract, specialization produces segregation. They also observed that most large cities, during the course of their growth, absorbed smaller, previously independent settlements which survived as 'multiple nuclei' in the larger places. We might expect each of these nuclei to have its own pattern of zones and sectors, much like the second market introduced by Von Thünen into his 'isolated state'.

We have seen that the traditional conceptual models of urban geographers, based on ecological and micro-economic theory, may provide reasonable summaries of the patterns that still dominate our cities, but are outdated with respect to the processes currently at work in them. Moreover, they offer interpretations of the city which may bear little resemblance to the 'mental maps' that provide the context in which politicians, businessmen and private individuals make decisions on where to invest or where to live.

## References and Further Reading

Valuable summaries of research in urban social geography include:
Herbert, D. T. (1972) *Urban Geography: A Social Perspective*, David & Charles, Newton Abbot.

Herbert, D. T. & Johnston, R. J. (eds.) (1976) *Social Areas in Cities* (two volumes), Wiley, London.
Robson, B. T. (1975) *Urban Social Areas,* Oxford University Press, London.
Timms, D. W. G. (1971) *The Urban Mosaic,* Cambridge University Press, Cambridge.

The social geography of cities is placed in the wider context of urban geography by:
Carter, H. (1975) *The Study of Urban Geography,* Arnold, London.
Scargill, D. I. (1979) *The Form of Cities,* Bell & Hyman, London.

The reaction against an ecological approach is reflected in:
Gray, F. (1975) Non-explanation in urban geography, *Area,* 7, 228–35.
Robson, B. T. (1975) The urban environment, *Geography,* 60, 184–8.

Several readers contain reprints of articles relevant to this and the following chapter:
Bourne, L. S. (1971) *Internal Structure of the City,* Oxford University Press, London.
Jones, E. (1975) *Readings in Social Geography,* Oxford University Press, London.
Lambert, C. and Weir, D. (1975) *Cities in Modern Britain,* Fontana, London.

On ecological theory, see the papers by Park, Burgess and McKenzie that comprise the first three chapters of:
Park, R. E. *et al.* (1925) *The City,* University of Chicago Press, Chicago.

Another important collection including the paper by Zorbaugh (1926) is:
Theodorson, G. A. (1961) *Studies in Human Ecology,* Harper & Row, New York.

Cultural influences on ecological patterns are illustrated by:
Cannadine, D. (1977) Victorian cities: how different?, *Social History,* 4, 457–82.
Firey, W. (1945) Sentiment and symbolism as ecological variables, *American Sociological Review,* 10, 140–8.
Gans, H. J. (1962) *The Urban Villagers,* Free Press, Glencoe, Illinois.

On the spatial structure of modern British cities, see:
Robson, B. T. (1969) *Urban Analysis,* Cambridge University Press, Cambridge.
Jones, E. (1960) *A Social Geography of Belfast,* Oxford University Press, Oxford.
Mann, P. H. (1965) *An Approach to Urban Sociology,* Routledge & Kegan Paul, London.

Classical economic theorists and their critics include:
Alonso, W. (1960) A theory of the urban land market, *Papers and Proceedings of the Regional Science Association,* 6, 149–58.
Alonso, W. (1964) The historic and the structural theories of urban form, *Land Economics,* 40, 227–31.
Evans, A. W. (1973) *The Economics of Residential Location,* Macmillan, London.
Harvey, D. (1973) *Social Justice and the City,* Arnold, London, Chapters 4 and 5.
Kirby, A. M. (1976) Housing market studies: a critical review, *Transactions, Institute of British Geographers,* New Series, 1, 2–9.

Studies of spatial variations in house prices include:
Ball, M. (1973) Recent empirical work on the determinants of relative house prices, *Urban Studies,* 10, 213–33.
Richardson, H. W. *et al.* (1975) Determinants of urban house prices, *Urban Studies,* 11, 189–201.

Among numerous studies of urban population density patterns, see:
Berry, B. J. L., Simmons, J. W. and Tennant, R. J. (1963) Urban population densities: structure and change, *Geographical Review,* 53, 389–405.
Berry, B. J. L. (1970) The geography of the United States in the year 2000, *Transactions Institute of British Geographers,* 51, 21–53.
Clark, C. (1951) Urban population densities, *Journal of the Royal Statistical Society Series A,* 114, 490–6.
Newling, B. E. (1969) The spatial variation of urban population densities, *Geographical Review,* 59, 242–52.
Warnes, A. M. (1975) Commuting towards city centres: a study of population and employment density gradients in Liverpool and Manchester, *Transactions Institute of British Geographers,* 64, 77–96.

Alternative models of urban structure are discussed in:

Hoyt, H. (1939) *The Structure and Growth of Residential Neighbourhoods in American Cities,* Federal Housing Administration, Washington.

Harris, C. D. and Ullman, E. L. (1945) The nature of cities, *Annals of the American Academy of Political and Social Science,* 242, 7–17.


On the social geography of London, see:

Ambrose, P. and Colenutt, B. (1975) *The Property Machine,* Penguin, Harmondsworth.

Clout, H. D. (ed.) (1978) *Changing London,* University Tutorial Press, London.

Hamnett, C. (1973) Improvement grants as an indicator of gentrification in Inner London, *Area,* 5, 252–61.

Hamnett, C. (1976) Social change and social segregation in Inner London, 1961–71, *Urban Studies,* 13, 261–71.

Jackson, A. A. (1973) *Semi-Detached London,* Allen & Unwin, London.

Mellor, R. (1973) Structure and process in the twilight areas, *Town Planning Review,* 44, 54–70.

Shepherd, J., Westaway, J. and Lee, T. (1974) *A Social Atlas of London,* Oxford University Press, Oxford.

Wilcox, D. (1977) *London: The Heartless City,* Thames Television, London.

Willmott, P. and Young, M. (1973) Social class and geography, in D. Donnison & D. Eversley (eds.), *London: Urban Patterns, Problems and Policies,* Heinemann, London, pp. 190–214.

# 7

# Segregation and Patterns of Behaviour in Urban Areas

### Residential Segregation

EVEN if we find it impossible to generalize about the spatial structure of English cities we cannot ignore the segregation of their inhabitants into distinctive social areas. In all but the smallest towns different social or ethnic groups occupy distinct and exclusive territories. But, as we saw in Chapter 5, the scale at which segregation occurs and the types of groups that are involved may change through time. A substantial literature in urban geography and sociology is devoted to the measurement of levels of segregation, often through the calculation of Indices of Dissimilarity ($I_D$) and Segregation ($I_S$) (Duncan and Duncan, 1955; Peach, 1975). The Index of Dissimilarity measures the difference between the distributions of two populations across a number of sub-areas, and represents the percentage of one population which would need to move areas for its distribution to coincide with that of the other population.

Consider the distributions of two socio-economic classes — manual workers and non-manual workers — in a town divided into five enumeration districts. Table 7.1 shows the percentage of each class living in each district. The Dissimilarity Index is calculated by summing the differences between the percentages resident in each district, and halving the total. In the example, $I_D = 50$, i.e. 50 per cent of manual workers must move to another district for their distribution to be the same as that of non-manual workers (30 per cent must move from area A, 20 per cent from B, redistributing themselves in areas C, D and E). The index can range from 0, where two populations have identical distributions, to 100, where there is no overlap between the populations. For instance, the dissimilarity index

TABLE 7.1. *An example of the calculation of the Index of Dissimilarity*

| Enumeration District | Percentage of Manual Workers in Each District | Percentage of Non-Manual Workers in Each District | \|Difference\| |
|---|---|---|---|
| A | 40 | 10 | 30 |
| B | 30 | 10 | 20 |
| C | 10 | 20 | 10 |
| D | 10 | 30 | 20 |
| E | 10 | 30 | 20 |
| Total | 100 | 100 | 100 |

$$I_D = \frac{|\text{Difference}|}{2} = \frac{100}{2} = 50$$

between blacks and whites in a city with a black ghetto would equal 100 if all the blacks lived in one district and none of the whites lived in that district.

The index is most frequently used to measure the dissimilarity in the residential patterns of different socio-economic, ethnic or religious groups. Among English studies, Jones and McEvoy (1978) have measured the segregation of Asian immigrants in Huddersfield, Collison (1967) the segregation of immigrant groups in Oxford, and Heraud (1968) the segregation of socio-economic groups in Crawley New Town. However, the index could equally well be applied to the distributions of different age groups or different types of housing, in fact to any pairs of distributions that are fixed in space.

In most cases more than two groups have been investigated: Collison worked with seven ethnic groups in Oxford, Heraud with five socio-economic groups in Crawley. Dissimilarity indices were calculated for each pair of groups and presented in a matrix, as in Table 7.2, which shows the dissimilarities between the distributions of different socio-economic groups in the outer London borough of Sutton in 1966. The final column of the matrix shows the Index of Segregation for each group, calculated in identical fashion to the Dissimilarity Index but measuring the difference between one group and all the remainder. For example, in Table 7.2 22 per cent of Class I would need to move wards for their distribution to coincide with that of the employed population as a whole.

The indices have obvious uses in measuring the extent of segregation at a moment in time, and in comparing levels of segregation through time or between cities. In Sutton the segregation index for Class I increased from 22 in 1966 to 26 in 1971. In the inner London borough of Lambeth, too, Class I became more segregated from the rest of the population, but the absolute level of segregation was lower than in Sutton (21 in 1966, 23 in 1971). Among similar uses of the index, Poole and Boal (1973) have demonstrated that the segregation of Protestants and Catholics in Belfast in 1969 was no greater than the segregation of the coloured population in Birmingham, and Heraud (1968) has argued that the planners' ideal of socially balanced neighbourhoods in Crawley New Town collapsed as segregation between social classes increased and each neighbourhood acquired a particular class identity.

The indices have also been used to test certain hypotheses about the nature of segregation. We might expect the spatial distributions of social classes ranked next to one another in the social hierarchy (e.g. semi-skilled and unskilled manual workers) to overlap, but the distributions of extremes in the hierarchy (professional and unskilled) to be mutually exclusive: unskilled workers may live in the same areas as the semi-skilled, but they rarely have professional households as their neighbours. In this case, the dissimilarity index for unskilled and semi-skilled would be much lower than for unskilled and professionals. When the values are arrayed in a data matrix, as in Table 7.2, we would expect them to increase away from the diagonal, confirming the hypothesis that the greater the social distance between

TABLE 7.2. *Segregation of socio-economic groups between wards in Sutton, 1966*

|  |  | Index of Dissimilarity | | | | Index of |
|  |  | I | II | III | IV | V | Segregation |
|---|---|---|---|---|---|---|---|
| Class | I | – | 13 | 30 | 40 | 37 | 22 |
|  | II |  | – | 20 | 30 | 33 | 13 |
|  | III |  |  | – | 17 | 21 | 19 |
|  | IV |  |  |  | – | 22 | 25 |
|  | V |  |  |  |  | – | 35 |

TABLE 7.3. *The ranking of dissimilarity indices in ten English and Welsh towns* (after Morgan, 1974)

|  | I | II | III | IV |
|---|---|---|---|---|
| Class I (professional-managerial) | – | 2 | 5 | 6 |
| II (lower non-manual) | 2 | – | 3 | 4 |
| III (skilled manual) | 5 | 3 | – | 1 |
| IV (semi-skilled and unskilled) | 6 | 4 | 1 | – |

1 represents the lowest index value, 6 the highest value.

two groups, the less similar their spatial distributions. Morgan (1974) examined the ranking of dissimilarity indices for sixteen English and Welsh towns in 1966, using a simplified class structure comprising four social classes: professional-managerial, lower non-manual, skilled manual, and semi-skilled and unskilled manual. For ten of the sixteen towns the indices were ranked in the same order (Table 7.3): the two classes with the most similar distributions were the two manual groups. The two non-manual groups also shared quite similar distributions. The finding that lower non-manual and skilled manual workers were the socially adjacent classes whose geographical distributions were least similar suggests that the divide between blue-collar and white-collar remains fundamental to English society.

It is also argued that segregation indices should follow a U-shaped distribution when presented graphically, with high values implying that the extreme social classes have very distinctive spatial patterns and low values showing that classes in the middle of the social hierarchy have distributions that overlap those of other classes. In practice, the distribution of segregation indices is often asymmetrical with Class I showing the highest degree of segregation, indicative of the greater freedom of professional households to choose their location.

Willmott and Young (1973) argued in the context of London that areas of older housing, usually in inner London, decline in class through time, but not at a uniform rate, so that at any moment they contain a mixture of land uses and social classes. In contrast, recently developed areas are more homogeneous and have not had time to evolve a pattern of uneven deterioration. Hence they will contain less variety of land use and population. This hypothesis was confirmed in a study carried out at University College London: it was found that dissimilarity indices for the distribution of socio-economic groups and housing classes by wards in Lambeth were generally lower than those associated with distributions at the same scale of analysis in Sutton. A higher degree of class mixing *within wards* was indicated for Lambeth than for Sutton, but had the scale of analysis been different — for example, if mixing within census enumeration districts had been considered — the conclusion might have been very different. Changing the scale of analysis may dramatically alter the values of segregation indices. In their study of Huddersfield, Jones and McEvoy found that at ward level the segregation index comparing Asians with the rest of the population was 55.1: in 1971 55 per cent of Asians needed to move *wards* for their distribution to correspond with that of the total population. But nearly 82 per cent needed to move *streets* for the two distributions to coincide at that more detailed scale.

Even an index of 100 can be ambiguous. Consider the situation illustrated in Fig. 7.1. In each of two towns, 50 per cent of enumeration districts are exclusively black, 50 per cent are exclusively white. But in A all the black districts lie in the same half of the city whereas in B alternate districts are black or white. In each case, the dissimilarity index, measured at the scale of enumeration districts is 100, but if the calculation was made at ward scale,

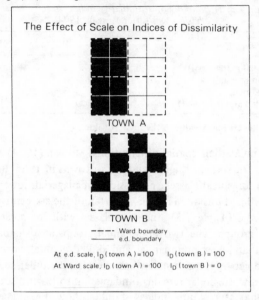

FIG. 7.1. *The effect of scale on indices of dissimilarity.*

where wards comprise blocks of four adjacent enumeration districts, the index for town B would be 0, for A it would remain at 100. How then, do we determine the most appropriate scale at which to measure segregation?

Figure 7.1 illustrates another deficiency of the Index of Dissimilarity. Two groups may have very different spatial distributions (i.e. a high value of $I_D$) yet the distance separating the homes of individual members of each group may be quite short. In A, only a few blacks living on the eastern edge of the black residential area, close to the town's central north-south axis, live next door to whites. In B, because black and white areas alternate throughout the town, there is a much longer black—white boundary and many more blacks live next door to whites. Yet, at enumeration district scale, $I_D$ takes the same value in each town.

Nor can the index tell us if the degree of segregation varies from one part of a city to another. Are there some areas with mixed populations and others dominated by a single group? Jones (1956) calculated a different form of segregation index to distinguish those areas of Belfast occupied by Protestants and Catholics in the same ratio as they inhabited the city as a whole, from those areas in which one group was relatively over-represented and the other correspondingly under-represented (Fig. 7.2).

But whatever technique we adopt, the level of segregation that we obtain will depend on the size of areas with which we work. If index values can vary so widely merely as a result of changing the scale of analysis, is it worth trying to *measure* segregation? And does it matter if two groups are segregated at one scale but not at another? What are the *consequences* of segregation?

We have already outlined some of the reasons *why* segregation occurs: the Wirthian argument that segregation is a reaction to the size, density and heterogeneity of urban society; the associated argument that segregation permits the use of residence as a status symbol, especially desirable in societies in which status is acquired rather than inherited; and

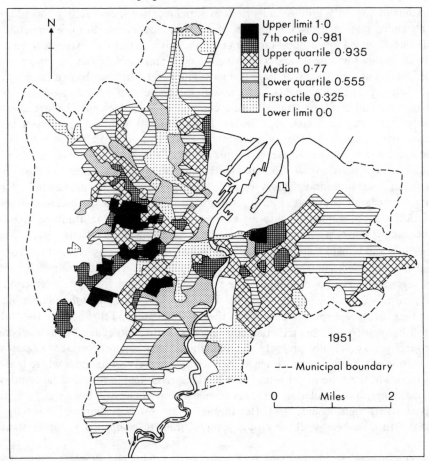

FIG. 7.2. *Levels of segregation in Belfast: areas shaded black are either exclusively Protestant or exclusively Catholic, stippled areas contain each group in the proportion in which they are represented in the city as a whole (after Jones, 1956).*

the economic argument based on the fact that people of different incomes can afford to live in different locations. To these we may add at least two further 'explanations' of segregation: the operation of a housing market in which dwellings are provided by a small number of large companies which develop large sites with identically sized or styled houses to be occupied by people of similar taste and income; and the desire for cultural solidarity and help in the process of assimilation among immigrant groups, resulting in ethnic segregation regardless of the exercise of racial discrimination. These processes may operate at different scales and we could justify our calculation of segregation and dissimilarity indices purely on the grounds of academic curiosity: we want to measure the results and relative importance of these hypothetical processes. But we can also use such calculations to justify (or attack) political or ethical arguments that segregation is 'good' or 'bad'.

The case against segregation and in favour of heterogeneous neighbourhoods is a strong one. It is claimed that heterogeneity promotes tolerance and understanding, helps the assimilation of minority groups and offers an enrichment of life as each group adopts the most attractive features from the cultures of other groups (Gans, 1961). Where communal facilities are financed out of local rates or taxes, there is a danger that exclusively poor areas with small incomes will be unable to provide the same range of facilities (e.g. sports centres, libraries, parks) as rich areas with large incomes. The differential may be overcome by resort to Rate Support Grants from central government, but this does not satisfy another objection that most political and community leaders come from the educated middle classes. Consequently there may be a lack of articulate leadership and an inability to exert political pressure among exclusively poor populations. It is also argued that children from deprived homes stand more chance of success if they attend the same schools as children from privileged backgrounds. Apart from residential mixing, the only other 'solution' to this problem has been the unsatisfactory one of 'bussing' children from homes in one neighbourhood to schools elsewhere. Finally, it has been suggested that the presence of middle-class facilities such as libraries, theatres and art galleries has an 'uplifting' or 'improving' influence on working-class families living in their catchment areas (Harris, 1973). Whether betting shops and billiard halls have a similar effect on the middle classes is not recorded!

Contrary to these arguments is the evidence of our own eyes that most people prefer to live in segregated neighbourhoods, for the sense of security and ease of interaction with like-minded people that segregation permits. The advocates of neighbourhood heterogeneity assume that because people are neighbours they will interact and that because they interact they will become friends. In fact, interaction may generate conflict as often as co-operation. Heterogeneity may actually promote discrimination. Thus support for racist organizations may be strongest in two types of neighbourhood: exclusively white areas where ignorance breeds racism in the guise of patriotism, and working-class areas of mixed racial composition where the indigenous population perceives immigrants as taking over houses and jobs that it regards as its own unalienable right. Heterogeneity may promote harmony, but only given an initial attitude whereby all the groups involved *want* to co-operate and understand one another.

One compromise is for planners to aim for only a moderate degree of heterogeneity mixing similar social or cultural groups but not the extremes of status or culture. This is the situation depicted by most matrices of dissimilarity indices with low values close to the diagonals and high values in the top right-hand corners of the matrices. We might argue, however, that *all* the values should be lower than they are.

Another common proposal is to maintain homogeneity at the scale of individual streets but plan for heterogeneity at the scale of political or economic communities, thus ensuring that all groups have access to the same political power and the same range of local amenities. The implication is that we should ignore high index values calculated at the level of separate streets, focusing instead on segregation at the scale of neighbourhoods or political wards. Even so, there will still be problems of interpretation. A high value could indicate discrimination and intolerance which have restricted a particular group to its exclusive territory in the city. Alternatively it could signify a cohesive minority group that has chosen to live apart, perhaps for religious reasons, but experiences little if any discrimination. The middle-class Jewish population in north-west London might fall into the second category, their nineteenth-century predecessors in the East End into the first.

**Neighbourhood and Behaviour**

Social geographers have also been interested in residential segregation for the association that it shows with other aspects of attitudes and behaviour. Is it the case that people who live in the same social area share the same life style and behave in similar ways? At one extreme is the caution expressed by Norman Dennis (1958), writing that:

"People seem to find it extraordinarily difficult to realize that mere living together in the same locality can result in a conglomeration of very little sociological importance" (p. 191). Dennis was particularly critical of the geographer's concept of social areas, observing that: "more than mere aggregation is needed to make a group, however homogeneous the aggregate may be" (p. 191). The opposite view is indicated by numerous attempts to identify common patterns of behaviour within neighbourhoods and differences between neighbourhoods.

One of the objectives of social area analysts in classifying districts according to their 'economic status' and 'family status' was to permit the selection of sample areas in which more detailed questionnaire surveys could be undertaken. For example, two districts similar in 'family status' but different in 'economic status' could be compared to assess the influence of 'economic status' on the attitudes or interaction patterns of residents. Herbert (1972) contrasted two areas of Newcastle-under-Lyme which differed in terms of social class and the mean rateable value of their housing but were otherwise similar. Both were inter-war estates, one developed by private enterprise, the other by the local authority. Herbert found that the majority of householders on the private estate belonged to local clubs or societies, whereas on the council estate less than 20 per cent were club members. Those council tenants who did attend local meetings usually mentioned organizations like the bingo club or a workingmen's club. The private householders were more likely to patronize the golf club or the Conservative association! The areas also differed in informal interaction. People on the private estate had plenty of friends, but many lived outside the area. The council tenants claimed fewer, but more local friends. However, this difference may reflect problems in the definition of 'friendship'. For example, if friendship is defined in terms of inviting folk into your home, or visiting them in their's, it is not surprising that the middle classes, involved in a round of coffee mornings and bridge evenings, seem more friendly than working-class families whose interaction is more spontaneous and centres on meetings in the local pub or club. Questionnaire surveys also generate problems caused by the misunderstanding and suspicion implicit in the relationship between an interviewer who is usually young, well-educated and familiar with the jargon of 'interaction' and 'neighbourhood', and respondents who may be of any age and educational background but almost certainly ignorant of the aims and techniques of social science research.

Nevertheless, some interesting results have emerged from attitudinal and behavioural studies in which the sampling frameworks have been defined by the boundaries of social areas. Robson (1969) investigated attitudes to education among the parents of children about to sit the 11+ examination in Sunderland and found significant differences between the aspirations of parents in middle-class and working-class areas. The findings raise the question whether such attitudes are associated with the areas or with the social groups to which the respondents belong. The two will not be synonymous since all but the most segregated populations contain some non-conforming cases: even for coloured or religious minority groups segregation indices rarely exceed 80. Areas are too easily stereotyped as 'working-class' or 'middle-class' and behaviour may be equally glibly dismissed as 'friendly'

TABLE 7.4. *Status and interaction in selected areas of Gloucester, 1978*

| Area | % households | | | % car owners | % households headed by | | | |
| | owner occupiers | l.a. tenants | other tenure | | non-manual | sk. manual | semi- & un-sk. manual | retired |
| --- | --- | --- | --- | --- | --- | --- | --- | --- |
| Beaufort | 94 | 0 | 6 | 79 | 30 | 40 | 12 | 18 |
| Heron Park | 100* | 0* | 0* | 90 | 84 | 11 | 3 | 2 |
| Linden | 73 | 0 | 26 | 49 | 14 | 34 | 21 | 30 |
| Matson | 12 | 87 | 1 | 39 | 9 | 30 | 31 | 30 |
| Tuffley | 37 | 60 | 4 | 67 | 18 | 50 | 21 | 11 |

| Area | % respondents | | Sample size |
| | with 'best friends' living outside Gloucester | belonging to at least one local organization | |
| --- | --- | --- | --- |
| Beaufort | 8 | 42 | 113 |
| Heron Park | 22 | 42 | 64 |
| Linden | 7 | 35 | 106 |
| Matson | 7 | 37 | 164 |
| Tuffley | 10 | 49 | 62 |

Note:    All figures are based on field-survey, April 1978, except 'housing tenure' which relate to the
entire population and are derived from 1971 Census. *Tenure figures for Heron Park are
estimated; the area had not been developed in 1971.

or 'unfriendly', 'active' or 'passive'. In a study undertaken by students at University College London into the social activity patterns of adult women in Gloucester, several distinctive social areas were identified and labelled as 'high-status' or 'low-status', 'elderly' or 'youthful', 'childless' or 'child-rearing'. But as Table 7.4 shows, the highest-status area (Heron Park) included some householders in manual employment and a low-status area (Matson) included a substantial minority of householders in non-manual work; and there were similar ranges in the age and stage of the life cycle of interviewees in the different areas. In fact the study showed that there *were* significant differences in patterns of friendship and club membership between the areas, much as Herbert had demonstrated in Newcastle-under-Lyme, but again it would be misleading to ignore the range of behaviour associated with each area.

Interestingly, in Sunderland, Robson (1969) found that the variations in attitudes within each class were greater than the variations between different classes living in the same area. Working-class parents living in middle-class areas held higher aspirations for their children than working-class parents living in working-class areas. We might argue that these results demonstrate the failings of a social classification that categorizes people merely on the basis of their socio-economic status. The fact that a family lives in a particular social area may be taken to imply its identity with the values of the area's dominant social group and its acceptance of the subculture associated with the area. In other words, 'working-class' families in middle-class areas are not working-class according to any useful definition of the term.

A subcultural explanation of behaviour has been advanced by Herbert (1976) in a detailed study of juvenile delinquency in areas of Cardiff. Herbert examined two clusters of enumeration districts which were allocated to the same social area type by a factor analysis of census data. Each cluster contained districts with a range of delinquency rates so that it was clear that the distribution of delinquents could not be explained solely by reference to the social and physical conditions of different districts, for example the occurrence of large families, broken homes, overcrowding or inadequate housing. A survey of parental attitudes and behaviour revealed that while parents in every district claimed to be concerned for their children's education and often held unrealistically high hopes for their children's academic attainment, those in delinquent areas showed less interest in practice (e.g. they attended meetings with teachers less often) and their children's actual level of achievement was lower. Parents in delinquent areas were less likely to condemn their children for what Herbert termed "less serious" offences such as truancy or cheating the bus company. They regarded detection and punishment of these offences as the responsibility of the school or the city corporation. Everybody condemned more serious crimes but parents in delinquent areas advocated physical punishment while those in non-delinquent areas preferred "verbal solutions". Herbert's conclusion was that certain areas retained a delinquent subculture which influenced the attitudes of all who live there.

If we accept a subcultural explanation of shared behaviour we can conclude that a lack of behavioural consensus — as in Gloucester — indicates the lack of territorially-based subculture. In these circumstances, a life-cycle approach to the analysis of behaviour may be more appropriate. Mann (1965) observed that the neighbourhood held different meanings for individuals at different stages in their life cycle. Young children, mothers with babies, and old age pensioners, particularly those without their own car, are more dependent upon their near neighbours than are teenage children, whose friendships may be made at a secondary school drawing its pupils from a wide catchment area, and women who are childless or whose children have grown up and who are not tied to the home or the school gates during the daytime. The local neighbourhood will mean more to women than to men, although that distinction may diminish as more women go out to work and more men stay at home. Formal associations will be most important for the lonely: single people, the widowed and recent arrivals, who join clubs in the hope of forging friendships which in time make their continued membership of the associations superfluous. For this reason, clubs often flourish in new communities, such as newly built housing estates, but gradually decline as residents make informal contacts and as the teething troubles of the new environment are ironed out and communal problems are replaced by individual problems.

## Residential Mobility

This chapter has concentrated on the nature of residential segregation and the patterns of association linking group or areal attributes to different forms of behaviour. But even in the studies of delinquency, attitudes and social interaction described above, little in the way of explanation was offered to account for the patterns of association that were identified. The process of decision-making was glossed over and analysis was still concerned with aggregative behaviour: 'middle-class' was contrasted with 'working-class', 'young' with 'old'. Many studies of residential mobility have been of this type and, in historical situations where information is limited to the act of mobility while the individual circumstances or motivation of movers remain unknown, our analyses cannot go beyond this (Dennis, 1977). Nevertheless, the limitations of aggregate analysis are obvious and dissatisfaction with this approach has led to the development of process-orientated models, influenced by psychological theory, in an attempt to portray the decision-making processes of individuals involved in various forms of spatial behaviour. In particular, both inter-urban migration and intra-urban mobility have received this treatment. The latter is of especial interest to us here since it provides the mechanism by which the population is distributed among the social areas whose patterns and properties have formed the concern of this and the preceding chapter.

Most moves may be important milestones in the lives of those doing the moving but they produce little change in the social geography of the city. In fact they serve to maintain the *status quo* by preserving the life-cycle characteristics of each area, with residents moving between areas as they move through successive stages of the life cycle. Other moves may be associated with stages in individuals' careers: a parallelism of social mobility and residential mobility. Again, the effect is to preserve the socio-economic status of different social areas.

In contrast, ecological theory emphasizes the minority of moves which contribute to processes of invasion or, at the individual scale, 'filtering', leading to the occupation of an area by a new status group. The ecologists assumed the invasion of high-status areas by low-status groups, or the filtering of properties down the social hierarchy, but the reverse of these processes — gentrification — is also a form of invasion and succession. Invasion is usually associated with suburbanization but, as in the expansion of immigrant ghettos, it could be multi-directional from the core of an existing immigrant area (Boal, 1976; Johnston, 1971) or, as with gentrification, it could involve moves towards the centre. Pritchard (1976) reckoned that in late nineteenth-century Leicester only about 200 moves per annum (2 per cent of all households) involved suburbanization. The majority of moves were made 'sideways' in the housing market, for example from one house rated at £10 p.a. to another £10 house. In addition, many other moves that did involve a change in house value, perhaps from a £5 house to a £10 house, must have been associated with social mobility or life-cycle reasons and did not contribute to ecological change.

In 1950, the American social psychologist Rossi undertook a survey of Philadelphian households to determine 'why families move'. He identified three types of change in the characteristics of dwelling and occupants that were liable to generate complaints about the suitability of the current residence (Rossi, 1955):

(i)  Changes in the state of either dwelling or neighbourhood. Rather than redecorate or repair his dwelling the occupier may prefer to move, especially if he is only renting the accommodation, has no power to enforce the landlord to make improvements and no incentive to undertake improvements himself, since they might only benefit subsequent tenants. Changes in the state of the neighbourhood may be either physical, as in the construction of a new road or housing estate adjacent to the dwelling, or social, as where the surrender of your neighbours to invasion by another group creates a bandwagon whereby you surrender too.

(ii) Changes in family structure, leading to changing space requirements: the birth of children or their attainment of an age at which it is unacceptable for them to share bedrooms, the departure of grown-up children from the home, or the arrival of elderly parents to live with their married children.

(iii) Changes in a family's values or aspirations, most commonly associated with social mobility.

A similar framework was adopted by Brown and Moore (1970) who considered residential mobility as one possible response to the development of stress (Fig. 7.3). 'Stress', equivalent to Rossi's 'changes causing complaints to arise', may generate one of three responses:

(i)  We lower our aspirations and come to terms with living in an unsatisfactory environment. In terms of action we do nothing.

(ii) We improve the existing environment to eliminate the stress, for example by installing

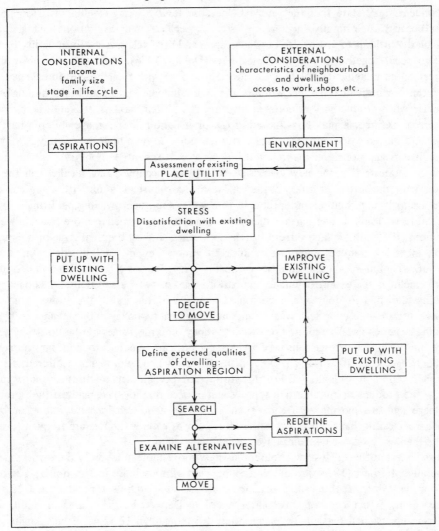

FIG. 7.3. *Brown and Moore's (1970) model of the decision to move.*

central heating, building an extension at the back of the house, or converting the loft. At neighbourhood scale, stress may be overcome by declaring the neighbourhood a General Improvement Area or by forming a tenants' association.

(iii) We decide to search for a new location. Even when this third strategy is adopted, residential mobility does not automatically follow. We may decide, after an unsatisfactory search, that our existing home is not so bad after all, given the range of vacancies within our finite financial resources. Since British surveys have shown that 30 per cent of the population would like to move at any time but only 10 per cent do so in the course of a year, it seems that many households choose or are forced to accept alternatives (i) and (ii).

A problem of classifying moves into the categories suggested by Rossi is that interviewees may express their complaint in the same way, whichever type of change has occurred.

Respondents may state that they moved "because their existing dwelling was too small", either because their family increased in size or because their aspirations changed. It is particularly difficult to distinguish between career and life-cycle reasons for mobility because the two occur together in many people's lives (Doling, 1976). The income of professional workers on an incremental salary scale increases in step with their progression through the life cycle. For individual manual workers, maximum income may occur in the middle of the life cycle when productivity or hours of overtime reach their maxima; for families of manual workers, peak income may be achieved in the brief period after teenage children have left school and started work, but before they have left home to raise their own family.

An American model of the relationship between residential mobility and the family life cycle suggests that the newly married couple will occupy a flat, ideally near the city centre. With the arrival of a family they move into a suburban house with a garden. They move again during child-rearing, probably to a larger suburban dwelling, and finally, when children leave home or one partner dies, there is a return to a smaller, more central dwelling (Simmons, 1968). But evidence from Britain contradicts at least the final stage of the model: people move less frequently in old age, unless they move beyond the limits of the urban area to a retirement home in the country or on the coast. Evidence for the immobility of the elderly includes the extent of under-occupation: one- or two-person households occupying dwellings designed for four or five persons. Doling (1976) has argued that moves from small to large private houses reflect wealth and building-society policy rather than family size. Building societies usually require borrowers to repay their mortgages by the time they retire. Since the standard mortgage runs for 25 years, societies are reluctant to grant new mortgages to clients aged over 40, although this is often the age when, with teenage children, demand for space will be at a maximum. For this group, mobility will depend on their ability to pay cash – the product of an inheritance, pools win or because they have paid off their previous mortgage and are moving to a cheaper area – or to acquire a loan elsewhere, probably through a clearing bank. In practice therefore, moves to large houses are frequently made *before* the family's space demands have reached a maximum.

It is also true that high-status households now move more frequently than working-class households. Herbert (1973b) found that 59 per cent of households in St. Thomas, a strongly working-class district of Swansea, had lived at the same address for more than 20 years whereas only 9 per cent of those interviewed in Derwen Fawr, an area of middle-class owner-occupiers, had lived in the same house for more than 10 years. Even allowing that many families could not have lived in Derwen Fawr for long as their houses were less than 10 years old, the difference between the two groups remained. Only 36 per cent of Derwen Fawr residents had lived anywhere in Swansea for more than 20 years. Studies of nineteenth-century mobility usually show the opposite relationship, the working classes moving more frequently – albeit over very short distances – than the middle classes (Pritchard, 1976). The explanation of this interesting reversal probably lies in the development of the welfare state. Council housing, unemployment and sickness benefits, retirement pensions and legislation protecting tenants from eviction have all contributed to the immobility of low-status groups. It appears then, that in the study of residential mobility, as elsewhere in urban geography, the structure of English politics and society has complicated the application of American models to English cities.

Further problems in deciphering the reasons for mobility lie in the links between life cycle, socio-economic status and housing tenure. It is often observed that private tenants in furnished accommodation move more frequently than owner-occupiers and that council tenants (and perhaps also *unfurnished* private tenants) form the least mobile tenure group. (Murie *et al.*, 1976). The reasons for this will be discussed in the next chapter. It is also true that each tenure is associated with particular status groups or stages in the life cycle. So it is difficult to decide whether the high mobility of young people results from their youth or their residence in privately rented, furnished rooms — the least secure form of tenure where eviction or frequent rent increase necessitate mobility. In contrast, old people, who move infrequently, occupy council housing where effective (although, at the time of writing, not legal) security of tenure is virtually guaranteed, or unfurnished tenancies with artificially low controlled rents, where a move would involve decontrol and an immediate increase in rent.

Brown and Moore's interpretation of mobility as a response to stress assumes that the decision to move is taken freely by the mover. In practice many moves are *forced* — as a result of eviction, slum clearance or in the sense that they inevitably follow from other decisions, to get married or divorced, to begin or end higher education. The Rowntree survey of Britain estimated that in 1962, 7 per cent of all moves resulted from eviction, 5 per cent from slum clearance. The first figure will have declined since 1962 as it has become harder for private landlords to evict tenants, but the latter figure may even have increased slightly.

Several British surveys have inquired into reasons for moving, but often the results are difficult to interpret. Robson (1975) reproduces a table of 'principal reasons' for moving, based on mortgage applications to the Nationwide Building Society, but it is difficult to separate reasons that accommodation was too small or too large from reasons that family size had increased or decreased.

Furthermore, applicants are unlikely to give their building society a frivolous reason for moving, or reveal a history of eviction which would cast doubts on their ability to make regular mortgage repayments. Despite these shortcomings there is no reason to doubt the survey's conclusions that most intra-urban moves are linked to the life cycle, most inter-urban or inter-regional moves to career or job reasons.

A second stage in Brown and Moore's model, after the decision to move has been taken, is the search procedure. The authors outline a sequence of search in which the mover compares the 'place utility' of his existing residence with the place utilities of dwellings in other areas. He has relatively complete and accurate knowledge about his present home, but less thorough and probably less accurate information about alternative residences. The mover's 'awareness space', the area within which he has sufficient information to choose between vacancies, will include some streets with which he is personally familiar — the streets adjacent to his present home, around his workplace, or along the routes from home to work, shops or friends — together with his 'indirect contact space' where information is derived from friends or the media.

In Swansea Herbert (1973b) found that less than half of his sample used newspapers or estate agents as sources of information on vacancies, although families looking for high-cost housing were more likely to use these sources than people looking for cheap housing. For both groups, 'looking around', friends and family were the most important sources. Herbert also asked about the effectiveness of different sources: which source had been instrumental in finding the respondent's present home? His results, which are reproduced in Table 7.5, paralleled Rossi's earlier findings in Philadelphia.

The consequence of dependence on 'looking around', family and friends is a short-distance pattern of movement, since most people 'look around' the area adjacent to their existing home or rely on friends and relatives who also live nearby and whose information fields are

TABLE 7.5. *Sources of information used by*
*households in Swansea to obtain their present*
*dwelling* (after Herbert, 1973b)

|  | % respondents in each area using each source | |
|  | High-cost area | Low-cost area |
| --- | --- | --- |
| 'Looking around' | 39 | 21 |
| Newspapers | 11 | 13 |
| Estate Agents | 17 | 8 |
| Family/friends | 25 | 58 |

equally restricted. Several North American studies have shown that the search space of inner-city residents tends to be circular, centred on their existing home, while that of suburbanites is elliptical, with a long axis linking home to city centre, indicating that people search only those areas with which they are already familiar (Adams, 1969; Brown and Holmes, 1971).

It seems likely that movers will become more dependent on estate agents for information on housing vacancies as owner-occupation increases in importance. A 1979 survey of 80 recent movers into an area of middle-income private housing in Gloucester showed that 63 per cent had found their new home through an estate agent, and only 13 per cent through friends or relatives.

A Nationwide Building Society survey of housebuyers in Britain in 1970 showed that 55 per cent moved less than 5 miles. Herbert's work in Swansea confirmed that high-status families moved farther than low-status families, but the mobility of both groups followed a distance-decay pattern (Fig. 7.4). But given the expense of moving house, the gain in 'place utility' may be insufficient to warrant a move to another house in the same street and there may be

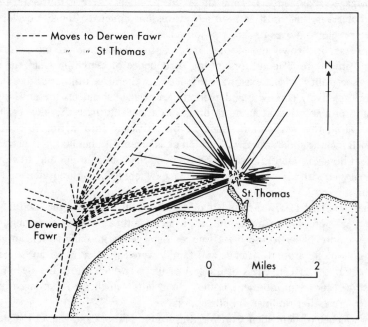

FIG. 7.4. *Intra-urban moves into Derwen Fawr (high status) and St.*
*Thomas (low status) in Swansea (after Herbert, 1972).*

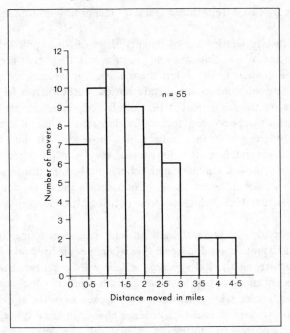

FIG. 7.5. *Intra-urban moves into Longlevens,
Gloucester, 1979.*

an inner cut-off to the distance-decay pattern (Fig. 7.5). This applies particularly to owner-occupiers, whose moves involve solicitors' fees, estate agents' fees, building-society fees, surveyors' fees, not to mention removal expenses. In May 1979 *Which* estimated the cost of moving house at £1,750. In contrast, families incur few costs in moving between tenancies and may still find it worthwhile to move between houses in the same street. Charles Booth observed frequent mobility at this scale among the East End poor in the late nineteenth century, while David Brindley, a docks porter in Liverpool in the 1880s, recorded twelve moves in his diary in the space of eight years, the longest less than 3 miles, the shortest 30 yards (Lawton, 1978).

Brown and Moore's model includes elaborate feedback-loops to allow for movers changing their aspirations (and perhaps deciding not to move after all) as they go about their search. Other theorists have considered the influences of time and competition on the decision to move. Vacancies must be inspected in a sequence and it is not always possible to return to a house to reassess it in the light of other houses seen subsequently — it may already have been bought by somebody else. Some people are searching against the clock, for example students who must find somewhere to live, however unsatisfactory, by the beginning of the academic year. So movers must decide when to stop searching and opt for a vacancy which may not be ideal (Flowerdew, 1976). Herbert found in Swansea that half his sample had not seriously considered any vacancy other than the one which they were occupying at the time of the interview. This result would seem to imply that:

(i)  The matching of supply and demand for housing is remarkably efficient — which seems unlikely;

(ii)  Most households cannot tolerate a long search and may make sub-optimal choices; or

(iii) The entire search and selection model in inappropriate for the majority of the population.

In the local authority sector, council tenants or waiting-list applicants may define their requirements in terms of dwelling size and location but they play no part in the search procedure until the council finally offers them a dwelling which they may feel obliged to accept, whatever its condition. In the private rented sector there is now so little accommodation on offer on the open market that most prospective tenants have effectively no choice. And in the owner-occupied sector the decisions of estate agents, surveyors and building-society managers may be more critical than those of the families engaged in moving.

Recent research has retained the behavioural emphasis on decision-making, but has turned from studies of how households make choices to how institutions allocate resources, constrain the behaviour of different classes of households and so shape the social geography of the city. This new emphasis, which we have entitled 'The Geography of Housing', is the subject of the next chapter.

It is clear that residential segregation is difficult to measure unambiguously and even more difficult to interpret, but it does seem that where people live and who their neighbours are has some influence on what they think and how they behave. Studies of residential mobility may have enhanced our understanding of how individuals choose, but institutional powers are such that choice takes place against the backcloth of the aggregate ecology of the city and only in a few cases does choice produce change in the city's spatial structure. To interpret the latter we need to understand more about the development process and the institutional and political environment which sets the limits on individual choice. Whether our interest lies at the level of the individual or with the ecology of the city as a whole, the way ahead may be through political economy as much as through social psychology.

### References and Further Reading

The use of dissimilarity and segregation indices originated in:
Duncan, O. D. and Duncan, B. (1955) Residential distribution and occupational stratification, *American Journal of Sociology*, 60, 493–503.

British studies of segregation include:
Collison, P. (1967) Immigrants and residence, *Sociology*, 1, 277–92.
Heraud, B. J. (1968) Social class and the new towns. *Urban Studies*, 5, 33–58.
Jones, E. (1956) The distribution and segregation of Roman Catholics in Belfast, *Sociological Review*, 4, 167–89.
Jones, T. P. and McEvoy, D. (1978) Race and space in cloud-cuckoo land, *Area*, 10, 162–6. This paper stimulated an extended debate on the subject of ethnic segregation: see *Area*, 10, 365–7 and *Area*, 11, 82–5 and 221–3.
Morgan, B. (1974) Social distance and spatial distance: a research note, *Area*, 6, 293–7.
Poole, M. A. and Boal, F. W. (1973) Religious segregation in Belfast in mid-1969: a multi-level analysis, *Institute of British Geographers Special Publication* 5 (Social Patterns in Cities), 1–40.

A useful reader, including several of the papers listed above, is:
Peach, C. (1975) *Urban Social Segregation,* Longman, London.

Qualitative discussions of residential segregation include:
Boal, F. W. (1976) Ethnic residential segregation, in D. T. Herbert & R. J. Johnston (eds.), *Social Areas in Cities Volume I,* Wiley, London, pp. 41–79.
Gans, H. J. (1961) The balanced community, *Journal of the American Institute of Planners*, 27, 176–84.
Harris, M. (1973) Some aspects of social polarization, in D. Donnison & D. Eversley (eds.), *London: Urban Patterns, Problems and Policies,* Heinemann, London, pp. 156–89.
Johnston, R. J. (1971) *Urban Residential Patterns,* Bell, London.

Willmott, P. and Young, M. (1973) Social class and geography, in D. Donnison & D. Eversley (eds.), *op.cit.*, pp. 190–214.

On the relationship between neighbourhood and behaviour, see:
Dennis, N. (1958) The popularity of the neighbourhood community idea, *Sociological Review*, 6, 191–203.
Herbert, D. T. (1972) *Urban Geography: A Social Perspective*, David & Charles, Newton Abbot, esp. pp. 222–5.
Herbert, D. T. (1976) The study of delinquency areas: a social geographical approach, *Transactions Institute of British Geographers*, New Series, 1, 472–92.
Mann, P. H. (1965) *An Approach to Urban Sociology*, Routledge & Kegan Paul, London, esp. pp. 149–82.
Robson, B. T. (1969) *Urban Analysis*, Cambridge University Press, Cambridge, esp. pp. 187–236.

Studies of past residential mobility include:
Dennis, R. J. (1977) Intercensal mobility in a Victorian city, *Transactions Institute of British Geographers*, New Series, 2, 349–63.
Lawton, R. (1978) Population and society 1730–1900, in R. A. Dodgshon & R. A. Butlin (eds.), *An Historical Geography of England and Wales*, Academic Press, London, pp. 313–66.
Pritchard, R. M. (1976) *Housing and the Spatial Structure of the City*, Cambridge University Press, Cambridge.

Among American mobility studies, see:
Adams, J. S. (1969) Directional bias in intra-urban migration, *Economic Geography*, 45, 303–23.
Brown, L. A. and Holmes, J. (1971) Search behaviour in an intra-urban migration context: a spatial perspective, *Environment and Planning*, 3, 307–26.
Brown, L. A. and Moore, E. G. (1970) The intra-urban migration process: a perspective, *Geografiska Annaler*, Series B, 52, 1–13.
Rossi, P. H. (1955) *Why Families Move*, Free Press, Glencoe, Illinois.
Simmons, J. W. (1968) Changing residence in the city: a review of intra-urban mobility, *Geographical Review*, 58, 621–51.

While British studies of residential mobility include:
Doling, J. F. (1976) The family life cycle and housing choice, *Urban Studies*, 13, 55–8.
Flowerdew, R. (1976) Search strategies and stopping rules in residential mobility, *Transactions Institute of British Geographers*, New Series, 1, 47–57.
Herbert, D. T. (1973a) The residential mobility process: some empirical observations, *Area*, 5, 44–8.
Herbert, D. T. (1973b) Residential mobility and preference: a study of Swansea, *Institute of British Geographers Special Publication* 5 (Social Patterns in Cities), 103–21.
Murie, A. *et al.* (1976) *Housing Policy and the Housing System*, Allen & Unwin, London, esp. pp. 35–61.
Pickvance, C. G. (1974) Life cycle, housing tenure and residential mobility, *Urban Studies*, 11, 171–88.
Robson, B. T. (1975) *Urban Social Areas*, Oxford University Press, London.
Short, J. R. (1978) Residential mobility in the private housing market of Bristol, *Transactions Institute of British Geographers*, New Series, 3, 533–47.

# 8

# The Geography of Housing in England and Wales

## The Provision of Housing

IN Chapter 5 the provision of housing was considered as an important mechanism behind the spatial structure of Victorian cities. We concentrated there on the roles of landowners, builders, financial agencies and government in influencing the types of housing that were provided and the locations in which they were situated. But we paid little attention to the mechanisms by which households were allocated to particular dwellings, apart from observing that the majority of households rented their accommodation from private landlords and that access to housing depended almost entirely on the ability to pay rent.

The same themes of landownership, building and government intervention recur in studies of the modern housing market. Several researchers have shown that residential land values peak in inner-city areas and decline with increasing distance from those areas, much as Alonso predicted, and that values are much higher in Greater London than in the rest of England and Wales. Whitehead (1974) found that in 1971 the cost of land for each new local authority dwelling averaged £1,800 in London but only £400 elsewhere in England and Wales. Furthermore, land values have risen more rapidly than building costs in recent years, so that they constitute an increasing proportion of the total cost of new housing.

Different types of builder have reacted in very different ways to the state of the land market. Large companies have opted for large but relatively cheap sites where they could gain economies of scale by building small houses to a limited number of standard designs. In the 1930s they selected sites on the edge of built-up areas, but the creation of Green Belts around major conurbations has restricted this form of development in recent years. They have turned instead to the construction of large estates of detached and semi-detached houses at medium densities (8–12 houses per acre) beyond the Green Belt, especially in parts of Kent, Sussex, Essex and Hertfordshire (Pahl, 1975).

Small building firms cannot afford (and do not particularly want) to buy large plots of land, but prefer infill sites where little has to be spent on building new roads or laying on water, gas or electricity supplies or mains drainage. Because these sites are expensive for their size, firms concentrate on high-density development (e.g. rows of 'town houses' or small 3- or 4-storey blocks of 'luxury flats') or expensive, high-quality, 'architect-designed' houses. The scarcity of infill sites has led to an increase in the *redevelopment* of suburban sites, as late-Victorian or Edwardian villas are first subdivided into flats for single people and young couples, and then demolished to make way for purpose-built flats or high-density, but still

124

middle-class, houses (Swann, 1975). This process has been particularly common in the vicinity of commuter railway stations, for example in Sutton, Croydon and Bromley in the suburbs of south London. In inner suburbs, however, land is so expensive that even this type of development is not viable. Thus, in the inner London borough of Lambeth developers in the early 1970s were willing to pay £35,000 per acre for residential land but available sites were valued at £60,000 per acre. There was little hope of attracting private builders even if the local council offered subsidies towards the purchase of land (Harloe *et al.*, 1974).

Other building sites that occasionally become available, for example abandoned railway yards and derelict industrial sites, often on poorly drained or polluted land, are cheaper to buy but may require major expenditure before they can accept buildings, and may also have undesirable neighbours such as transport routes or continuing industries. As a result they are left to the local authority to develop for council housing, as are areas of old poor-quality housing deemed unsuitable for gentrification.

The effect of private and public developers adopting these strategies is generally to reinforce the *status quo,* intensify existing patterns of residential segregation and make invasion and succession of the type outlined by Burgess even less likely to occur in the future. New middle-class housing is built in or adjacent to traditionally middle-class areas, working-class housing in working-class areas. On the urban fringe, however, the activities of large and small building firms have contributed to a reversal of Burgess' model: the edge of the continuous built-up area includes the stockbroker belt, where upper middle-class families live in expensive, 'architect-designed' houses constructed by small builders, while poorer or younger middle-class households become 'reluctant commuters' living in smaller, cheaper houses on large estates beyong the Green Belt (Pahl, 1970).

The way in which builders are financed contributes to a mismatch between supply and demand at least as serious as occurred in the nineteenth century. A large proportion of house-building is undertaken by small firms with few capital assets, and dependent on short-term bank loans to finance each new scheme. Little more than 20 per cent of work in the British construction industry is carried out by firms employing more than 1,000 workers, while 90 per cent of firms employ less than 25 workers (Murie *et al.*, 1976). The fortunes of these small firms are strongly affected by general monetary policy and there is a very high bankruptcy rate among them. Banks are prepared to lend money to builders only at the height of a boom, so that in periods when the economy picks up and demand for private housing increases there is a time-lag of perhaps a year before builders can obtain credit, and of another year before the additional houses are completed. The gap between supply and demand widens and the usual result is house price inflation. The trend is reinforced because during such periods building societies receive greater investments and may offer more and bigger mortgages, thus increasing the competition among a large number of prospective buyers for a limited supply of new and vacant dwellings. For example, in 1972 house prices increased by 31 per cent although retail prices rose by only 7 per cent and average earnings by 13 per cent. By the time the supply of new housing has increased, a mortgage famine may have set in, demand declined, and builders left with houses that they cannot sell. In fact, government intervention to damp down inflation usually takes the form of reducing demand rather than stimulating supply. Thus, if the bank rate is increased investors may transfer their savings from building societies to other institutions, societies then have less money to lend and choose to increase the mortgage rate to maintain their share of the investment market, and so house purchase becomes more expensive.

**Changes in Tenure**

While economists and a few geographers have researched the topic of housing provision, more attention has been focused on the allocation procedures whereby dwellings of different types are occupied by different socio-economic, age or ethnic groups. Housing allocation has assumed a more central role than it had in the nineteenth century because of the diversity of tenures that are now available, and the apparently close association between tenure and the characteristics of occupants.

At the beginning of this century approximately 90 per cent of households rented their accommodation from private (including philanthropic) landlords. Tenants had no security of tenure, no protection against rent increases and no social security system to support them in times of illness, unemployment or old age. It is not surprising, therefore, that the rate of residential mobility was high, especially among the working classes who moved frequently but over as short distances as possible, matching their dwellings to the rents that they could afford to pay at any time. No more than 2 per cent of households lived in council housing and there was no formal system of council house allocation (through a waiting list and points system) as exists today. Roughly 10 per cent of households were owner-occupiers, mostly the rich except in skilled working-class areas where building clubs and self-help organizations had flourished. Many wealthy people rented their accommodation and even some private landlords did not own the houses they lived in themselves.

By 1977 the proportion of households in privately rented (including housing association) dwellings had declined to only 14 per cent, compared to 53 per cent in the owner-occupied sector and 32 per cent in local authority or new town housing. Of course, these proportions vary widely between different parts of the country. In 1971 19 per cent of households in England and Wales fell into the 'privately rented and other' category but in Greater London the figure was 34 per cent and even higher in some inner-city areas (e.g. Kensington and Chelsea 75 per cent). There are more council tenants in cities in the north and north-east of England (e.g. Sunderland 53 per cent, Gateshead 45 per cent), and more owner-occupiers in rural areas and in south-east England. Nevertheless, it is clear that there has been a dramatic reorganization of housing provision in Britain since World War I (Table 8.1).

*Private Renting*

Rent control was first introduced in 1915 in response to a wartime crisis. The shortage of labour and materials for non-military activities during the war exacerbated an existing housing shortage, forcing the government to freeze rents to prevent the exploitation of

TABLE 8.1. *Housing tenure in the United Kingdom*

| Date | owner-occupied | % dwellings rented from l.a. or new town | privately rented or other |
|------|------|------|------|
| 1914 | 10 | 1 | 90 |
| 1947 | 26 | 13 | 61 |
| 1960 | 42 | 26 | 32 |
| 1966 | 47 | 29 | 24 |
| 1971 | 50 | 31 | 19 |
| 1977 | 54 | 32 | 14 |

tenants. The extent of rent control varied between the wars but cheap housing had not been decontrolled by the outbreak of World War II, when a new freeze was imposed on all low- and middle-value housing. So there was little incentive to build new housing for rent, except in the exempt high-value category. Most private landlords were keener to sell than to expand their activities, but since nobody else wanted to acquire their property the inter-war period was principally one of stagnation. The oldest privately rented houses were demolished in slum clearance programmes, a few dwellings were bought by sitting tenants and so passed into owner-occupation, but most survived unchanged.

After World War II government activity concentrated first on building new council houses to replace the private housing that had been bombed and to catch up on the shortage that had been created by another period of wartime inactivity. But in 1955 a new programme of slum clearance began, directed at unfit private dwellings, usually late-Victorian terraced houses owned by private landlords. The survival of a viable privately rented sector was still considered desirable and the Conservative government introduced successive Rent Acts allowing for rent decontrol on vacant possession and for rent increases associated with repairs. However, landlords judged that their most profitable course of action was to obtain vacant possession — by harassment, bribery or violence if necessary — and then to sell to individual owner-occupiers or to property developers.

Subsequent legislation did little to redress the balance. In 1965 the Labour government introduced the nebulous concept of 'fair rents' in which the size and frequency of rent increases was limited but rents were permitted to rise following improvement. In conjunction with the offer of Improvement Grants some landlords modernized their properties only to relet to higher-income tenants. More often, landlords and developers took advantage of Improvement Grants to modernize their property at the government's expense and then sell it to middle-class owner-occupiers at a substantial profit (Merrett, 1976).

Most of this legislation applied only to *unfurnished* rented accommodation, so that another response of landlords was to convert their property to a 'furnished' state in which it was easier to evict tenants or obtain rent increases. Since many of the people seeking furnished lodgings do not intend staying long, for example students, young single professional people and foreign visitors, a landlord was likely to gain vacant possession of his property quite frequently, even without recourse to harassment or eviction.

The point of such conversions was nullified by the 1974 Rent Act which extended the rights enjoyed by unfurnished tenants to furnished tenants. Some landlords evaded this Act too by converting their flats into 'bed and breakfast' hotels or by offering only short lets (of less than 6 months) which were outside the compass of the Act: hence the advertizing of so-called 'holiday lets' in such exquisite tourist areas of London as Neasden, Willesden and Acton (see the London *Evening Standard* any night)! Other landlords sold their property on vacant possession or kept it vacant in the hope of a repeal or amendment of the Act in their favour in the future.

*Owner-Occupation*

As private renting has declined so owner-occupation has flourished. The 1920s witnessed a rapid decline in building costs, a fall in bank rate from 7 to 3 per cent which heralded an era of cheap mortgages, and a transfer of investment from industry to building societies. For example, the assets of the Woolwich Building Society rose from £3,600,000 in 1925 to

£30,100,000 ten years later. In 1920 a 3-bedroom house in London might cost about £930. By the late 1930s suburban semi-detached houses were on offer at £300—400 (Jackson, 1973). The purchaser required only a 5 per cent deposit, and the remainder was generously provided by a building society mortgage repayable at an interest rate as low as 4.5 per cent. From financing builders and landlords, the role of building societies became one of financing owner-occupation for the lower-middle classes.

Since the 1950s owner-occupation has expanded rapidly with the encouragement of both Conservative and Labour governments. Owner-occupiers with mortgages obtain income-tax relief on the interest payments that they make, and since 1967 other housebuyers, on too low an income to pay much tax and therefore unable to benefit from tax relief, have qualified for 'option mortgages' whereby the buyer foregoes any tax relief but repays the mortgage at a specially low interest rate. Local authority mortgage schemes were introduced as long ago as 1899 but have achieved significance only in the last twenty years. They have been used to allow low-income households to buy older properties on which building societies often refuse to lend (frequently properties that had been owned by a private landlord). Finally, Conservative councils have encouraged the sale of council houses to sitting tenants. Thus, the Greater London Council sold about 16,000 houses between 1967 and 1973, and the return of a Conservative GLC in 1977 and a Conservative government in 1979 has led to a renewal of council-house sales on an even bigger scale. Before 1979 the Labour government permitted limited sales to sitting tenants in areas where there was no serious housing shortage. Since then the Conservative government has encouraged the sale of new council houses to families on local authority waiting lists and given all tenants the right to buy their homes, often at a substantial discount.

## Council Housing

Council housing assumed significance in the housing crisis that followed World War I. It was estimated that 610,000 new homes were needed in 1919, plus a further 100,000 p.a. thereafter to keep up with the replacement of slums, the growth in the number of households and the growth in the total population. These figures may appear quite modest by comparison with rates of new construction of 3—400,000 in the 1960s and 1970s, but they signified a mammoth task compared with an average net increase of dwellings of 76,000 p.a. during the 40 years prior to the war. Labour and materials were scarce in 1919 and building costs at four times their pre-war level. If the government was to honour its pledge of 'homes fit for heroes' it had to build them itself. The first phase of 200,000 dwellings, built under the Addison Act of 1919, were to generous standards on small and pleasant suburban estates, but it was quickly recognized that the country could not afford such luxurious subsidized housing and subsequent Housing Acts carefully limited the level of subsidy that local authorities could claim for each new dwelling. Some very large council estates were built (e.g. the London County Council accommodated 80,000 people on its Becontree estate) and standards of design and construction, while far superior to anything achieved for the working classes by private enterprise, did not match those obtained on Addison Act estates.

In the 1930s attention turned from building suburban 'cottage estates' to replacing inner-city slums with blocks of flats, but in 1947 council housing still constituted only 13 per cent of dwellings in Great Britain. Local authorities were most active in the provision of housing immediately after World War II: for example, in 1951 89 per cent of all new dwellings were built by local authorities or new town development corporations, but that figure declined to 35 per cent in 1960 and the emphasis again shifted from suburban estates to inner-area redevelopment. The 1960s witnessed the construction of high flats (26 per cent of all dwellings in council schemes in 1966 were in blocks more than five storeys high, and 10 per cent in blocks of more than 15 storeys) and experiments in system-building, industrial building and the use of unconventional building materials (Sutcliffe, 1974).

The local authority sector has also expanded through the acquisition of properties in other tenures. Philanthropic agencies that operated as non-profit-making trusts (e.g. the Peabody and Guinness Trusts) have survived in the guise of 'housing associations', but properties owned by '5 per cent' companies have generally passed into the hands of local authorities. Other privately rented accommodation has been 'municipalized' by councils anxious that it should not be sold to the professional middle classes and so deprive low-income groups of valuable inner-city accommodation. Some local authorities have acquired dilapidated property several years prior to demolishing it and, in the interim, have administered it in the same way as their purpose-built council housing. Other, more doctrinaire, Labour councils have deliberately bought houses in areas of predominantly middle-class owner-occupation. On the other hand many Conservative councils have advertized 'sales of the century', offering tenants the opportunity to buy their homes at a discount, while one of the first actions of the incoming Conservative government in 1979 was to curb the municipalization policies of Labour local authorities.

## Other Tenures

The 1970s witnessed the spawning of alternative solutions to the housing problem: squatting, co-ownership and tenants' co-operatives. As yet these forms of housing accommodate only a few tens of thousands, and even housing associations account for only 2–3 per cent of the population. Such alternatives have arisen in an attempt to plug the gap in the housing market left by the demise of the conventional privately rented sector. As we shall see later in this chapter, private landlords have an important role to play in housing many different groups who do not want or cannot afford to buy and do not qualify for council housing: students, young single people, one-parent families, ex-prisoners and immigrants. Housing associations have adopted the mantle of Victorian philanthropists in providing cheap accommodation, ostensibly by private enterprise. In practice, most associations draw their funds from government agencies (much as companies like the Improved Industrial Dwellings Co. depended on the loans offered by the Public Works Loan Commissioners in the late nineteenth century) and critics have argued that they represent an inefficient use of public money which would be better spent in extending local authority involvement in housing (Swann, 1975). But as long as most local authorities adhere to allocation schemes that discriminate – however unintentionally – against the unconventional and frequently most needy cases, housing associations will have the advantage of flexibility of action in housing single people, unmarried mothers, the elderly and special categories like released prisoners.

Following the 1974 Housing Act and a switch in government policy from slum clearance to rehabilitation, housing associations assumed a more important role in improving dilapidated properties, especially in urban areas, and letting them to tenants drawn mainly from local authority waiting lists. They have switched from 'special needs' to 'general needs', but they remain subject to the criticism that they are not accountable to the electorate in their use of public money in the way that local authorities are.

In a tenants' co-operative each tenant has an equal, usually nominal (e.g. £1) share in the freehold of the properties owned by the co-operative, and the level of rents, repairs, improvements and new tenants are decided upon at regular meetings of the shareholders. If they vacate their dwellings tenants usually resell their shares to the co-operative for the purchase price and any profits are spent on reducing rents or acquiring additional properties.

While housing associations and tenants' co-operatives provide alternative forms of renting for low-income groups, co-ownership societies offer an alternative to conventional owner-occupation for the better-off. Finally, there are an estimated 25,000 squatters in London (mid-1978), with another 20,000 in the rest of Great Britain. It is claimed that the 'average squatter' is most likely to be a manual worker with a family, squatting simply because of the lack of anything better, contrary to the popular image of squatters as students or drop-outs seeking an alternative life-style.

All the changes outlined above are very interesting but the reader may be left wondering what relevance they have to social geography! They are important because:
(a)  different forms of tenure are associated with particular socio-economic, family or ethnic status groups; and
(b)  different forms of tenure are associated with particular locations, for example most privately rented accommodation is in inner urban areas, most modern owner-occupied housing is suburban.

So housing constitutes an explanatory variable linking status to residential location, an alternative explanation of segregation to the preference-focused socio-psychological theories outlined in the previous chapter. It is also argued that 'housing class' is related to the rate and extent of residential mobility and to other aspects of social interaction and community formation.

### Tenure and Status

Some forms of tenure are more desirable than others. The financial incentives offered to owner-occupiers have already been mentioned and, even if owning one's home is not always the personal solution to inflation that it is sometimes made out to be (since the inflated value of a house can only be realised by selling it, which generally means buying another at an equally inflated price), it does offer a sense of security and independence. Council housing is also a relatively attractive tenure. Despite recent rounds of rent increases, council house rents are still below free-market levels, as reflected in the 'fair rents' set for privately rented accommodation. Many tenants are enjoying increasing control over the management of their homes and in practice are more secure than private tenants, who may still suffer the unpleasantness, if not harassment, of an inhospitable landlord. Some unfurnished tenants, usually elderly, who have lived for a long time in dwellings with controlled rents, may pay very little, but most tenants, especially those in furnished accommodation, pay more rent than council tenants and receive less in return: levels of overcrowding and sharing of amenities for cooking and washing are highest in the furnished sector (Table 8.2).

Not surprisingly, therefore, competition is most intense to gain access to owner-occupancy or a local authority tenancy, and privately rented accommodation forms a residual tenure for all but a few young, temporary residents (e.g. students) who may actually prefer to share

TABLE 8.2. *Overcrowding and the provision of amenities, by tenure, 1976*
(after the General Household Survey, 1976)

| % households | With no use of bath | Sharing use of bath | With no inside w.c. | Sharing use of w.c. | Below bedroom standard | No central heating |
|---|---|---|---|---|---|---|
| Owner-occupied (outright) | 6 | 1 | 7 | 1 | 2 | 51 |
| Owner-occupied (with mortgage) | 1 | 1 | 1 | 0 | 3 | 30 |
| Rented from l.a. or new town | 1 | 1 | 3 | 0 | 7 | 58 |
| Privately rented unfurnished | 27 | 6 | 30 | 7 | 5 | 85 |
| Privately rented furnished | 5 | 47 | 38 | 50 | 12 | 77 |
| Rented from housing association | 6 | 10 | 14 | 12 | 9 | 53 |

Note:   'Bedroom standard' compares the number of bedrooms per household with the desirable number, assuming that each married couple is given one bedroom, single persons aged 21+ each occupy one bedroom, and children aged 10—20 are segregated by sex at no more than 2 per bedroom.

a rented flat. Success in the competition for housing depends partly on the ability to pay, but also on various tests of suitability imposed by 'gatekeepers' such as building society managers and council officials.

## Owner-occupation

The fundamental requirement of a prospective owner-occupier is access to sufficient capital. Of the 53.5 per cent of U.K. dwellings owner-occupied in 1977, only 44.3 per cent (23.7 per cent of *all* dwellings) were owned outright, 43.1 per cent were owned with a building-society mortgage and 12.6 per cent with another form of loan — from a local authority, bank or insurance company. But many of those who now own outright only do so because they have repaid the building-society mortgage they obtained ten, twenty or more years ago. It is clear, therefore, that the building-society mortgage is the usual means of access to the owner-occupied sector. Lending figures for two recent years are shown in Table 8.3.

In 1972 societies made over 680,000 loans worth £3,649,000,000. By 1977 the number of loans had reached 737,000 worth £6,705,000,000. The building-society movement is dominated by a few very large societies and this pattern has been accentuated in recent years by mergers and take-overs reducing the number of societies from over 700 in 1959 to 364 by 1977. Of the total assets of the movement, estimated at £28,000,000,000 in 1977, over half are held by the five largest societies.

Despite their variation in size, most societies follow the same, basically conservative, path

TABLE 8.3. *Sources of loans for house purchase in the United Kingdom*
(from Housing and Construction Statistics No. 28, 1978)

| Date | % loans granted by: | | | | Total Advanced |
|---|---|---|---|---|---|
| | Building societies | Local authorities | Insurance companies | Banks | |
| 1975 | 81 | 14 | 4 | 1 | £6,117,000,000 |
| 1978 | 89 | 6 | 3 | 3 | £9,854,000,000 |

Note:   Figures are based on 'gross advances' except for banks, for which only a 'net advance' is recorded.

necessitated because they contradict the normal rules of banking: they borrow from investors who may withdraw their money at any time and they lend over periods of 20–30 years at rates little higher than they pay to investors. So they must ensure that the people to whom they lend are not going to default on their repayments. If they do default, or die before repaying the mortgage, the society must be sure that the property will resell for at least the value of the mortgage. Seen in this context, the cautious policy of societies towards both borrowers and dwellings is understandable.

Most societies will lend up to 90 per cent of their own surveyor's valuation (not necessarily equivalent to the sale price) of a recently built, freehold house. On pre-war properties and flats the maximum loan may be a smaller percentage of the valuation, although the figure may be increased by insuring the extra percentage: in effect the borrower pays a higher interest rate. Although societies prefer houses to be freehold, flats and maisonettes should be leasehold, to avoid problems of assigning responsibility for the common parts, communal gardens, foundations or roof. If there is nobody legally responsible, a block of flats may deteriorate and each dwelling may decline in value or prove impossible to resell. Most societies will lend only if the lease has at least 50 years to run, so that it has not expired by the time the mortgage has been repaid. Again, the intention is to ensure that the property will still have some value should the borrower decide to resell or the society acquire the property by default.

Societies are most cautious of lending on old (pre-1919) or converted properties (e.g. a Victorian house converted into self-contained flats), or on properties of unconventional materials (e.g. timber). Since builders only construct dwellings that they can be sure of selling, and since most prospective purchasers will require a mortgage, the effect is to standardize new housing. Since demand for mortgages invariably exceeds supply and societies allocate all but a small proportion of funds to low-risk properties, the prospects for older housing, especially in 'decaying' inner-city areas, remain bleak, however sincere the assurances of society officials acknowledging their social responsibility.

Boddy (1976) found that in Newcastle-upon-Tyne most building-society mortgages went to new detached and semi-detached houses on suburban estates; very few went to terraced houses in General Improvement Areas near the city centre where prospective buyers had to apply to the council for mortgage assistance (Fig. 8.1). In Saltley, an inner area of Birmingham, only 7 per cent of housebuyers obtained building-society mortgages, 22 per cent bought outright, 50 per cent borrowed from a clearing bank and 14 per cent used other, invariably more expensive, forms of 'back-street finance' such as moneylenders and private finance companies (Williams, 1978). These figures stand in stark contrast to the national statistics quoted at the beginning of this section.

To the extent that certain clients prefer particular types of dwelling, society policy towards property may affect the types of people who become owner-occupiers: tenants offered the opportunity of buying their home from their landlord may not be interested in buying any other property, single people may prefer flats to equally priced small houses. But a more direct sanction on potential homebuyers lies in the earnings rule that societies apply. Most societies will lend between two and a half and three times the annual salary of the applicant, perhaps with a further allowance for a spouse's earnings. This rule arose from the belief that repayments should not exceed a quarter of gross salary. Even this is a very high figure compared to the amount that most continental families spend on housing or the 14–20 per cent that was considered excessive in Victorian England. Societies also prefer clients with secure jobs, good prospects or salaries with annual increments. Thus a

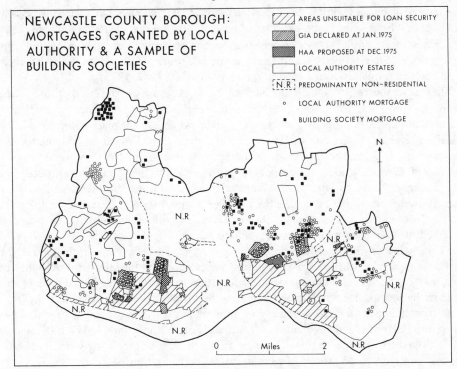

NEWCASTLE COUNTY BOROUGH:
MORTGAGES GRANTED BY LOCAL
AUTHORITY & A SAMPLE OF
BUILDING SOCIETIES

AREAS UNSUITABLE FOR LOAN SECURITY
GIA DECLARED AT JAN.1975
HAA PROPOSED AT DEC.1975
LOCAL AUTHORITY ESTATES
N.R  PREDOMINANTLY NON-RESIDENTIAL
o   LOCAL AUTHORITY MORTGAGE
■   BUILDING SOCIETY MORTGAGE

FIG. 8.1. *The Pattern of mortgage finance for home ownership in Newcastle-on-Tyne*
*(after Boddy, 1976).*

professional person may be preferred to a manual worker even though at the time of application the latter earns more; his earnings may depend on overtime and he may have less security against future redundancy or unemployment.

Not all professional workers requesting less than three times their annual salary for sound properties will receive a mortgage offer. There are always more 'safe' applicants than there is money available. Societies may defer a mortgage offer for several months, so reducing the overall level of residential mobility. For many people, caught in a 'housing chain' whereby they must complete the sale of their present dwelling on the same day that their vendor completes the purchase of his future home, the offer of a mortgage "in x months time" is equivalent to a refusal, and several households may be frustrated in their attempts to move. In addition, societies give priority to first-time buyers and especially to applicants who have invested their savings with them over the preceding years.

Of course, there are ways of 'beating the system' and these tend to accentuate the middle-class bias in owner-occupation. For example, mortgages linked to life-assurance policies and arranged by insurance brokers are more accessible to the middle classes, who may also receive financial aid from their employer (e.g. removal or conveyancing expenses) or a bridging loan from their bank to help overcome the problem described in the previous paragraph. An estate agent may use his business connections to obtain a mortgage for a potential purchaser whom he regards as a 'good customer'. Likewise, solicitors receive mortgage quotas from societies in which they advise their clients to invest and then use their quotas to arrange mortgages for other clients. Since middle-class people are more likely to use solicitors in the course of their everyday business, know them personally or at least know about them, the resulting middle-class bias is only to be expected. In fact it has been argued that building society managers are less significant 'gatekeepers' than solicitors, surveyors or estate agents. Surveyors filter out unsuitable properties, and estate agents and solicitors filter out undesirable clients often before a formal mortgage application has been made (Ford, 1975).

Alternative sources of home loans include banks, insurance companies, private finance companies and local authorities. The major clearing banks are increasingly financing the purchase of expensive properties while, at the other extreme of the market, local authorities are often regarded as 'lenders of last resort' to buyers turned down by building societies because they had insufficient status or the property they hoped to buy was too old or dilapidated. Obviously, local authorities also pay attention to the condition of property, but they are more likely to lend on dwellings in General Improvement Areas or in cases of 'homesteading', where the council sells a dwelling in a poor state of repair on condition that the purchaser undertakes renovation. Different local authorities may also impose other tests of eligibility: mortgages may be granted only to married couples with children, or to people who already live or work locally. Since funds come from central government their availability fluctuates in accord with public expenditure policy. Some authorities try to stabilize the condition of old but structurally sound properties inside their area by facilitating their purchase by low-income households. Others use their lending provisions to reduce the length of their waiting list for council housing by granting mortgages to waiting list families even for properties outside their administrative area. For example, the London Borough of Lambeth granted mortgages to residents of Lambeth who wanted to buy houses in outer London, so stimulating a process of working-class suburbanization.

Boddy found that in Newcastle the average income and socio-economic status of local authority mortgagees was slightly lower than that of building-society borrowers (Fig. 8.2), but there was a greater difference in the types of dwelling that each institution financed (Fig. 8.3). In Huddersfield, Duncan (1976) observed that the council was more sympathetic than building societies to applications from Asian families, perhaps because Asians requested mortgages to buy late-nineteenth-century terraced houses that opened directly on to the street without front gardens — properties that building societies would have rejected whoever the applicant. However, a survey of immigrant housing demonstrated that throughout Britain immigrants were less likely than the white population to own a house with a building-

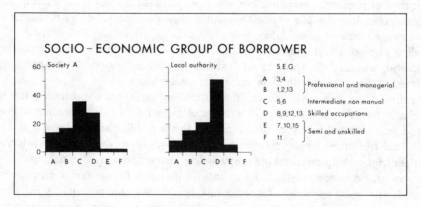

FIG. 8.2. *The allocation of mortgages in Newcastle, by socio-economic status (after Boddy, 1976).*

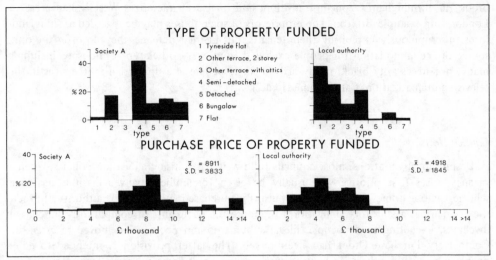

TYPE OF PROPERTY FUNDED

1 Tyneside flat
2 Other terrace, 2 storey
3 Other terrace with attics
4 Semi-detached
5 Detached
6 Bungalow
7 Flat

PURCHASE PRICE OF PROPERTY FUNDED

Society A    x̄ = 8911    S.D. = 3833

Local authority    x̄ = 4918    S.D. = 1845

£ thousand

FIG. 8.3. *The allocation of mortgages in Newcastle, by type and cost of property (after Boddy, 1976).*

society mortgage, but more likely to borrow from a local authority (Smith, 1977). Interestingly, Asian households — especially those with low incomes and little command of the English language — are much more likely than the general population to be owner-occupiers (Table 8.4). Nine-tenths of Asian-owned dwellings are terraced houses, two-thirds built before World War I. Many are owned outright, bought by pooling the savings of friends or relatives. The Asian experience is a sobering reminder that owner-occupancy embraces some of the poorest as well as the richest members of society, and some of the worst as well as the most luxurious housing.

Duncan's study also emphasized that local authorities are not, in fact, 'lenders of last resort'. This role is played by finance companies that lend over shorter terms (5–10 years) at higher interest rates (15–20 per cent). It is ironic that many immigrants are forced to depend on expensive 'back-street finance' because building societies reckoned them too poor or unreliable to repay an ordinary mortgage. Back-street moneylenders are often the only source of funds for the purchase of large inner-city properties, once the homes of servant-keeping middle-class families but now dilapidated. Exorbitant rates of repayment can be met only by subdividing houses into lodgings let at high rents and ignoring their maintenance or improvement. Rex and Moore (1967) observed this process operating in Spark-

TABLE 8.4. *Ethnicity and housing tenure, 1974*
(after Smith, 1977)

| Tenure | % in each tenure | | |
|---|---|---|---|
| | West Indians | Asians | General Population (1972) |
| Owned outright | 4 | 23 | 22 |
| Owned with mortgage | 45 | 53 | 28 |
| Total owner-occupied | 50 | 76 | 50 |
| Rented from l.a. | 26 | 4 | 28 |
| Privately rented | 24 | 19 | 22 |

brook, in Birmingham's zone-in-transition, and it also characterizes West Indian areas of London, for example Brixton. The proprietors of such houses may be regarded as slum land-lords unscrupulously exploiting their tenants, but in their defence, they do offer the only source of accommodation for people excluded from every other type of housing, including many, not necessarily black, newly arrived single people and unmarried mothers (as in the television dramatization 'Cathy Come Home').

### Council Housing

Despite local variations, most councils follow similar housing allocation policies. When a vacancy arises first priority will usually be given to families involved in slum clearance schemes whose homes have been compulsorily purchased by the local authority. In fact, the council has a statutory obligation to rehouse the occupants of compulsorily purchased dwellings, excepting single people, illegal subtenants and people who moved in *after* the Compulsory Purchase Order had been served. The latter provision is intended to deter people who would otherwise have to wait several years to be rehoused from moving into slum properties in the hope of jumping the queue.

Local authorities are also obliged to rehouse homeless families and those who have been recommended for rehousing on medical grounds by the local health authority. Again, pre-cautions may be taken to limit the number of officially recognized 'homeless' and to allocate them to poor-quality council housing (e.g. pre-World War I properties, dwellings acquired from '5 per cent' or private landlords) or even to hostel accommodation in which parents and children may be split up; otherwise a council with a generous policy of rehousing the homeless may find it attracts more than its fair share of homeless families.

In inner-city areas the majority of vacancies that arise will be allocated to the homeless, the sick or displaced slum dwellers, and although a waiting list will also operate, in practice very few people on the waiting list will be rehoused. For example, in Hull families whose homes had been compulsorily purchased waited on average only two to three months between being interviewed by a housing official and moving into council accommodation, whereas waiting-list families averaged more than ten years between registering their name on the list and being allocated a dwelling (Gray, 1976b). The only statutory obligation of local authorities is that they should give 'reasonable preference' to persons in insanitary or over-crowded houses, with large families or in unsatisfactory housing conditions. But 'large', 'insanitary' and 'unsatisfactory' have never been precisely defined and in Hull, the Housing Manager argued that there could be no waiting-list families in unsatisfactory housing who would not qualify for rehousing under slum clearance schemes. Hence, the slow movement of the waiting-list queue was not a special cause for concern.

In rural and suburban areas more vacancies will go to families on the waiting list. Most local authorities use some kind of points system whereby applicants receive points for the time they have spent on the list, their age, marital status, family size, present housing con-ditions, ill health, etc., and vacancies are offered to those with most points, assuming of course that the vacant dwellings are of an appropriate size. Murie *et al.* (1976) have suggested that whatever the points system the same people will be rehoused. What is more important is the supply of housing and most local authorities have concentrated on building 2- and 3-bedroom houses, with very few 1-bedroom flats (except for the elderly) or houses with 4 or more bedrooms. In 1971 37 per cent of all housing in Great Britain but only 21 per cent of council housing comprised 6 or more rooms. What often happens, therefore, is that large families rapidly accumulate sufficient points to reach the top of the waiting list, but remain there while families with fewer points leapfrog over them into council housing, simply because there are so few large council houses that vacancies arise infrequently. It follows that efforts to reform the council-housing system must be directed at the construction of new housing as much as at the bureaucratic machinery that matches families to houses.

Those with most chance of council housing are young married couples with one or two children, living in overcrowded, privately rented rooms and requiring 2- or 3-bedroom dwellings. They will have lived and/or worked in the local authority area for several years, and will have registered on the waiting list as soon as they got married, but only acquired sufficient points to qualify for housing with the birth of children. Single people unless of pensionable age, newcomers including immigrants, and former owner-occupiers are under-represented among council tenants.

The allocation system encourages abuse. Households may deliberately move to poor privately rented housing in anticipation that it will be designated a General Improvement Area or Housing Action Area, whereby their housing will be improved partly at government expense, or more likely that a Compulsory Purchase Order for demolition will be served and they will automatically be rehoused. Newly married couples may choose to continue living with parents or start a family, in order to exacerbate their level of overcrowding and so qualify for rehousing. Most local authorities also require applicants to rank their choice of housing. There is little to lose by opting for a flat (which is less popular than a house) in an older or less attractive and therefore less popular area, since this strategy will provide speedier access to the public housing sector, and once inside a family can always apply for a transfer to a more desirable property.

This consideration raises the point that waiting list applicants compete for vacancies with families already in council accommodation applying for transfers, usually to bigger or better dwellings, on more modern or attractive estates. When new dwellings are completed, or when tenants die, move out of the area or out of the public housing sector, the vacancies are more likely to be offered to transfer applicants than to waiting list families. Both prospective tenants and transfer applicants are interviewed in their homes by council officials and subjectively assessed for cleanliness, reliability in rent-paying, nuisance to their neighbours, and the general quality of their housekeeping. Only households rated 'good' will be allocated to good-quality properties. Households rated 'fair' or 'poor' will be offered only older or less popular dwellings. Unfortunately, it is difficult for a housing visitor to divorce his or her judgement of a family from its present housing conditions. If you live in overcrowded conditions in an old house in a vandalized neighbourhood it may be impossible to convince an official that you are honest, respectable and deserving!

The allocation system has a number of important geographical consequences:

(1) A cycle develops, whereby waiting list applicants would prefer houses but are only offered flats. Soon after moving into a flat they apply for a transfer to a house, thus increasing the demand for houses for transfer applicants and reducing still further the chances that a waiting list applicant will receive a house. Murie noted that in one local authority in 1972–3 flats constituted only 9 per cent of the housing stock but 29 per cent of new lettings, in another the proportions were 30 per cent and 54 per cent.

(2) 'Good' tenants are more likely than 'poor' tenants to receive a transfer. Gray found that in Hull in 1972, 98 per cent of successful transfer applicants were graded 'fairly good' or better. Low-status tenants were likely to have their applications rejected, except in cases of

statutory overcrowding or family break-up. Council tenants can also move by arranging an exchange, whereby two households simply swap accommodation with the approval of the council(s) involved, but low-status tenants concentrated in low-quality accommodation are even less likely to manage an exchange than a transfer: nobody wants to exchange a modern house in an attractive area for a pre-war flat in a poor area! Overall, therefore, the effect is to permit the residential mobility of 'good' tenants and restrict the mobility of 'poor' tenants, a reversal of the pattern that prevailed in the nineteenth century.

(3) The most obvious geographical consequence is the development of residential segregation within the public housing sector. By concentrating all their low-status tenants or problem families on particular estates local authorities have been accused of creating council slums at the same time as demolishing privately owned slum housing! In Hull, Gray found that 63 per cent of tenants graded 'poor' or 'fair only' were allocated housing built before 1945 and none received new accommodation, whereas 43 per cent of 'very good' or 'excellent' tenants moved into new housing and only 11 per cent into pre-war dwellings.

From the viewpoint of housing management the policy is a sensible one. It is undesirable for new housing to be vandalized or ill-maintained by 'poor' families. In terms of the provision of specialist social services, too, the concentration of problem families may be preferred. But the undoubted effect is to maintain a local subculture of failure and depression from which it is even more difficult for the next generation to escape, especially if children are segregated in schools that acquire 'good' or 'bad' reputations.

Ethnic minority groups may also suffer discrimination. Robson (1975) recorded that in seven inner London boroughs in 1966, 33 per cent of English but only 5 per cent of coloured households lived in council accommodation. By 1971 West Indian households in England and Wales were almost as likely as the general population to occupy council housing, but Asians were still under-represented. However, since the majority of West Indians are manual workers, and since manual workers predominate in council housing, it is still the case that West Indians are relatively under-represented in the local authority sector. To some extent, under-representation reflects ignorance (not all immigrants know that they can apply for accommodation), the registration system (in the 1960s many immigrants had not lived in British cities for long enough to qualify) and the lack of large housing (immigrant households are, on average, larger than English households and there are not enough large council houses). But those Asians and West Indians who have received council properties also appear to have suffered discrimination, albeit unconscious in most cases. A survey of 'Westhorpe', a borough in the north of England, showed that minority tenants were concentrated on 'undesirable' estates (Table 8.5); in 'Woodley', a Midlands town, 25 per cent of lettings to coloured families involved acquired, rather than council-built, properties, compared with 8.4 per cent of lettings to white families. This could be explained by the above average size

TABLE 8.5. *The distribution of coloured tenants on council estates in 'Westhorpe'* (after Smith, 1977)

| Type of estate | Mean date of construction | No. of coloured tenants (a) | No. of 2+ Bed properties (b) | a/b % |
|---|---|---|---|---|
| Very desirable | 1955 | 2 | 470 | 0.4 |
| Quite desirable | 1955 | 92 | 2406 | 3.8 |
| Rather undesirable | 1940 | 293 | 2525 | 11.6 |
| Very undesirable | 1936 | 14 | 54 | 25.9 |

of both acquired properties and immigrant families. But the effect was to put immigrants into older, poorer-quality accommodation. Finally, because immigrants tend to be in more immediate need than white families on the waiting list, and because immigrants lack any intimate knowledge of the different council estates in the town to which they have moved, they tend to accept whatever is offered to them, while local white families can express their preferences more positively and refuse to accept second-rate accommodation (Smith, 1977).

*Private Renting*

Private renting is more important than its small share of the present-day housing market would suggest, since many young households pass through the tenure on their way to a local authority tenancy or a mortgage. In 1971, 11 per cent of households in England and Wales outside Greater London occupied unfurnished privately rented dwellings, but 18 per cent of newly formed households (e.g. newly married couples, young single people living away from their parents for the first time) lived in unfurnished accommodation. Only 2 per cent of households occupied furnished dwellings, but 13 per cent of new households lived in furnished accommodation. Within Greater London the figures were 20 per cent of all households, but 26 per cent of new households in unfurnished dwellings, 8 per cent of all households but 28 per cent of new households in furnished accommodation (Murie, 1976).

For nearly a third of the population (and more in London), therefore, renting from a private landlord remains an essential first step, while residence requirements are fulfilled or sufficient points are acquired to obtain council housing, or while savings are invested with a building society until a deposit has been raised and the society is prepared to grant a mortgage. As private renting declines alternative arrangements must be made for households who would otherwise pass through the sector: local authorities must house more single people or short-stay residents; government, builders and building societies must co-operate to make first-time buying easier for young people without savings; and more encouragement will have to be given to alternative tenures such as housing associations and tenants' co-operatives.

Some categories of private tenant have no prospect of ever obtaining a mortgage or a council house and are even more dependent on the continued existence of privately rented accommodation:

(1) Established households — elderly people with controlled tenancies, who have spent most of their lives in the same unfurnished dwelling, paying the same (now very low) rent.

(2) Immigrants with young families, often sharing furnished accommodation with resident immigrant landlords. In inner London in 1966, 6 per cent of English but 48 per cent of immigrant households lived in furnished accommodation (Robson, 1975). A survey of racial disadvantage in Britain showed that at every job level (non-manual, skilled, semi-skilled and unskilled manual) West Indians were more likely than the general population to be renting from a private landlord, Asians in manual work and especially unskilled Asians were less likely to be renting, but Asians in white-collar and professional jobs were twice as likely as whites to rent privately (Smith, 1977).

(3) 'Problem families' — for example, one-parent families or families experiencing chronic unemployment — living in areas of 'housing stress', where they pay high rents for very poor accommodation. They find it impossible to save and so have no prospect of moving up-market into an unfurnished flat or their own house, for either of which a deposit and references would be required.

The first of these three groups may be expected to disappear with the passing of the present generation of elderly households but the other two groups experience increasing pressure from two different sources:

(a) The diminishing quantity of privately rented accommodation due to gentrification and slum clearance.

(b) Increasing competition for the remaining privately rented accommodation from students and young workers who are prepared to share housing. Since each member of a shared flat is in receipt of earnings or a grant, their combined income is much higher than that of a one-parent or unemployed family dependent on social security payments, or even a nuclear family in which only one member is earning. The result is that young households outbid poorer families, and rents rise beyond the level that poorer families can afford to pay. The effects of competition are most evident in small university towns with limited supplies of privately rented housing (McDowell, 1978).

In summary, therefore, the elderly are over-represented in unfurnished and the young in furnished accommodation. In 1971, 12 per cent of all household heads but 54 per cent of furnished tenants were aged under thirty. But in housing stress areas furnished tenants were older, often coloured, often semi-skilled or unskilled, and often living with children in overcrowded conditions (Adams, 1973; Mellor, 1973). At the other extreme are very luxurious furnished tenancies, occupied by visiting, usually foreign, businessmen, for example in parts of Mayfair and St. John's Wood in London.

Despite their best intentions housing associations have had limited success in catering for those most in need. Because the value of improvement grants is based on the number of separate dwellings after conversion, associations prefer to convert large old properties into several small flats. This may satisfy the demand for one-bedroom dwellings but it does nothing to alleviate the shortage of accommodation for large families. Nor, because of their small scale of operations, can associations tolerate as large rent arrears as some councils do. Consequently they cannot risk accommodating too many problem families of unproven reliability. In Lambeth in 1971 only 47 per cent of household heads rehoused by the London Housing Trust but 60 per cent of Lambeth council tenants earned less than £20 per week, and most housing association families included only one or two children (Harloe et al., 1974).

Although unfurnished dwellings still outnumber furnished, it is much easier to gain access to the latter. Unfurnished tenants rarely move and when they do, the landlord is less likely to fill their vacancy than to sell the property to the local authority, an owner-occupier or a property company. Before the 1974 Rent Act was passed, furnished tenants moved frequently, either because they were evicted or out of choice (e.g. students at the end of each summer term) and it was relatively easy to gain entry to the sector. Since 1974 many landlords have chosen not to fill vacancies, but to sell with vacant possession or keep their rooms empty in the hope of a change in the law. Furnished tenancies have become more precious possessions as opportunities for mobility have declined, and it seems likely that ease of access to the sector has decreased significantly since 1974.

Because housing associations derive much of their funds from local authorities they are obliged to grant them allocation rights, often to half the vacancies that arise in housing association properties. The associations have limited funds for the purchase of properties and frequently buy houses with sitting tenants, since such dwellings are much cheaper than houses with vacant possession. Until these tenants choose to leave, therefore, the new landlords have no opportunity to install tenants of their own choice.

TABLE 8.6. *Tenure and socio-economic status: Great Britain, 1971* (after Murie *et al.*, 1976)

| | Profess-ional | Employers and Managers | Int'mediate and Junior Non-manual | Skilled Manual | Semi-skilled | Unskilled |
|---|---|---|---|---|---|---|
| | | | % household heads in each tenure | | | |
| Owner-occupied | 85 | 74 | 59 | 45 | 31 | 21 |
| Rented from l.a. or new town | 3 | 10 | 20 | 38 | 44 | 56 |
| Privately rented unfurnished | 2 | 7 | 11 | 11 | 16 | 18 |
| Privately rented furnished | 3 | 2 | 5 | 2 | 2 | 3 |
| Other | 6 | 8 | 6 | 5 | 7 | 3 |

| | Owner-occupied | Rented from l.a. or new town | Pr. rented unfurnished | Pr. rented furnished |
|---|---|---|---|---|
| | | % household heads in each socio-economic group | | |
| Professional | 7 | 0 | 1 | 4 |
| Employers and managers | 22 | 5 | 9 | 9 |
| Intermediate and junior non-manual | 24 | 13 | 19 | 34 |
| Skilled manual | 30 | 41 | 31 | 20 |
| Semi-skilled | 12 | 28 | 26 | 14 |
| Unskilled | 3 | 12 | 10 | 7 |
| Others* | 3 | 2 | 4 | 12 |

* e.g. members of armed forces and students

## A Theory of Housing Classes

From our survey of the means of access to different types of housing it may appear that the relationship between status and tenure is not so close after all (Table 8.6). Owner-occupiers are *usually* middle-class or middle-aged, but they may be younger or poorer families living in General Improvement Areas with the aid of local authority mortgages, or poor, unskilled Asians living in the worst remaining housing, purchased outright for only a few thousand pounds. Private tenants, too, may be rich visiting businessmen, young and potentially well-off single people sharing a furnished flat, elderly folk who have chosen to live in the same terraced house that they have rented all their adult lives, or a residuum of the poor and unemployed who have no choice but to accept overcrowded and insanitary shared accommodation in housing stress areas. Local authority tenants are a more homogeneous bunch — few young single people or childless couples, a predominance of middle-aged manual workers and their families — but here too, distinctions are made between 'good' and 'poor' tenants and between waiting-list families and rehoused slum dwellers. So it is desirable to refine our classification of housing tenures into a larger number of housing classes. For example, Rex and Moore (1967) identified seven housing classes which they used in a study of race, community and conflict in Sparkbrook, part of the transition zone of the Birmingham conurbation:

(1) outright owners of large houses in desirable areas,

(2)  owner-occupiers with mortgages,

(3)  council tenants in purpose-built council flats and houses,

(4)  council tenants in slums awaiting demolition,

(5)  tenants of private landlords,

(6)  resident landlords who take in lodgers to help repay the loans they raised to buy their houses,

(7)  their lodgers in rooms.

In the light of our preceding discussion it would be desirable to subdivide class (5) to distinguish between furnished and unfurnished tenants who possessed different legal rights at the time of the study, and to include an additional class of immigrant owner-occupiers who have paid cash for rundown properties in decaying areas. We could also increase the number of housing classes to include groups and types of housing not found in Sparkbrook, but this would be to miss the point of Rex and Moore's argument. They used their theory of housing classes to understand the relationships between different groups and the types of conflict or co-operation that characterized life in Sparkbrook. For example, conflict could arise between respectable owner-occupiers and lodging house keepers, whose activities reduced the value of property in the area. Owner-occupiers and respectable council and private tenants may also share an antipathy towards the less respectable tenants, especially those in lodging houses or those considered undeserving of any council accommodation, however poor, while conflicts and jealousies between the two types of council tenants may divide them in negotiations with the council. The division of the population into housing classes is also useful for highlighting competition within classes, for example between private tenants competing for a limited number of privately rented dwellings, between council tenants competing for transfers to better dwellings, between whites, West Indians and Asians in any of the classes.

The theory has also been applied by Pahl (1970) to the rural—urban fringe where conflicts involve the traditional rural population and newcomers seeking a retirement home, second home or dormitory suburb. Pahl's classes include large property owners; salaried in-migrants with capital and pretensions to acquiring a 'heritage home'; spiralists who view the area as a temporary stop on the promotion ladder towards their own 'heritage home' later in life; reluctant commuters with limited income or capital seeking a home where they can bring up their children in a pleasant environment but who can only afford to do so where property prices are low at a considerable distance from the city in which they work; the retired; local council tenants; tied cottagers and other private tenants; and local tradesmen and businessmen. Newcomers and locals may compete for the same housing (e.g. local businessmen and spiralists, local tradesmen and reluctant commuters), but conflicts between housing classes also extend beyond the issue of housing itself. The owners of 'heritage homes' have moved to the countryside to escape urban life and want to conserve the rural environment, but reluctant commuters and local working-people will be less interested in conservation, more interested in improving local services. Reluctant commuters will also be interested in educational provision, while the retired will seek good health services and reasonable public transport.

In fact the zone-in-transition and the urban fringe are two of the few types of area where several housing classes occur together or compete for the same housing stock. In general, owner-occupiers, local authority tenants and private landlords and their tenants are clearly differentiated in space, and different groups within each tenure are also geographically segregated.

**Tenure and Location**

We have seen that purpose-built privately rented accommodation predates purpose-built council or owner-occupied housing. Other things being equal, therefore, we would expect to find privately rented dwellings concentrated in inner-city areas developed prior to areas of owner-occupation or council housing in the suburbs. But this simple model makes no allowance for a number of complicating factors:

(i)  the clearance and renewal of inner areas involving the replacement of privately rented dwellings by other tenures;

(ii) the absorption of older nuclei, which may contain some pre-war, privately rented housing, in suburban expansion;

(iii) the transfer of properties from one tenure to another: from unfurnished private renting to local authority tenure by municipalization or compulsory purchase; from furnished tenancies to owner-occupation as part of the process of gentrification; or from council housing to private ownership in recent campaigns to sell council houses.

Inner-city renewal involving completely new construction is too expensive for private enterprise to contemplate unless it comprises *very* high-status housing (e.g. West End flats for Arab sheikhs) or non-residential land uses. Consequently, most residential redevelopment in inner cities is council-controlled, often in the form of medium- or high-rise blocks of flats. Local authority redevelopment schemes have concentrated on areas of small terraced houses, previously let unfurnished to working-class families. Such houses were often shoddily built in the late nineteenth century and lacked amenities such as a fixed bath or indoor toilet: they were genuinely in need of renewal. They lay in traditional working-class areas where the demand for council housing was greatest and where the local authority was probably Labour-controlled and committed to the extension of public ownership at the expense of private landlords; and they offered the best opportunities for councils to achieve 'housing gains'. These occur when the number of people rehoused on a site exceeds the number living there before redevelopment. It is easier to achieve a housing gain where each house has been occupied by only one family than where properties have been multi-occupied, which is usually the case with the other type of inner-city privately rented accommodation: houses designed for occupation by middle-class families and their servants and subsequently sub-divided and converted to furnished tenancies. In London examples of this type of housing include large terraced houses in Earl's Court, divided into bedsitters for students, secretaries and overseas visitors, and mid-Victorian villas in Brixton, each occupied by several West Indian families renting from a West Indian landlord. This type of housing has often been ignored by local authorities in designating redevelopment areas for at least three reasons. Firstly, it is more difficult to achieve a housing gain unless redevelopment is at high densities, which implies expensive and unpopular high-rise construction. Secondly, if a local authority was to enforce regulations limiting overcrowding of dwellings with inadequate amenities it would increase the numbers of 'homeless' that it would be morally, if not statutorily, obliged to rehouse. Thirdly, although multi-occupied houses may be overcrowded with respect to the facilities they possess, they are rarely structurally unsound, and are considered ripe for rehabilitation rather than clearance.

At the least, rehabilitation will be associated with rent increases, resulting in a change in the status of tenants. More probably, rehabilitation will be associated with the sale of the dwelling either direct to an owner-occupier who undertakes his own programme of improvement or to a property developer who then resells the converted accommodation, usually to young single people or childless couples, invariably middle-class. This is the process known as gentrification.

The extent of inner-city owner-occupation depends upon the attitudes of building societies. While local authorities may finance working-class owner-occupation, especially in General Improvement Areas, the amount of money available for local authority mortgages is small compared to the resources of building societies. We saw earlier in the chapter that building societies are reluctant to lend on old properties, especially prior to their renovation and especially in 'decaying' inner-city areas. Societies generally assert that they consider each property on its merits, but it has also been claimed (e.g. by Duncan (1976) working in Huddersfield) that societies 'redline' entire areas in which they refuse to lend (Williams, 1978). It is difficult to prove the case conclusively, beyond demonstrating the difference between the number of mortgages granted on houses in suburban areas and the number allocated to inner-city properties. For instance, a 5 per cent sample of all societies lending in Greater London in 1970 recorded 1,539 mortgages in outer London boroughs but only 325 in inner London, but this bias may result purely from decisions not to lend on individual, high-risk houses, most of which are concentrated in inner London (Harloe *et al.*, 1974).

Even if individual societies redline particular districts, as Williams (1976) showed in his study of Islington, it is unlikely that all societies will adopt the same policy. Williams contrasted the attitudes of large, national and small, local societies towards gentrification in Islington in the 1950s and 1960s. Large societies ignored the area because they received plenty of applications for loans for 'safe' houses elsewhere, they had no branch offices in the area (and therefore no obligation to grant mortgages to local investors) and no first-hand sources of information on the likely success of rehabilitation schemes. In contrast small, locally-based societies were obliged to lend in the area to keep faith with local investors and were confident that their local knowledge was sufficient for them to minimize their risks in lending on unmodernized properties. Moreover, the directors of local societies were often solicitors or estate agents with businesses in Islington, so it was in their own interest to ensure that mortgages were available for their clients. Since local societies generally offered less favourable terms to mortgagees (smaller percentage loans at higher interest rates) their activities only assisted high-income purchasers who could afford an expensive mortgage and a large deposit. By the 1970s major societies were also prepared to lend in Islington, but by then property prices had risen beyond the resources of low-income households.

In recent years more local authorities have been prepared to undertake rehabilitation of municipalized dwellings, especially in Housing Action Areas established under the 1974 Housing Act. Policy has moved in favour of rehabilitation partly in response to criticisms of the characterless and depressing appearance of most blocks of council flats, but also in line with reductions in government expenditure and the recognition that, in the short term, rehabilitation is cheaper than redevelopment. Housing associations have also played a significant part in the rehabilitation movement.

The overall effect of these changes has been to produce areas of unfurnished privately rented houses mixed with a few very poor-quality owner-occupied dwellings and with purpose-built council flats and municipalized houses awaiting demolition or rehabilitation; and areas of large, old houses, subdivided into furnished flats, often with shared facilities, mixed with gentrified properties in owner-occupation. The two types of area correspond to the contrasting eastern and western inner-city sectors identified by Mann (1965) in his model of the typical English city that we outlined in Chapter 6. In both types of area some properties will have been taken over by housing associations or tenants' co-operatives. Squatters will most probably be located in municipalized properties awaiting conversion or demolition by the council.

In suburban areas there are several kinds of privately rented accommodation, none of much significance quantitatively and all declining in importance. In older nuclei, developed as free-standing towns before their absorption into suburbia, the same types of dwelling as occur in the inner city are present on a smaller scale. In addition, between the wars, blocks of 'mansion flats' were built for letting to middle-class households, especially in locations convenient for commuting — along main roads or near suburban railway stations. Many of the property companies who owned these flats are now selling them on long leases, either to sitting tenants, or by advertizing to the general public when the tenants leave. The result is a change in tenure from unfurnished renting to owner-occupation, but there is rarely any change in the status of residents. The new owner-occupiers, if not the same people as the old tenants, are of the same type. A few suburban houses, normally owner-occupied, may be let while their owners are abroad or working elsewhere in the country for one or two years. This type of letting is diminishing as estate agents who administered such lets now find them more trouble than they are worth, and as successive Rent Acts have made it more difficult for an owner to regain occupation of his own property from a tenant.

Most suburbs, therefore, are split between owner-occupied and local authority dwellings and, except where council houses have been sold to their occupants, the two occur in geographically distinct areas. For instance, in the London Borough of Sutton new council housing has been restricted to the traditionally working-class northern parts of the borough. Southern wards are almost exclusively owner-occupied, except for a few small estates dating from the 1950s and the Roundshaw Estate, developed jointly by the local borough and the GLC between 1967 and 1971 on the site of Croydon Aerodrome. This constitutes a 'windfall' site for the local authority and even though it lies in the south of the borough it is clearly physically isolated from surrounding areas of semi-detached suburbia (Dennis, 1978).

The balance between owner-occupied and local authority housing in a suburb will reflect its political history. Families who would be council tenants in a Labour-controlled town may necessarily become owner-occupiers in Conservative towns, where the stock of council housing is actually diminishing as the most attractive council dwellings are sold to tenants, leaving the council with the least attractive properties to let, and where owner-occupancy may be encouraged by generous local authority mortgage schemes.

The fact that some households can change their housing tenure without changing their house may appear to weaken the claims of a close correlation between housing and status. However, we would still expect a close relationship between status and tenure at the time the household moved to its present address. Clearly, the relationship varies through time as owner-occupation has become possible for lower-status groups and through space as some areas are biased towards public ownership, others towards private housing. Nevertheless, the links between socio-economic, family and ethnic status and housing tenure remain strong.

To conclude this discussion some evidence from Greater London will be presented. The spatial pattern by wards is shown in Fig. 8.4. There is the expected concentration of owner-occupation in outer London with generally low levels in inner areas. If more recent information or data at a more detailed scale had been available, the effects of gentrification in such areas as Islington, Stockwell and Fulham would be apparent. Council housing shows a more even distribution, although predominating in inner London and especially in the East

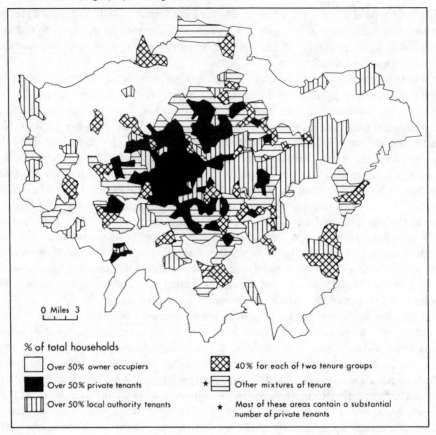

FIG. 8.4. *Housing tenure in Greater London, 1971, by wards.*

End where slum clearance and renewal have proceeded farthest. Suburban 'cottage estates' such as St. Helier, on the boundaries of Sutton and Merton, and Becontree, extending through much of Barking, show up clearly as islands of council housing in a sea of owner-occupancy. Furnished private tenancies are concentrated in inner north and west London and parts of south London, but there are few furnished tenancies in the East End, where the small amount of housing not in public ownership remains in the form of unfurnished tenancies. Unfurnished renting shows a wider distribution than furnished tenure but is still restricted to inner suburbs built before World War I (Shepherd *et al.*, 1974).

These patterns are confirmed by Table 8.7 which reproduces the distribution of different tenures in selected London boroughs. One outer borough, Harrow, has a substantial majority of owner-occupiers; another, Sutton, has a greater leavening of council tenants reflecting the incorporation of part of the St. Helier estate within its boundaries; Tower Hamlets in the East End has very few owner-occupiers or furnished tenants, an overwhelming majority of council dwellings and a residue of small houses let unfurnished by private landlords; Kensington and Chelsea in inner west London has more of a mixture of housing classes, but the largest tenure group in 1971 comprised furnished tenants.

Within each borough the segregation of tenure groups is usually greater in outer than in

TABLE 8.7. *Housing tenure in selected London boroughs, 1971*

| Borough | owner-occupiers | % households renting local authority | renting private unfurnished | renting private furnished |
|---|---|---|---|---|
| Harrow | 70 | 11 | 14 | 5 |
| Kensington and Chelsea | 16 | 8 | 37 | 38 |
| Lambeth | 20 | 31 | 33 | 15 |
| Sutton | 63 | 20 | 13 | 4 |
| Tower Hamlets | 2 | 67 | 26 | 3 |
| GREATER LONDON | 40 | 25 | 24 | 11 |

inner boroughs, reflecting the more recent and homogeneous development of the outer areas by comparison with the mixture of original development, changed tenures and post-war renewal that characterizes inner London. Table 8.8 shows the levels of segregation in Sutton and Lambeth in 1966, using the dissimilarity indices described in Chapter 7. Particularly noticeable are the high degree of segregation of council housing in Sutton (indices of 61, 63 and 75) and the contrast in the relationship between council housing and unfurnished private renting in the two boroughs (indices of 63 in Sutton and 21 in Lambeth). In Sutton most council housing was built on greenfield sites. In Lambeth local authority property included municipalized unfurnished tenancies and modern council flats built on the sites of former, and in the midst of surviving, terraced houses let unfurnished by private landlords.

## Location and Status

So far we have argued that there are close links between tenure and socio-economic, family and ethnic status, but not so close that each tenure is associated with only one socio-economic group or stage in the life cycle. This is partly because each tenure includes some housing that was purpose-built for that tenure and other housing that has been converted from other tenures, and the purpose-built and converted dwellings rarely accommodate the same types of people. Dwellings bought by a local authority from private or philanthropic landlords usually accommodate lower-status tenants than purpose-built council dwellings; houses designed for owner-occupation satisfy the lending criteria of building societies and attract middle-income, middle-class households, whereas houses converted from privately rented dwellings attract either the rich (in the case of gentrification) or young, low-income families (in General Improvement Areas) or low-status, low-paid immigrants (in old, un-modernized properties).

TABLE 8.8. *The segregation of tenure groups in the London Boroughs of Sutton and Lambeth, by wards, 1966: indices of dissimilarity, Sutton values above diagonal, Lambeth values below diagonal*

| | Owner-occupied | Local authority | Private unfurnished | Private furnished |
|---|---|---|---|---|
| Owner-occupied | | 61 | 23 | 39 |
| Rented from l.a. | 43 | | 63 | 75 |
| Rented pr. unfurnished | 30 | 21 | | 32 |
| Rented pr. furnished | 24 | 32 | 18 | |

We have also argued that there are close links between tenure and location, again not so simple that each tenure is associated with only one type of location. In fact it may be preferable to define relationships *exclusively,* in terms of the status groups or locations that are not associated with a particular tenure: private renting is *not* usually suburban, council tenants are *rarely* young, single people.

The next stage in the argument is to complete the triangle of relationships by accounting for the spatial distribution of social, demographic and ethnic groups in terms of the structure of the housing market. But an insoluble problem in such an explanation lies in our dependence on ecological correlations. The data available to us here relate at best to enumeration districts, at worst to entire London boroughs. Even if we demonstrate that a particular district has relatively high proportions of New Commonwealth immigrants, over-crowded dwellings, households without exclusive use of all amenities (fixed bath, indoor WC, hot water) and privately rented accommodation, we cannot be sure that these charac-teristics all relate to the same people – that immigrants live in overcrowded, privately rented accommodation without their own private sanitary amenities. The printed census does not allow such precise identification.

Nevertheless, ecological correlations – sometimes of a negative character – hint at the explanatory role of housing in accounting for the residential segregation of status groups. Dividing Greater London into its 33 boroughs (including the City of London) we can see that the distribution of men with professional or managerial occupations in 1971 was associated with an *absence* of council housing ($r = -0.70$); the distribution of car-owning households (another indicator of high social rank) was positively associated with owner-occupied housing ($r = +0.92$) and with high-quality housing ($r = +0.88$ with 'percentage of households with exclusive use of all amenities') and negatively associated with overcrowding ($r = -0.88$). Family life, as indicated by high percentages of children, high fertility rates and large households, was negatively associated with privately rented accommodation ($r = -0.73$ between 'percentage of the population aged 5–14' and 'percentage of dwellings unfurnished, privately rented', and $r = -0.57$ for the relationship with furnished dwellings). Low family status, indicated by one-person households and high proportions of women in the labour force, was associated with overcrowding, both types of private renting and the sharing of amenities by two or more households. Persons of New Commonwealth origin also lived in boroughs with high levels of overcrowding, multiple-occupancy and large numbers of dwellings lacking all amenities, while persons of neither British nor New Commonwealth parentage (e.g. of European origin) were especially associated with areas of furnished accommodation ($r = +0.91$), overcrowding ($r = +0.75$) and shared toilet facilities ($r = +0.85$).

At a more detailed scale Robson (1969) in Sunderland and Pritchard (1976) in Leicester have undertaken factorial ecologies of 1961 census data. In Sunderland the first principal component identified enumeration districts with high numbers in socio-economic classes I (professional and managerial) and II (intermediate non-manual), relatively few adults who had left school by their sixteenth birthday and relatively many owner-occupiers. The second component grouped together privately rented dwellings, shared dwellings with inadequate facilities, a lack of council housing and a lack of families. In other words, variables associated with social rank and family status loaded on the first two components, in accordance with social area theory, but each was associated with other variables relating to housing tenure or quality. Likewise in Leicester, the second principal component linked owner-occupation, large dwellings (of more than 6 rooms), dwellings with all amenities, dwellings with garages, car-owners, and socio-economic classes I and II, while the third component brought together ethnic (Irish-born) and life-cycle (low family status) variables with measures of privately rented furnished accommodation and shared amenities.

In Table 8.9 we have attempted to summarize our findings on housing tenure, age and quality and the characteristics of residents. We do not claim the table to be comprehensive: the critical reader will find exceptions to the classes listed there and will think of additions that apply in his or her own town. But if it does nothing else, the table exemplifies the complexity of the housing system and warns against oversimplifying generalizations. The final column lists some typical locations of the different housing classes in Greater London including, for example, the development of 'tower blocks' by local authorities in areas such as Canning Town in London's Dockland in the 1960s and more recent, low-rise but high-density flats by the borough of Southwark in Bermondsey in south-east London; the rehabilitation of dwellings built by the Improved Industrial Dwellings Co. in the 1860s south of King's Cross by the Camden borough council, and their administration of East End Dwellings Co. flats in nearby Cromer Street. In contrast, the blocks erected by the Peabody Trust in North Southwark in the 1870s continue under their original administration (Table 8.9). Readers should consider the history and location of different housing classes in their own towns in the same way.

## Housing and Mobility

In Chapter 7 we referred briefly to the relationship between housing tenure and residential mobility. We saw that in the late nineteenth century the working classes moved more frequently, especially over short distances, than the middle classes, whereas in the 1970s they moved less often. Pritchard (1976) has calculated that in Leicester, 22 per cent of households moved in the course of a year in the 1870s but only 9 per cent in the 1960s. He attributes the change to the shift from insecure private renting to the security of owner-occupation and council housing; to the increase in life expectancy and continued independence of the elderly, resulting in an increasing proportion of households with elderly heads; and to the decrease in vacancies, partly a function of the unstable financial basis of the building industry, whereby supply never anticipates demand, and partly a self-perpetuating problem: fewer vacancies means less mobility means fewer vacancies. . . . Overall, mobility in England is approximately half that in the United States, where 20 per cent of households move in any year, a difference that should act as a further warning against the uncritical application of American models to English situations.

The statistics should not be interpreted as meaning that every household in England moves once every ten years. The General Household Survey (1972) showed that 47 per cent of household heads had not moved in the previous 10 years, 35 per cent had moved at least once in 5 years and 1 per cent had moved at least 5 times in that period. Even among private tenants, whom one would expect to have moved frequently, there was a substantial population of non-movers: for example, 61 per cent of furnished tenants in London in 1970 had moved in the preceding 18 months but 10 per cent had been at the same address for more than 5 years.

Another difference between Britain and North America concerns the length of vacancy chains: for every 10 new housing units constructed in the United States in 1966, 35 moves occurred (the 10 families moving into those units, plus 25 households shuffling along the chain into vacancies created by the movement of the first 10 families), whereas a survey of

TABLE 8.9. *Housing, status and location*

| Tenure | Age and Dwelling Type | Location | Special Characteristics | Socio-economic Status | Family Status | Ethnic Status | Examples in London |
|---|---|---|---|---|---|---|---|
| Rented from local authority | Flats, purpose built since World War II | Inner city, often on the site of 19th-c. working-class housing | | Low | Childless couples, young families; old people | Some immigrants | Inner south and east London |
| | Houses built since 1919 | Low-status sectors of suburbia, 'windfall' sites | Some under-occupation | Low-middle, esp. skilled manual | Families with children; couples whose children have left home | Very few coloured families | Becontree, Watling, St. Helier |
| | Houses, built before 1919 for private renting, now municipalized and awaiting demolition or improvement. Some already improved. | Inner city, usually traditional working-class areas | Some overcrowding and lack of amenities, except in improved properties | Low; some tenants from previous landlord; some tenants ranked 'poor' by housing visitors | Single people; elderly couples; households of unrelated adults | Quite large numbers of coloured persons, esp. West Indians | Stockwell |
| | Flats, built before 1919, often by philanthropic agencies | Inner city, often on 19th-c. slum clearance sites | Some sharing of amenities | " | " | " | King's Cross |
| Owner-occupied | 'Town houses', semi-detached and detached houses and bungalows built since 1919 | Suburbia and beyond | Some under-occupation | Middle-high | Young and middle-aged families with children; couples whose children have left home | A few high-status minority-group members, loosely clustered, e.g. Jews | Outer north-west and south London |
| | Modern flats | Suburbia, esp. where convenient for public transport, on sites of Victorian and Edwardian villas | | Middle | Young singles; childless couples; small families | | Beckenham, Sutton, Stanmore, Edgware |
| | Inter-war mansion flats, previously let by property companies, but now more often owner-occupied | City centre and inner suburbs, along main roads | | Middle-high | Very few children | Some foreign visitors | Maida Vale, Finchley Road |

| | | | | | | | |
|---|---|---|---|---|---|---|---|
| | Large houses, dating from Edwardian times or earlier, often leasehold. | Inner suburbs, often near open space or on higher ground | | High | Mature families | A few foreign businessmen and their families | Hampstead, Dulwich |
| | Pre-1919 houses, originally rented, now gentrified and often converted into flats | Inner city, 18th- and 19th-c. middle-class suburbs | | Middle-high | Young and middle-aged couples and small families | | Islington, Chelsea, Kennington |
| | Pre-1919 houses, originally rented, still unimproved | Inner-city, decaying neighbourhoods | Overcrowding, sharing and often lack of amenities | Low | Some old people, but mostly families | Many immigrants, esp. Asians | Few examples in London; even these houses too expensive |
| Privately rented (unfurnished) | Pre-1919 by-law terraced houses, unimproved in anticipation of compulsory purchase | Inner city | Some lacking in amenities | Low | Many elderly people | Some Irish and coloured, often renting from minority gp. landlord | Hackney, Brixton |
| Housing Assn. | Pre-1919, now improved | Inner city, often in GIAs or HAAs | | Low | Singles, large families, special groups in need, l.a. waiting-list families | Some immigrants | Holloway, Lambeth, Notting Hill |
| | Pre-1919 Housing Trust flats | Inner city, often on 19th-c. slum clearance sites | Some sharing of amenities | Low | Mixed | | Peabody, Guinness, Sutton Trusts, e.g. North Southwark, Pimlico |
| | Modern flats or sheltered housing | Suburban | | Low-middle | Elderly | | Harrow, Sutton |
| Privately rented (furnished) | Any property normally owner-occupied, rented while owner is away | Mostly suburban | | Middle-high | Temporary residents, esp. families | European and American visitors | Any middle-class suburb |
| | Pre-1919 houses subdivided into flats and bedsitters | Inner city, usually 19th-c. middle-class areas | Overcrowding, multiple occupancy, sharing of amenities | Low (except students and young professionals) | Problem families; older singles; students and young singles sharing | Large numbers of immigrants | Camden, Clapham Earls Court |

vacancy chains in west central Scotland revealed that 10 new private dwellings facilitated 21 moves, 10 new council dwellings only 16 moves. However, we should not conclude that the relative immobility and apparent ineffectiveness of new construction at generating mobility in Britain are less desirable that the state of affairs in the U.S.A. Shorter chains among council tenants reflect more slum clearance, so that no vacancies are created when slum families are rehoused. Shorter chains also reflect the construction of more new dwellings for relatively low-income first-time buyers in Britain, so that new dwellings are filled by new households (e.g. newly weds, or young people moving out of their parents' homes). In America, more new housing is designed with the richest members of society in mind, and the *only* way in which low-income families can benefit is by 'levelling up' or 'filtering' into the housing vacated by the rich. So it could be argued that high mobility rates in North America are a consequence of inefficient provision for the mass of the population.

Nevertheless, the change in British mobility since the nineteenth century has been so great that it is fair to argue that in the past people moved *more* often than they would have liked, while today they move *less* frequently than they would prefer. At any time, one-third of British households express a desire to move, but only one in ten manages to move in the course of a year. The remainder are frustrated, either by the breakdown of housing chains described earlier in this chapter, or because they set their sights unrealistically high given their income and status, or because of the inefficiency of local authority transfer procedures.

Given the links between tenure and the life cycle, it is not surprising that some tenures are over- or under-represented in the mobility statistics. Many furnished tenants are young people whose incomes, if not their jobs and workplaces, are liable to change frequently, and whose household circumstances also change as they make new friends or get married. Such people would move frequently regardless of the characteristics of their housing tenure. Likewise, elderly people in controlled tenancies or council flats would be unlikely to move even if they could take their artificially low rent with them, or even if it was easier to transfer from one council flat to another. But some variations in mobility *can* be directly attributed to the characteristics of different tenures.

*Owner-occupiers*

Moves within owner-occupation are most amenable to the theoretical treatment provided by Brown and Moore (1970) described in Chapter 7. Households choose their dwelling subject to the constraints of their own capital resources, the availability of a mortgage, the vacancies that are available at the time of search, the time that they can spend in the search, and the frustrations incurred by the breakdown of housing chains. Very few people move out of owner-occupation into another tenure. In the National Movers Survey (1972), 33 per cent of all moves by continuing households were from one owner-occupied dwelling to another, in the majority of cases into a more expensive house; 3 per cent of all moves were from owner-occupation into a council tenancy, often by the owners of small, unfit terraced houses subject to slum clearance; and a further 3 per cent were from owner-occupation into private renting, including long-distance labour migrants taking temporary accommodation at their destination before moving back into owner-occupation after a more thorough search of vacancies than they could have undertaken from their former home (Short, 1978).

*Council Tenants*

We noted earlier that a household can move within the local authority sector by applying for a 'transfer' or arranging an 'exchange' and that 'good' households are more successful in this competition than households whose housekeeping and appearance is rated 'poor' by housing officials. It is in this sector that desired mobility most clearly exceeds actual mobility. More than one in five GLC tenants apply to move during any year, but only about 3 per cent of tenants do actually move (Bird, 1976). The demand for transfers is greatest where most waiting list families are allocated flats rather than houses, so the mobility rate among council tenants would probably be even lower if they were more efficiently allocated on first entering the sector. It seems, therefore, that there are few opportunities to move between council dwellings for other than vital reasons (e.g. overcrowding, under-occupation, divorce, health reasons).

Except for 'key workers' and labour migrants moving to new or expanded towns, there is − at the time of writing − no national system facilitating moves between council properties in different areas. Coupled with the residence qualification that most local authorities require before considering an application for housing, the effect is to deter the migration of manual workers between towns. A council tenant living and working in 'A' will think twice before accepting a job in 'B' if it means a return to the bottom of the queue for council housing and the prospect of several years in privately rented accommodation, which in any case is difficult to obtain.

*Private Tenants*

Although there were only two furnished dwellings for every five unfurnished, mobility in 1972 was almost as great within the furnished sector as between pairs of unfurnished dwellings. Unfurnished tenants were often old and rarely moved (or wanted to move), often in controlled tenancies and unlikely to find anywhere that was as good value for money, and often in properties that were either sold or demolished when they left.

We have already commented on the continuing role of the private sector in accommodating new households setting up their first homes. In 1958 63 per cent and in 1972 31 per cent of new households moved into privately rented dwellings, in each year substantially more than the proportions of all households in private tenancies. It follows that there are also large numbers of families moving out of the sector, typically, low-income families moving from unfurnished private to council tenancies (10 per cent of all moves in 1972), and young middle-class households moving from furnished rooms into owner-occupation (6 per cent of all moves).

**Some Final Comments**

It seems likely that recent trends in the housing market have fostered conservatism among householders. The extension of owner-occupation to lower-income groups has created a corps of working-class capitalists, a new type of property-owning petty bourgeoisie. Household heads who acquire a financial stake in their homes become more resistant to any changes that might adversely affect the value of their property. In the past a private tenant who disapproved of changes in his environment, such as the invasion of his home area by another social or ethnic group, simply moved elsewhere: it was his landlord who suffered if he was unable to relet the dwelling or had to accept 'inferior' tenants or lower the rent. But the owner-occupier is his own landlord: he will be more careful in selecting where to live, most probably moving to a 'safe' area and subsequently defending its character by supporting local residents' associations and conservation societies. So the spread of owner-occupancy (and council housing as currently administered) has produced both the immobility of individual households and a reinforcement of the characteristics of different areas. Middle-class areas become even more middle-class. Areas perceived as decaying actually do decay.

A social structure based on relationships to the means of production has been complicated by a system of classes based on access to housing, a form of consumption. Marxists have argued that the promulgation of a theory of housing classes, in which council tenants, private tenants and mortgagees are assigned to different classes, obscures their communality of interests. Local authorities, private landlords and building societies are all different manifestations of the property-owning elite, while council tenants, private tenants, lodgers and mortgagees are all constrained in where they can live and what they can do with the property they occupy. Moreover, it is easier to move from one housing class to another than it is to change from employee to employer, from working-class to middle-class. In practice, however, the differences in location, behaviour and membership of different housing classes are sufficiently great for some form of housing class theory to remain fundamental to the social geographer's understanding of segregation and mobility in contemporary England.

## References and Further Reading

A comprehensive guide to the British housing system in the 1970s is provided by:

Murie, A., Niner, P. and Watson, C. (1976) *Housing Policy and the Housing System,* Allen & Unwin, London.

while a radical critique of the system appears in papers that make up:
Housing Workshop of the Conference of Socialist Economists (1975) *Political Economy and the Housing Question,* School of Cultural and Community Studies, University of Sussex.

An easier introduction to some of the complex ideas contained in this collection is:
Community Development Project (1976) *Profits Against Houses,* CDP, London.

New books on housing are appearing frequently, for example:
Cullingworth, J. B. (1979) *Essays on Housing Policy,* Allen & Unwin, London.
Lambert, C., Paris, C. and Blackaby, B. (1978) *Housing Policy and the State,* Macmillan, London.
Lansley, S. (1979) *Housing and Public Policy,* Croom Helm, London.

The British scene is contrasted with continental experience in:
Duclaud-Williams, R. H. (1978) *The Politics of Housing in Britain and France,* Heinemann, London.
Hallett, G. (1977) *Housing and Politics in West Germany and Britain,* Macmillan, London.
Headey, B. (1978) *Housing Policy in the Developed Economy,* Croom Helm, London (deals with Britain and Sweden).

Geographical introductions are offered by:
Bassett, K. and Short, J. (1980) *Housing and Residential Structure,* Routledge & Kegan Paul, London.
Robson, B. T. (1975) *Urban Social Areas,* Oxford University Press, Oxford.

For an econometric approach to the housing market, see:
Whitehead, C. M. E. (1974) *The UK Housing Market: An Econometric Model,* Saxon House, Farnborough, Hampshire.

Land development and housing construction are discussed by:
Jackson, A. A. (1973) *Semi-Detached London,* Allen & Unwin, London.
Pahl, R. E. (1975) *Whose City?,* Penguin, Harmondsworth, esp. chapters 5–6.
Sutcliffe, A. (1974) *Multi-Storey Living,* Croom Helm, London.
Swann, J. (1975) The political economy of residential redevelopment in London, in Housing Workshop, *op.cit.,* pp. 104–15.

A theory of housing classes is developed in:
Pahl, R. E. (1970) *Patterns of Urban Life,* Longman, London, esp. chapter 4.
Rex, J. A. (1968) The sociology of a zone of transition, in Pahl, R. E. (ed.), *Readings in Urban Sociology,* Pergamon, Oxford, pp. 211–31.
Rex, J. A. and Moore, R. (1967) *Race, Community and Conflict,* Oxford University Press, Oxford.

The owner-occupied sector and the role of building societies are considered by:
Boddy, M. J. (1976) The structure of mortgage finance: building societies and the British social formation, *Transactions Institute of British Geographers,* New Series, 1, 58–71.
Duncan, S. S. (1976) Self-help: the allocation of mortgages and the formation of housing sub-markets, *Area,* 8, 307–16.
Ford, J. (1975) The role of the building society manager in the urban stratification system, *Urban Studies,* 12, 295–302.
Short, J. R. (1978) Residential mobility in the private housing market of Bristol. *Transactions Institute of British Geographers,* New Series, 3, 533–47.
Williams, P. R. (1976) The role of institutions in the inner London housing market, *Transactions Institute of British Geographers,* New Series, 1, 20–33.
Williams, P. R. (1978) Building societies and the inner city, *Transactions Institute of British Geographers,* New Series, 3, 23–34.

On local authority housing see:
Bird, H. (1976) Residential mobility and preference patterns in the public sector of the housing market, *Transactions Institute of British Geographers,* New Series, 1, 20–33.
Community Development Project (1976) *Whatever Happened to Council Housing?,* CDP, London.
Damer, S. (1976) A note on housing allocation, in Political Economy of Housing Workshop, *Housing and Class in Britain,* School of Cultural and Community Studies, University of Sussex, pp. 72–4.
Gray, F. (1976a) The management of local authority housing, in Political Economy of Housing Workshop, *op. cit.,* pp. 75–86.
Gray, F. (1976b) Selection and allocation in council housing, *Transactions Institute of British Geographers,* New Series, 1, 34–46.
Paris, C. and Lambert, J. (1979) Housing problems and the state: the case of Birmingham, England, in D. Herbert & R. J. Johnston (eds.), *Geography and the Urban Environment Volume II,* Wiley, Chichester, pp. 227–58.

The privately rented sector is considered by:
Adams, B. (1973) Furnished lettings in stress areas, in D. Donnison & D. Eversley (eds.), *London: Urban Patterns, Problems and Policies,* Heinemann, London, pp. 354–82.
McDowell, L. (1978) Competition in the private-rented sector: students and low-income families in Brighton, Sussex, *Transactions Institute of British Geographers,* New Series, 3, 55–65.
Mellor, R. (1973) Structure and process in the twilight areas, *Town Planning Review,* 44, 54–70.

Its fate, in terms of clearance, improvement and gentrification, is discussed in:
Dennis, N. (1978) Housing policy areas: criteria and indicators in principle and practice, *Transactions Institute of British Geographers,* New Series, 3, 2–22.
Duncan, S. S. (1974) Cosmetic planning or social engineering: improvement grants and improvement areas, *Area,* 6, 259–71.
Hamnett, C. (1973) Improvement grants as an indicator of gentrification in inner London, *Area,* 5, 252–61.
Merrett, S. (1976) Gentrification, in Political Economy of Housing Workshop, *op. cit.,* pp. 44–9.
Swann, J. (1975) Housing associations: a socialist critique, in Housing Workshop, *op. cit.,* pp. 116–22.

On the situation of immigrants in the housing market, see:
Burney, E. (1967) *Housing on Trial,* Oxford University Press, London.
Smith, D. J. (1977) *Racial Disadvantage in Britain,* Penguin, Harmondsworth.

A comprehensive case study of the various sectors of the housing system is:

Harloe, M., Issacharoff, R. and Minns, R. (1974) *The Organization of Housing: Public and Private Enterprise in London,* Heinemann, London.

More general geographical perspectives on the London housing market are included in:

Dennis, R. J. (1978) Changing South London, in Clout, H. D. (ed.), *Changing London,* University Tutorial Press, London, pp. 88–98.

Shepherd, J., Westaway, J. and Lee, T. (1974) *A Social Atlas of London,* Oxford University Press, Oxford.

while an important geographical study of housing in a provincial city is:

Pritchard, R. M. (1976) *Housing and the Spatial Structure of the City,* Cambridge University Press, Cambridge.

Finally, all these studies of housing should be considered in the context of ecological and behavioural approaches to urban structure, as illustrated by:

Brown, L. A. and Moore, E. G. (1970) The intra-urban migration process: a perspective, *Geografiska Annaler,* 52B, 1–13.

Mann, P. H. (1965) *An Approach to Urban Sociology,* Routledge & Kegan Paul, London.

Robson, B. T. (1969) *Urban Analysis,* Cambridge University Press, Cambridge.

# 9

# The Inner City

## Recognizing the Problems

IN the last chapter we observed that two of the most mixed and socially unstable types of area in contemporary England are inner-city zones of transition and urban fringe belts, each characterized by a multiplicity of social and housing classes. The next two chapters examine these areas in more detail and extend the discussion beyond the single issue of housing that formed the focus of Chapter 8.

The most fundamental characteristic of all inner urban areas in England is population decline. Between 1961 and 1976 inner Manchester lost 20 per cent of its inhabitants, inner Liverpool 40 per cent. In the decade 1961–71 the population of Greater London declined by 7 per cent, but the rate of change was much higher in inner London (−13 per cent) than in outer boroughs (−2 per cent). In itself, such a decline may be no bad thing. It reflects the out-migration of families from overcrowded Victorian slums to suburban estates, migration that is often accompanied by a change in status from tenant to owner-occupier. It also means that redeveloped slum-clearance areas or rehabilitated old housing need accommodate persons at much lower densities than previously. In fact, the demand for housing has not decreased in proportion to the decline in population because average household size has also decreased: a smaller population requires the same number of dwelling units and housing stress continues to characterize inner areas. Even more disturbing is the context in which population decline has occurred. Employment in manual occupations, especially of an unskilled nature, has rapidly contracted; the most able have moved out and the least able, often including large numbers of immigrants, have been left behind.

In recent years the 'problem of the inner city' has become a popular topic for conferences, symposia, television documentaries, newspaper and magazine features and political activity. In the wake of major speeches in 1976 and 1977 by Peter Shore, Minister for the Environment, the publication of three *Inner Area Studies* and a white paper entitled *Policy for the Inner Cities,* the Inner Urban Areas Bill was introduced in December 1977 and became law in June 1978. Inner-city partnerships have been established to co-ordinate the activities of local and central government and to involve local pressure groups in decision-making. Regular announcements of the allocation of additional financial resources to inner-city areas have been made, although it is worth noting that the money granted to local authorities to alleviate urban problems is less than the sum denied them by cuts in public expenditure. The granting of 'development area' status to inner areas has been advocated so that they might more easily attract new industrial and office developments; and the role of the Location of Offices Bureau was altered from one of directing offices out of London to one of 'providing the facts', thus permitting the relocation of offices in inner London as well as in the provinces.

157

Contrary to the impression that this frantic burst of activity may have given, government attempts to resuscitate inner-city areas actually have a much longer history (CDP, 1977). For example, in 1965 the Milner Holland Report on *Housing in Greater London* identified areas of bad housing to be designated as areas of special control. Subsequently, the Greater London Development Plan identified areas of 'housing stress', using ward data from the 1966 census to rank areas according to their levels of overcrowding, multiple occupancy, and access to basic amenities (Fig. 6.3). The worst 10 per cent were designated 'stress areas'. Many of these areas also fared badly with respect to numbers of evictions, homeless people and children in care, and were dominated by the survival of privately rented accommodation (Knox, 1975). The Francis Committee (1971), reporting on the operation of the Rent Acts, also recommended that local authorities should designate areas of 'housing stress' to ensure the proper functioning of the Rent Acts where tenants were still charged excessive rents and were subject to harassment and unlawful eviction (Adams, 1973).

Other responses to the problem of bad *areas,* as opposed to individual poor houses, included the establishment of General Improvement Areas (1969) and Housing Action Areas (1974). In the former, householders could receive grants towards the cost of home improvements and the local authority undertook environmental improvements, such as traffic management schemes, the planting of trees and replacement of unfit houses or wasteland by landscaped parks and play areas. The designation of a GIA guaranteed a life of at least 30 years for improved housing within its boundaries. Housing Action Areas are intended to include districts where housing problems are compounded by other circumstances, such as a concentration of immigrants, one-parent families or the unemployed. In practice, local authorities have designated HAAs, if at all, on much the same lines as they selected GIAs.

Government activity has not been confined to problems of housing. In 1966 the Plowden Report on *Children and their Primary Schools* proposed positive discrimination to favour schools in neighbourhoods where children were most severely handicapped by home conditions. The criteria considered important by the Plowden Committee included the number of retarded, disturbed or handicapped pupils on the register of each school, the truancy rate and the numbers of pupils from one-parent families, large families, families of low socio-economic status or dependent on different forms of state aid (e.g. supplementary benefits), and from families in shared or overcrowded dwellings. It was assumed that children from large families often received insufficient attention from their parents, and that children living in overcrowded conditions had too little privacy to read or study on their own. The number of pupils unable to speak English and the turnover rates of both pupils and teachers at each school were also taken into consideration. Much of this information was available only from the census, and enumeration districts were assumed to match the catchment areas of schools: hence the construction of an educational priority index by the Inner London Education Authority for each of its 600 schools, based partly on school records and partly on the census. The outcome was the designation of 'Educational Priority Areas', although 'area' is something of a misnomer, since the beneficiaries of the financial aid recommended by Plowden were individual schools rather than geographical areas (Knox, 1975; Herbert, 1976).

None of the activities discussed so far was specifically directed at the inner city, but it happens that inadequate and badly managed housing, poor schools and disadvantaged children are concentrated either in inner-city areas or on those suburban council estates that local authorities have used as dumping grounds for those perceived as 'poor' tenants. The recognition of 'multiple deprivation' in areas of bad housing, bad education, bad health services, inadequate employment opportunities, poor recreation facilities ... led in 1968 to the initiation of an Urban Aid Programme to finance nursery schools, housing and neigh-bourhood advice centres, play schemes and other communal activities in the poorest and most overcrowded urban areas. In 1969 twelve Community Development Projects were established, mostly in inner-city areas (e.g. in Southwark and Canning Town in London, Saltley in Birmingham, Hillfields in Coventry and Benwell in Newcastle), but also in some small mining settlements, then suffering from high rates of unemployment and lack of new investment (e.g. Glyncorrwg in South Wales, Cleator Moor in Cumbria). According to CDP workers it was assumed:

"Firstly, that it was the 'deprived' themselves who were the cause of 'urban deprivation'. Secondly, the problem could best be solved by overcoming these people's apathy and promoting self-help. Thirdly, locally-based research into the problems would serve to bring about changes in local and central government policy" (CDP, 1977, p. 4).

The projects included action teams, which promoted community participation in local government and mobilized local tenants and action groups, and research teams which evaluated the work of action teams and made policy recommendations to central government. But the scheme quickly turned sour as project workers grew frustrated by slow progress, and parti-cularly by the government's lack of interest in their invariably radical critiques of land and housing markets and local government policy. Local authorities resented the criticism of CDP workers in their employ, and some projects were closed down prematurely. The unpala-table conclusion of CDP workers was that the problems of deprived people in depressed areas lay neither in the people nor in the areas, but in the capitalist system of which they were part.

## Social Disorganization in the Inner City

Urban geographers and sociologists have long been aware of the distinctive characteristics of inner-city areas. The majority of case studies by the Chicago group of human ecologists focused on groups or areas associated with the inner city (e.g. Wirth, 1928; Zorbaugh, 1929; Reckless, 1926). A further series of ecological studies demonstrated the concentration of criminals (especially delinquents) and the mentally ill (especially schizophrenics) in inner-city zones, most particularly in areas characterized by sub-standard housing, poverty, large foreign-born populations and high rates of residential mobility (Dunham, 1937; Shaw and McKay, 1942). These studies from the 1930s have been replicated for more recent times by many American researchers. For example, Mintz and Schwarz (1964) endorsed Dunham's conclusion that while the distribution of manic depressives in Chicago was random, schizo-phrenics were concentrated in unstable inner-city districts. Collectively, crime, delinquency, suicide, mental illness and family problems have all been labelled as aspects of 'social dis-organization' (Giggs, 1970) or 'social deviance' (Herbert, 1976), or as 'social defects' (Castle and Gittus, 1957). These terms should not be regarded as carrying any pejorative meaning. Criminals, the mentally ill, unmarried mothers and divorcees are 'deviant' only insofar as they form minority groups in society and their behaviour differs from the norm.

Among British studies, Castle and Gittus (1957) found that in Liverpool both the mentally *deficient* (persons certified as handicapped) and the mentally ill (persons treated for mental illness during 1952–3) were concentrated in commercial and business wards and inner residential areas, especially in the zone-in-transition, as were cases of suicide, child neglect and juvenile crime. They suggested that neurotic disorders might follow a different distribution, perhaps similar to that of manic depressives in Chicago or concentrated on suburban housing estates where housewives experienced social isolation in unfamiliar and often unfriendly surroundings. Timms (1965) found that in Luton schizophrenics lived in areas of sub-standard housing and lodging houses, but also on local authority estates, while neurotics were randomly distributed.

In Greater London, both schizophrenic and non-schizophrenic patients admitted to psychiatric hospitals are drawn disproportionately from the inner boroughs, although the pattern is clearer for the former group (Fig. 9.1). There is also a bias towards higher rates in the more socially mixed boroughs of west London and lower rates in solidly working-class East End boroughs. For example, schizophrenia admissions per 100,000 inhabitants numbered 160 in Kensington and Chelsea, 156 in Westminster, 152 in Hammersmith, compared to 139 in Tower Hamlets and 104 in Hackney. Typical outer suburban rates were less than half these values; 50 in Bexley, Bromley and Harrow, 64 in Barnet (*Evening Standard*, 27 January, 1976). These variations may also reflect spatial differences in the availability of and response to diagnostic facilities.

The better-off inner city is also relatively more important for suicides, the extreme outcome of mental illness (Howe, 1979). Living in areas of comfortable material prosperity,

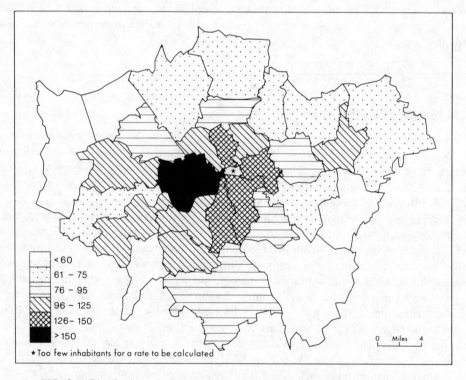

< 60
61 – 75
76 – 95
96 – 125
126 – 150
> 150
★ Too few inhabitants for a rate to be calculated

0    Miles    4

FIG. 9.1. *Distribution of patients admitted to psychiatric hospitals suffering from schizophrenia, Greater London, by borough. Figures refer to the numbers of patients per 100,000 inhabitants (based on figures published in the* Evening Standard, 27 January 1976).

those who commit suicide are often relatively poor, and we might attribute suicide to change in family or economic status. The geography of suicide is the geography of perceived personal failure, in marriage, family life, social relationships or business; and in the last case failure is rendered all the more distressing by living in the midst of material success. Inner areas accommodate large numbers of unattached, widowed or divorced people, especially young adults and the elderly, who may be more likely to experience social difficulties or mental illness or even be driven to suicide. It is possible, therefore, that the spatial concentration of social problems in inner areas reflects no more than the spatial concentration of age or status groups that are especially subject to such problems, and that there is nothing inherently geographical about the phenomenon (Fig. 9.2).

Investigation of the geography of crime may focus on either areas of criminal residence or areas in which most crimes are committed. If our concern is for the quality of life for all people, we will concentrate on the latter, delimiting districts in terms of safety; if our objective is a biological or environmental explanation of criminal activity, we will be more interested in who criminals are and where they live. But the reliability of maps showing the occurrence of crime depends on the comprehensive reporting of criminal offences and there is evidence to suggest that in the case of juvenile delinquency the punishment of middle-class offenders may be left to their parents, while working-class delinquents are more frequently reported and arrested (Herbert, 1976). If we are interested in where offenders live, then we must assume that the distribution and characteristics of convicted criminals

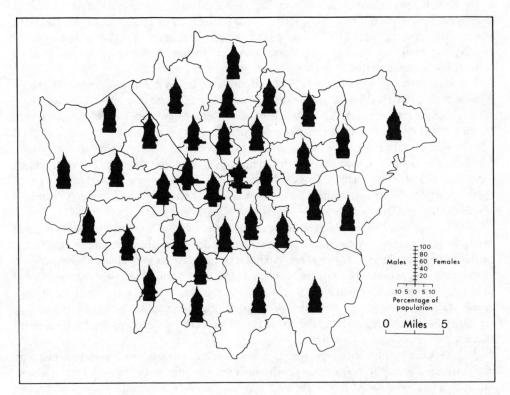

FIG. 9.2. *The age–sex structure of borough populations in Greater London, 1971 (after Shepherd et al., 1974).*

correspond to those of offenders who are never caught. We must also distinguish between different types of crime. Most geographical studies have focused on relatively minor offences such as car theft or delinquency, where the districts of residence and occurrence frequently coincide and where sufficient offences are committed to make statistical analysis feasible; but other types of crime, such as fraud and tax-evasion, may be economically more significant despite their relative rarity, and may exhibit very different spatial patterns from those made by petty crime (Pahl, 1975)!

British studies of patterns of criminal residence have revealed a more complex geographical distribution than that found in American cities, but some similar patterns of ecological correlation. In Greater London high rates of juvenile delinquency were correlated at borough scale with overcrowding, substandard housing, a predominance of manual workers, increasing numbers of non-whites and an overall declining population (Wallis and Maliphant, 1967, reported in Herbert and Johnston, 1976). However, the correlation with housing conditions is unlikely to be causal since high delinquency rates are also recorded on suburban housing estates where the built environment is satisfactory, but the population retains many of the social and economic characteristics that it possessed before removal from the inner city: low incomes, high levels of unemployment, large numbers of broken homes. In fact, almost every form of social disorganization that was associated with the zone-in-transition in pre-war American studies is associated with both inner-city areas and peripheral local authority estates in English cities, indicating the role of public intervention in the English housing market in redistributing individuals who experience different forms of social disorganization but not really solving their problems. For example, at the scale of the enumeration district, Giggs (1970) found that in Barry high rates of physical illness (tuberculosis), financial problems (rent arrears), criminal offences and marital disorganization (divorce) were concentrated in the same areas, central and peripheral.

The association of the inner city with problems of family life is also demonstrated by figures on the distribution of one-parent families. In this case the lesser significance of suburban areas may reflect the inability of many one-parent families to obtain council housing and their consequent dependence on the inner-city privately rented housing market. Of the twenty local authorities with the highest proportions of one-parent families in Britain, fourteen are Greater London boroughs including every Inner London borough except Newham. The other six include five city authorities with severe inner-city problems (Manchester, Salford, Liverpool, Bradford and Newcastle) and only one smaller place (Rochdale) (*Evening Standard*, 3 July 1978).

Despite the coincidence of high levels of crime, mental illness, bad housing and immigrant residence at the scale of enumeration district and London borough, we must not assume the existence of causal links between these variables, nor imply that individuals who experience one social problem also suffer from others, live in bad housing and have only recently moved to the city. A plausible explanation of spatial patterns is that criminals, the mentally ill, one-parent families and immigrants are all disadvantaged groups suffering discrimination, especially in the housing market, and so are forced to accept accommodation in the zone-in-transition or in poor-quality council housing.

At face value, evidence on the spatial concentration of people with social problems in inner-city areas seems to point to an 'environmental' explanation of crime or mental illness. But such an analysis would ignore the vast majority of inner-city residents who are neither schizophrenic nor delinquent! At most, therefore, physical or social environmental factors provide only a partial explanation of deviant behaviour and we must search for alternative or additional causes at either the individual level or the scale of the social group. An environmental explanation of mental illness also assumes that patients developed their condition *after* settling in the inner city. But it is just as likely that their problem arose in other areas and that they registered their illness with the authorities only after moving to the zone-in-transition. We may also question whether the 'environmental' part of the explanation concerns the physical or the social environment, the neighbourhood and housing conditions in which a person lives, or the people among whom he lives. Any amount of environmental improvement, by creating Housing Action Areas or Educational Priority Areas or pursuing other forms of positive discrimination in favour of inner-city areas, is unlikely to eradicate problems of crime, mental illness and family disorganization.

With regard to crime, Herbert concluded that "it is not urban environments *per se* but social characteristics of the group which are the 'real' correlates of delinquent behaviour" (Herbert and Johnston, 1976, p. 105). Herbert tested his concept of the deviant sub-culture by comparing areas of Cardiff with similar socio-economic and demographic structures, but significantly different levels of delinquency. He found that attitudes towards education, crime and punishment also differed significantly between delinquent and non-delinquent areas (Table 9.1).

Yet another interpretation of deviant behaviour is based on Wirth's theory of urbanism, and especially his concept of 'anomie', the loss of values said to typify heterogeneous societies. Lander (1954, reported in Herbert and Johnston, 1976) found that delinquency rates were highest in the most mixed areas of Baltimore, where whites and blacks lived in approximately equal numbers. All-white or all-black areas had lower delinquency rates. Similarly, we might explain high levels of deviance in zones-in-transition in English cities in terms of the normlessness associated with social and ethnic mixing. Alternatively, the high levels of violence in mixed districts, whether in Baltimore or Brick Lane (in London's East End) may reflect their status as disputed territories. Even within the transition zone different ethnic minorities possess their own territories (Suttles, 1968; Ley and Cybriwsky, 1974), the borders of which are jealously guarded. Violence is most likely to occur when one group attempts to penetrate the territory of another, for example in a National Front march through an immigrant area.

TABLE 9.1. *Attitudes to crime and education in delinquent and non-delinquent areas of Cardiff* (after Herbert, 1976)

|  | Non-delinquent area | | Delinquent area | |
|---|---|---|---|---|
|  | % parents hoping children obtain | % children actually attaining | % parents hoping children obtain | % children actually attaining |
| At least CSE or trade qualification | 100 | 55 | 100 | 27 |
| At least GCE or OND | 86 | 40 | 86 | 14 |
| At least A level or HND | 56 | 17 | 71 | 3 |
| At least College or Degree | 41 | 7 | 71 | 2 |
| Reactions to misbehaviour | % parents approving | | % parents approving | |
| Physical punishment | 17 | | 38 | |
| Verbal solution | 64 | | 48 | |
| Withdraw privileges | 48 | | 12 | |
| Ignore | 0 | | 10 | |

## Well-Being

Not only mental but also physical illnesses are more common in inner-city areas. Howe (1979) showed that mortality rates in general, and deaths from cancers and bronchitis in particular, are higher in Inner London, especially the East End, than in the suburbs, while at a national scale, death rates are higher in north-west England than in the south-east. We could explain these patterns in socio-economic terms: the residents of London's East End (or of north-west England) are less affluent, less well housed, less well fed and subject to greater stress from overcrowding at home and noise or monotony at work than the residents of London's suburbs (or of south-east England in general). Some of the variance unexplained by this purely socio-economic analysis may be attributed to higher mortality rates among those members of higher socio-economic groups who live or work in poor areas and suffer the effects of traffic fumes, smoke pollution or restricted access to a wide range of amenities, from recreational open space to hospital beds. While the very rich minority living in such areas can overcome problems of access by resorting to private transport, private schools or private health care, the situation of the majority remains one of multiple deprivation.

It is not surprising, therefore, that interest in individual aspects of social welfare has broadened into a more general concern for the quality of life in urban areas, often by extending the technique of factorial ecology to include additional variables, unrelated or only indirectly related to the social area dimensions of economic, family and ethnic status. Smith (1973) sounded the clarion call for this type of study, writing that "it is time for a humane human geography (p. 14) . . . it cannot be claimed that the factorial ecology approach is identifying basic dimensions of spatial variation when some important conditions of human existence are not included" (p. 43). Smith suggested that if regional or intra-urban variations in social deprivation were depicted three-dimensionally, their topography might be "just as dramatic as the physical and economic surfaces to which we attach so much importance" (p. 14). In Smith's view, social well-being has three major components: income, in the broadest sense of that term (i.e. an individual's or an area's access to all forms of resources, including not only money but all the various provisions of a welfare state); physical health; and 'state of mind'. Unfortunately, such nebulous concepts do not translate easily into precise statistical indices. The links between dimensions of social well-being and specific variables for which information is available may be as tenuous as those we observed between three aspects of increasing societal scale and the variables of social area analysis.

Studies of well-being based on factor analysis are subject to the same criticisms as factorial ecology. It is assumed that each variable included in the analysis is equally important since, in factor analysis, each variable contributes the same amount of variance. But do we really consider it as important to have access to a cinema as to have exclusive use of your own fixed bath (two variables that are weighted equally in Knox's (1975) study of levels of living in England and Wales)?

Interpretation of the output is also hindered if variables are not *normative*. We would probably agree that the higher the crime rate or the greater the degree of overcrowding, the lower the level of well-being in an area, but it is harder to judge whether high proportions of doctors or old people in the population denote high or low levels of well-being. The presence of large numbers of pensioners may be interpreted as a sign of health and longevity, or as an additional tax burden on those who are gainfully employed and who have to pay for the health and welfare facilities required by their dependants. Likewise, the desirability of large numbers of doctors depends on whether their abundance denotes a high quality of service (good) or a high level of need (bad).

Ideally, social indicators should be related to outputs, like health or educational attainment, rather than inputs, like health care or expenditure on schools. It is also easier to work with normative, weighted variables where the object of study is limited to one aspect of well-being, as in the multivariate studies of educational priority and housing stress outlined earlier in this chapter. Unlike the purely descriptive 'informative indicators' of geographers such as Coates and Rawstron (1971) and Knox (1975), these studies have been commissioned by politicians and administrators and involve the use of 'problem-orientated indicators'. But neither type of indicator has any practical relevance unless we can define the form of desirable or 'just' distributions. We cannot assume that an unequal distribution of resources, whether of schools or teachers, hospitals or doctors, is necessarily an inequitable or unfair distribution. Nor, at the level of outputs rather than inputs, can we assume that because one area performs less well than others, in terms of educational attainments or morbidity, the situation is 'unjust' and requires a re-allocation of resources.

At an individual level, Runciman (1966) suggested that resources should be allocated to individuals according to their need, their contribution to the common good and their merit. Harvey (1973) extended these criteria to apply to areas, so that we should allocate resources to different parts of the city according to the needs and special merit of local residents and the spread effects to neighbouring areas that would follow from positive discrimination. Following this argument, Smith suggested that inner-city residents receive less resources than they deserve, given the extent of their contribution to the common good (e.g. their operation of such vital services as street- and office-cleaning and public transport, which benefit mainly suburbanites). Perhaps too, inner-city residents deserve 'merit' payments such as the provision of extra police protection or health facilities to compensate for having to live in areas with high crime rates and an unhealthy environment.

Most attention has been focused on the problem of defining *need*. We cannot assume that need is the same for all people everywhere. Where spatial, as distinct from individual, variations in need exist, the extent to which the allocation of resources should correspond with those spatial variations must depend on the freedom that people have to choose where to live. Since many people, especially in inner areas, have little real choice in where they live, it seems fair that different areas should attract different levels of resource allocation. But we cannot always employ independent 'experts' to define need, since they may well come from a different social or cultural background and rank resources differently from local inhabitants. Nor can we obtain a fair assessment of need by asking residents to express their 'felt needs'. The deprived, especially the elderly and immobile, often show surprisingly little awareness of the extent of their deprivation, presumably because they rarely visit affluent, suburban neighbourhoods or come into regular contact with people very much better off than themselves. There is considerable truth in the adage that "what you've never had, you'll never miss". Furthermore, we cannot equate need with demand. For example, every household needs a home but not all households have sufficient income to exert an economic demand for a home.

Our suspicion that attempts to define a 'just distribution' in spatial as well as individual terms may be misguided is increased by recent empirical studies. The final reports of Inner Area Studies in Birmingham (Small Heath) and London (Stockwell) suggest that while areas may experience multiple deprivation in the sense that they accommodate a range of social, economic and environmental problems, surprisingly few residents in these areas are themselves deprived on more than one or two indicators. Added to this evidence is the argument that "most of the deprived live outside inner areas and most of those living in inner areas are not themselves deprived" (Robson, 1978, p. 515).

Interestingly, Smith's (1973) study of variations in social well-being in Tampa, Florida also cast doubt on the validity of the concept of multiple deprivation. By means of factor analysis, Smith identified four inter-related dimensions of the social geography of Tampa:

(1) A 'social problems' dimension, identifying areas with high death rates, high crime rates, low incomes, heavy dependence on government welfare and high rates of drug-taking and venereal disease.

(2) A 'socio-economic' dimension, picking out areas of poor housing and education, low incomes and manual workers.

(3) A 'racial' dimension, associating areas of Negro residence with overcrowding, many residents in receipt of welfare, and few in white-collar jobs or with experience of further education.

(4) A 'social deprivation' dimension, associated with high unemployment, VD, drugs and poor housing.

Comparing the problem areas defined by this analysis with those designated under various urban aid programmes, Smith was able to recommend changes in the distribution of aid. In particular, he noted that at the scale of the census tract, the incidence of social problems was partly independent of socio-economic status and racial composition, and that there was no necessary correlation between problems of the physical environment and problems of the social environment. Smith's research casts further doubt on the efficacy of 'physical' solutions to social and economic problems. Even where extra resources for the improvement of the physical environment are successful in achieving that objective, they may not benefit deprived households, either because the genuinely deprived do not live in the action areas or because the effect of physical improvement is to displace the genuinely deprived — as in the case of gentrification — into new areas of deprivation.

Harvey (1973) has argued that further empirical investigations of deprived areas are unnecessary and may actually divert attention from action, especially on a theoretical plane, to eliminate the causes as well as the consequences of deprivation. However, both Smith's study of Tampa and the Inner Area Studies demonstrate that neither the coincidence of problems in space nor the scale at which they should be tackled are so self-evident.

### Race and the Inner City

In 1971 the 'coloured' population of Great Britain (including all people of West Indian, Asian or African origin) numbered approximately 1,500,000, including at least 500,000 children born in Britain to immigrant parents. It is estimated that by 1978, 45 per cent of the coloured population was British-born, while by 2000 this figure will have increased to 65—70 per cent. It is no longer acceptable to regard 'black', 'brown' or 'coloured' as synonymous with 'immigrant'. In fact the number of coloured immigrants recorded by the 1971 census was little higher than the number of Irish-born. There were 347,000 from the West Indies, 264,000 from India and 173,000 from Pakistan and Bangladesh, compared to 721,000 born in the Irish Republic (Peach, 1975).

The concentration of the coloured population in metropolitan and especially inner-city areas has a long history. Immigrants entered Britain as a replacement population at times of relatively full employment, filling labour shortages in public transport and the health service. They were required particularly in areas from which the white population was moving out, especially inner-city districts. Understandably, they congregated in a few areas where they could find support from fellow-migrants. They experienced discrimination in the private housing market from both landlords and estate agents and were initially unsuccessful in the competition for council housing. A West Indian solution to this dilemma was the rise of the slum landlord, while Asian families with a tradition of self-help and private enterprise in Asia or East Africa preferred to buy cheap terraced houses. In recent years West Indians have had more success in the local authority sector, although they are still over-represented on less popular council estates, while Asians have obtained council mortgages to buy nine-teenth-century terraced houses, better in quality than their earlier cash purchases, but still in inner suburban areas, such as Handsworth in Birmingham (Rex, 1978).

In 1971, 55 per cent of West Indians in Britain lived in London and a further 13 per cent in Birmingham. Little (1978) noted that 80 per cent of the coloured population lived in only 15 per cent of census enumeration districts. Despite the beginnings of dispersal and suburbanization, immigrants and their children are becoming relatively more concentrated in inner areas because the white population is decentralizing even more quickly. For example, between 1961 and 1971 the population of Greater London declined by 11.5 per cent, but the West Indian population in the same area increased by 80 per cent, the Indian population doubled and the Pakistani population quadrupled (Peach, 1975). Jones (1976) identified those parts of Birmingham most associated with the coloured population. The total population of these areas fell from 166,000 (1961) to 140,000 (1971), but this decline was made up of a substantial decrease in the number of British-born (including second-generation immigrants) from 149,000 to 99,000, a slight increase in the West Indian population from 12,000 to 14,000, and a dramatic rise in the Asian-born population from 5,000 to 24,000. In 1961, the most West Indian enumeration district in Birmingham was 36 per cent West Indian; in 1971, 61 per cent of the population of the most West Indian district had been born in the West Indies and the proportion of West Indian origin was 91 per cent.

The areas occupied by the coloured population contain the poorest housing and the worst employment prospects; 80 per cent of coloured people live in enumeration districts where overcrowding and multiple occupancy are three times the national average. Education clearly has a vital role to play in enabling coloured children to escape from the cycle of deprivation experienced by their parents, but so long as educational opportunities and levels of achievement are least in areas of bad housing and poor job prospects, the problem will intensify. In the area controlled by the Inner London Education Authority, only 10–12 per cent of immigrant children fell into the top quarter of all London schoolchildren at age 11 on tests of English, Mathematics and Verbal Reasoning. Moreover, there was little sign of improvement in the success rate between 1966 and 1971. But there was a significant difference between children of Asian and West Indian origin. Asian children did as well as white children in Maths and Verbal Reasoning, but had a poorer command of the English language. West Indian children achieved only one-third of the success rate of white children in all three subjects. The indications were, therefore, that Asian children would do as well as (and might do better than) white children once they had mastered the language, whereas West Indian children continued to under achieve (Little, 1978).

In other respects, however, the differences between Asians and English are greater than those between West Indians and English, but again the difference may work to the advantage of Asian children. Indians and Pakistanis are ethnic groups, differing from their hosts in language, religion, culture and social organization, but most West Indians are distinct only racially. They share the language, religion and social aspirations of their hosts and have developed much less of their own institutional life. It is possible, therefore, that Asians are better able than West Indians to resist or ignore discrimination. While both Asian and West Indian children may aspire to the culture of their white classmates, the Asians can find security in their own culture and, if necessary, make a virtue out of their distinctiveness, but West Indian children have less to fall back on if they are rejected by white society. One reaction has been their attempt to create a culture, for example by the adoption of Rastafarian philosophy.

Asians and West Indians occupy different parts of British cities except where new arrivals have been forced to share the common deprivation of the worst parts of the transition zone (Fig. 9.3). But levels of segregation may be as great between different West Indian or different Asian groups, for example between Indians, Pakistanis, Bangladeshis and East African Asians, or between Muslims, Sikhs and Hindus, as between each racial group. Peach (1975) found that Jamaicans formed 51 per cent of London's West Indian population in 1971, but 80 per cent of the West Indian population of Ferndale Ward in Lambeth. One consequence of the residential solidarity of island groups has been the development of long-distance commuting as immigrants obtain better jobs but retain their allegiance to their ethnic group. Commuting by West Indians from homes in Brixton to jobs in car factories in Luton, or to office employment in outer London has been widely noted (Peach, 1975).

In Birmingham, West Indians and Indians predominate in clusters north and west of the city centre, while Pakistanis dominate the immigrant areas of south Birmingham (Fig. 9.4). The concentration of Bengalis in Spitalfields and Bethnal Green in London's East End attracted publicity following physical as well as verbal attacks from National Front supporters. The response of the Bengali community was to request greater police protection *en route* from home to work, but also greater segregation in blocks of council flats. Their request represents a retreat into a 'community of conflict' (Boal, 1972) in which a besieged group can benefit psychologically by identifying with a particular locality, and can ensure security for its members so long as they remain within the area. A similar

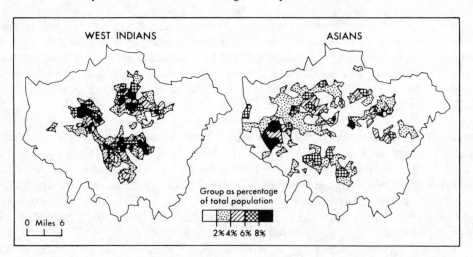

FIG. 9.3. *Residential patterns of West Indians and Asians in Greater London, 1971 (after Shepherd et al., 1974).*

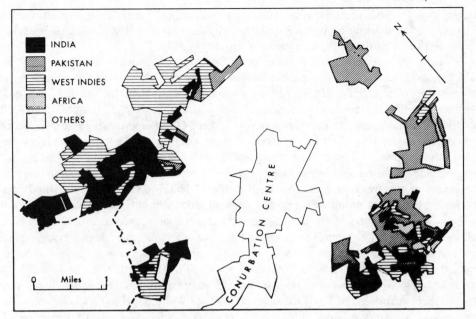

FIG. 9.4. *The first ranking New Commonwealth-born population group in areas of coloured population in Birmingham, 1971 (after Jones, 1976).*

process of increasing segregation characterized the residential mobility of Protestants and Catholics in working-class areas of Belfast following the outbreak of violence in 1968. Such segregation may be an effective means of restoring peace and personal safety in the short term, but only by storing up trouble for the future of race or sectarian relations in urban areas.

A more optimistic prediction of the future of Asian groups depends on parallels between Asian immigration in the 1960s and 1970s and Jewish immigration in the late nineteenth and early twentieth centuries. In East London, Bengalis inhabit exactly the same area as earlier Jewish refugees from Eastern Europe. In exceptional cases, the same building has been successively a Huguenot church, a Jewish synagogue and Muslim temple (Huddleston, 1978). More generally, both Asians and Jews entered the occupational hierarchy at or near its foot, both show a concern for education, and both have preferred self-help to state welfare. Despite continuing residential and cultural segregation of the Jewish population there is little anti-Jewish discrimination today and it may be anticipated that the same traits will characterize the situation of more recent immigrant groups by the twenty-first century.

This sanguine forecast of future prosperity for recent immigrants must be tempered by the recognition that there are far wider variations among them than there were among Jews arriving in England after 1880. The parallel with the Jewish population may be valid for educated or self-employed Asians. Although their initial employment in England was often on a lower income and with less responsibility than their education or entrepreneurial skill justified, many Asians have ascended the ladders of economic status and housing class, moving within the owner-occupied sector from inner-city terraces to suburban detached or semi-detached houses. In contrast, the parallel may be less apt for low-income, unskilled

Asians, such as those in Spitalfields. Moreover, as Peach (1975) reported, "paradoxically, the first generation seems more integrated into British society than the second. The evidence of disaffection of British-born black youth is strong" (p. 377).

In theory we can distinguish between ethnic, racial or religious 'enclaves', the products of cohesion within minority groups, and 'ghettos', where external pressures prevent dispersal and enforce concentration. Peach (1975) commented that "Ghettos are bad, but concentrations and polarizations of minorities are not necessarily so" (p. 377). But in practice it is very difficult to separate the two concepts, except by observing changes in patterns of concentration over time. In England most minority ethnic groups have become less segregated through time, or have at least moved out from close-knit concentrations in inner areas to less dense, and probably less cohesive, clusters in suburban districts, indicating the predominance of enclaves over ghettos in English cities. Boal (1976) refers to 'full assimilation' where the pattern of group residence has changed from concentrated to dispersed, most common where members of the minority group share the same language or follow the same religion as the majority and are prepared to intermarry among them. 'Occupational assimilation' occurs where the minority obtains housing and jobs as good as, if not better than, those of their hosts, but where there is no cultural assimilation. In England the classic example is the upward social and outward geographical mobility of the Jews, from the clothing sweat-shops of Leylands in inner Leeds or Whitechapel in east London, to the prosperous high-status suburbs of Alwoodley (Leeds), Golders Green and Edgware (north London) (Fig. 9.5). Most coloured immigrant groups are experiencing slow dispersal, but often slower than the out-migration of indigenous populations from inner-city areas. Several studies have concluded that while West Indian populations are now less segregated than they were in the 1960s, Asian-born groups are becoming more segregated (Dalton and Seaman, 1973; Jones, 1979; Lee, 1977).

The problem with a term like 'assimilation' is that it implies assimilation *to* a host culture, but most indicants of assimilation used by sociologists measure nothing of the sort. For example, desegregation may be accompanied by a greater determination on the part of a minority group to maintain its cultural uniqueness once it has lost its geographical distinctiveness. Assimilation to the occupational or educational standards of the host population is better termed 'equalization', and perhaps the only satisfactory quantitative measure of assimilation is the rate of intermarriage. Furthermore, in the process of assimilation most minority groups will contribute something of their own culture to that of their hosts: white youths acquire a liking for reggae or soul music, university students practise transcendental meditation and we all grow accustomed to a diet of curry, chop suey and canneloni.

**Economy and Environment**

The continued segregation of immigrant groups would be less disturbing if the areas they inhabit were flourishing economically. There is a rapidly expanding literature on the economic problems of inner-city areas (e.g. Kirby, 1978; IBG, 1978; CDP, 1977). Here we consider the effects of economic change on the social structure of inner areas.

An exceptionally large proportion of the male workforce resident in inner areas is semi-skilled or unskilled. For example, 35—40 per cent of adult males in Stockwell in inner south London fell into these categories in 1971, compared to an average for Greater London of only 24 per cent. Between 1961 and 1971 the number of economically active males in ten inner London boroughs fell from 1,057,000 to 859,000. The number of unskilled workers

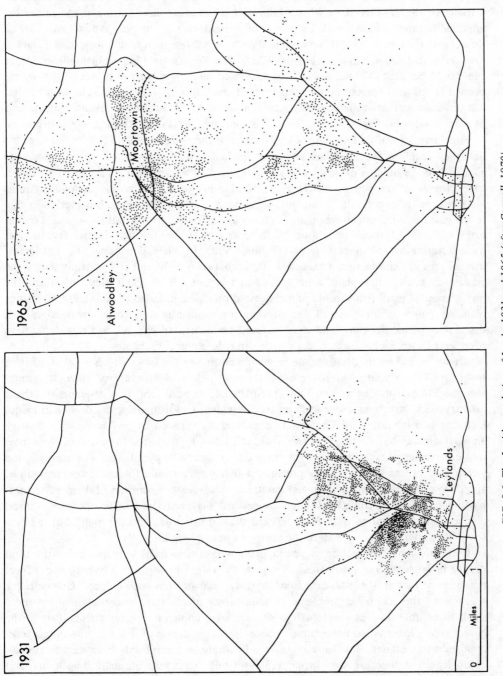

FIG. 9.5. The Jewish population of Leeds, 1931 and 1965 (after Connell, 1970).

declined not only absolutely (from 119,000 to 82,000) but also relatively (from 11 per cent to 10 per cent of the total workforce). However, this decline was slower than for unskilled workers in the country as a whole, indicating a relative concentration of the remaining unskilled in inner London during a period of upward shift in the occupational structure of the country (Hamnett, 1976). The decline was also much less than that among skilled manual workers, who decreased in number from 370,000 to 269,000, and in proportion from 35 per cent to 31 per cent. Manual workers accompanied their employers in moves to new or expanded towns, or obtained council tenancies or mortgages on outer London housing estates, but unskilled workers were generally viewed as less desirable tenants by the housing officials of outer London boroughs, who vetted GLC or inner borough nominations to suburban estates.

Firms moving out of London took advantage of the move to update their technology, so that they required fewer unskilled workers in their new locations. New town houses were allocated to the holders of new town jobs, so unskilled workers, denied access to the latter, were effectively trapped in their present housing in inner London. Unemployment rates increased, partly as a result of this out-migration of thriving businesses, but even more due to the closure of manufacturing plants in inner areas. Between 1966 and 1974 inner London lost 94,000 jobs through the closure of factories and 46,000 through the net migration of manufacturing out of inner London (Dennis, 1978). In inner Manchester, the net loss of manual jobs in manufacturing exceeded 40,000 between 1966 and 1975, mainly due to the closure of small, single-plant firms (Lloyd and Mason, 1978). Plant closures reflect the inefficiency of small firms in old and congested premises, but also the effects of insensitive planning policy whereby small factories in predominantly residential areas have been designated 'nonconforming land uses', refused permission to expand, and sometimes have been served with compulsory purchase orders in redevelopment schemes.

It may be argued that the decline in manufacturing in the inner city is no worse than in the country as a whole, given the age-, size- and industrial-structure of inner-city manufacturing. It can also be argued that "industry knows best" and that attempts to attract industry back into inner-city locations are misguided. Unfortunately, the decline in manufacturing and labouring jobs has rarely been counterbalanced by any increase in tertiary employment, as has occurred in suburban and outer metropolitan areas; and where new jobs *are* created they seldom benefit the existing inner-city population. For example, the location of offices in inner areas provides skilled work, mainly for suburban commuters, apart from a few jobs for cleaners, caretakers and canteen workers. Likewise, science-based industry (e.g. computers, micro-processors) may suit the land-use policies of local planners and the limited bulk-carrying capacities of urban transport systems, but it offers few jobs to anybody, least of all to the inner-city unemployed.

It is true that the decline in employment opportunities has only paralleled the total decline in population in inner areas, but while the ratio of people to jobs may not change, the range of jobs available to each inhabitant who remains has been reduced. One tentative solution to the economic problems of inner areas involves the encouragement of more small firms, following in the footsteps of successful immigrant entrepreneurs. Part of the government's Inner Areas Programme finances the construction of new factories on purpose-built industrial estates. But many immigrant firms are successful only because they employ cheap labour or because the owner and his family work exceptionally long hours, and arguably it should be no part of government policy to encourage such sweated labour. Keeble (1978) has argued that policy should not try to attract new or mobile firms into inevitably uneconomic inner-city locations. It is more important to assist existing firms, again by the provision of new premises and an appropriate infrastructure. Perhaps the only long-term solution lies in education and retraining, so that the number of unskilled, illiterate and innumerate workers is reduced. Or perhaps policy should not try to reverse the loss of population and jobs from inner areas, but should concentrate on *planned* dispersal and planned education for long-term unemployment or underemployment, whether in inner city or suburb.

The physical environment of industrial decline is derelict land. The environment of new council housing in the inner city is often little better (DoE, 1977). Tower-blocks that rise from a sea of concrete, that suffer from elementary design and construction faults manifest in damp, noise and a perpetual 'out of order' sign on the lift, and that provide 'dwelling units' rather than homes are a far cry from the landscaped paradise envisaged by Le Corbusier and his disciples. Many residential redevelopment schemes, not only high-rise and not only inner-city as the depressing experience of Liverpool (Kirkby) and Tyneside testifies, lack private gardens, open spaces where children can play safely, or any kind of 'defensible space' for which residents feel personally responsible. Inevitably, the public environment is subject to vandalism, or becomes unsafe for law-abiding passers-by, and a new cycle of physical neglect and decay is created. It may be too deterministic to argue that an improved built environment would mean an eradication of social problems, but some improvement in the quality of life would surely follow if the environment did not encourage abuse.

In the 1970s the worst excesses of comprehensive redevelopment gave way to rehabilitation, partly in response to the criticisms of high-rise flats and partly for reasons of economy. The impersonality of block living is often contrasted with the close-knit community structure that typified inner-city areas in the past and it is suggested that planned dispersal is unsatisfactory because many people will not want to move away from communities they have known all their lives. But it is easy to over-romanticize such communities which were really only a "mutuality of the oppressed" (Williams, 1973, p. 104). In fact, most inner-city residents are there by necessity not by choice, and well-planned, low-rise houses and flats are preferable to rehabilitated nineteenth-century housing on almost all grounds except historical interest. Neil McIntosh, director of 'Shelter' and formerly chairman of a London borough housing committee, has been reported as saying that "We are rehabilitating housing and dwellings which should not, to my mind, be rehabilitated. They should be knocked down" (*Evening Standard*, 15 March 1978).

## Government Policy

We began this chapter by describing some past attempts to aid inner-city areas and their inhabitants. It is appropriate to conclude by reviewing more recent government activity. The consultants employed by the Department of Environment in three inner area studies in Liverpool, Small Heath (Birmingham) and Stockwell (south London) all emphasized the inter-related nature of social and economic problems and the previously fragmentary form of government policy. For example, the Liverpool consultants commented that:

"Until very recently departments have pursued apparently independent policies. Some have operated in the inner areas through special projects (Department of Education and Science, Home Office); through social policies (Department of Health and Social Security); or through concern with housing and local government finance (Department of the Environment). But for two key departments (Industry and Employment) the inner area perspective has been missing. The weaknesses of this fragmentation have become clear as each special project in turn demonstrated the inter-relatedness of economic and social issues, of community, housing and education questions" (DoE, 1977, p. 13).

Government ministers also stressed the need for a comprehensive policy, founded on improving local economies, and administered through the normal channels of government, including the Rate Support Grant. Peter Shore, then Secretary of State for the Environment, commented in 1977 that:

"If we are to make real headway in improving the conditions of our inner-city areas we must use the main programmes of central and local government. We need to get an inner-city dimension into these programmes, at central and local level alike. By main programmes I mean education, social services, housing, transport, planning, industry, manpower and the various environmental services. We cannot rely solely, or even mainly, on extra initiatives such as the Urban Programme or Educational Priority Areas. These provide valuable topping up, and help to ameliorate problems. But if we are to get to grips with the underlying economic and social forces, we must deploy the major instruments of public policy."

In practice, the Labour government established seven inner-city partnerships — in Manchester/Salford, Liverpool, Newcastle/Gateshead, Birmingham and three in London: Docklands, Lambeth, Hackney/Islington — in which local and central government programmes are co-ordinated and leavened by a generous helping of public consultation, and fifteen Programme Authorities, with lesser powers mainly in provincial cities such as Leeds, Wolverhampton, Hull and Sunderland (Fig. 9.6). As an example, the Lambeth partnership committees include representatives from central government departments, from the regional health and education authorities, from the Greater London Council (GLC) and from the local borough. These committees have the task of preparing and implementing inner-area programmes. Unfortunately, the impression from outside is of too many committees with too little money, frequently required to reach decisions after insufficient time for consultation and analysis. The partnerships have been frustrated by conflict at several levels. When it was established, the Lambeth partnership involved a Labour Government, a Conservative GLC and a borough council controlled by the extreme left of the Labour Party. Within central government, the Department of Environment was committed to giving all the designated areas, including those in London, the same powers of attracting employment and investment as assisted areas throughout Britain, but the Department of Industry continued to favour decentralization away from the whole of south-east England, including inner London. At a local level it was often impossible to reconcile the conflicting demands of different interest groups: conservation societies, trades unions and tenants' associations, for example. It is not easy to improve the physical environment at the same time as attracting industry.

Until the return of a Conservative Government in May 1979 the assumption that we need area-based policies at all went virtually unchallenged. Conservative policy provides fewer special grants or incentives directed solely at the inner city, but greater freedom for private initiatives that are likely to replace derelict industrial sites and slum housing with tourist hotels, offices and other high-rent activities. Inner-city finance may suffer from reductions in the size of the Rate Support Grant, but benefit from the introduction of land uses that increase the local rate income. This type of redevelopment, like much urban aid — especially that directed at housing improvement — has an undoubted cosmetic effect in enhancing the physical and visual quality of our cities, but it is less clear whether those most in need are the people who benefit. It seems probable that as areas are improved, so the poorest residents

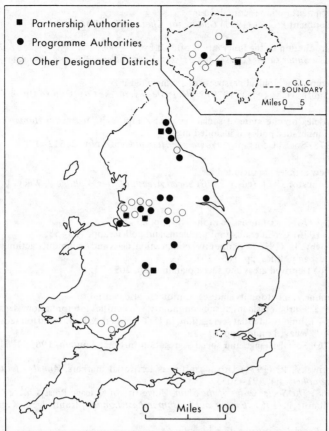

■ Partnership Authorities
● Programme Authorities
○ Other Designated Districts

G.L.C
BOUNDARY
Miles 0   5

0   Miles   100

FIG. 9.6. *Districts designated under the Inner Urban Areas
Act, 1978.*

migrate to other, unimproved districts. For example, as private housing is gentrified or municipalized, problem families are forced into scarcer and usually more expensive, un-modernized, privately rented accommodation, much as casual labourers in Victorian London were forced to make new and worse slums by the 'cleansing' agencies of new roads, railways and model housing. In these circumstances, 'upgrading' (the replacement of low-rent land uses like housing by high-rent uses like offices) is acceptable only if provision is made to rehouse the former residents in areas where they can find employment, and if services such as schools and shops are maintained for the smaller number of inner-city residents that remain; and areal policies are effective only if they bring *all* areas, not just a few experimental districts, up to an acceptable minimum standard.

## References and Further Reading

Among government publications on the problems of inner-city areas, see:
Dept. of the Environment (1977) *Inner Area Studies.*
H.M.S.O. (1965) *Report of the Committee on Housing in Greater London* (Milner Holland Report), Cmnd. 2605.
H.M.S.O. (1977) *Policy for the Inner Cities,* Cmnd. 6845.

A critique of government policy is contained in:
Community Development Project (1977) *Gilding the Ghetto,* CDP, London.

A geographical introduction to the inner city is offered by:
Kirby, A. (1978) *The Inner City – Causes and Effects,* Retailing and Planning Associates, Corbridge.

while several different geographical perspectives are included in:
Herbert, D. T. & Smith, D. M. (eds.) (1979) *Social Problems and the City,* Oxford University Press, Oxford.

Annual review articles on the state of social geography appear in *Progress in Human Geography,* and a brief discussion of inner-city policy is included in:
Robson, B. T. (1978) Social Geography, *Progress in Human Geography,* 2, 512–17.

Several longer review articles are included in:
Herbert, D. T. & Johnston, R. J. (eds.) (1976) *Social Areas in Cities, Volume 2,* Wiley, London.

In particular see:
    Herbert, D. T. (1976) Social deviance in the city, pp. 89–121.
    Herbert, D. T. (1976) Urban education: problems and policies, pp. 123–58.
    Bell, C. and Newby, H. (1976) Community, communion, class and community action: the social sources
       of the new urban politics, pp. 189–207.
    Gittus, E. (1976) Deprived areas and social planning, pp. 209–33.

Concepts of community, territoriality and segregation are also central to:
Boal, F. W. (1972) The urban residential sub-community – a conflict interpretation, *Area,* 4, 164–8.
Boal, F. W. (1976) Ethnic residential segregation, in D. T. Herbert & R. J. Johnston (eds.) *Social Areas in Cities, Volume 1,* Wiley, London, pp. 41–79.
Hamnett, C. (1976) Social change and social segregation in Inner London, 1961–1971, *Urban Studies,* 13, 261–71.
Ley, D. and Cybriwsky, R. (1974) Urban graffiti as territorial markers, *Annals of the Association of American Geographers,* 64, 491–505.
Suttles, G. D. (1968) *The Social Order of the Slum,* University of Chicago Press, Chicago.
Young, M. and Willmott, P. (1957) *Family and Kinship in East London,* Routledge & Kegan Paul, London.

American studies of social disorganization include:
Dunham, H. W. (1937) The ecology of functional psychoses in Chicago, *American Sociological Review,* 2, 467–79, reprinted in G. A. Theodorson (ed.) (1961) *Studies in Human Ecology,* Harper & Row, New York, pp. 62–71.
Mintz, N. L. and Schwarz, D. T. (1964) Urban psychology and psychoses, *International Journal of Social Psychiatry,* 10, 101–17.
Reckless, W. C. (1926) The distribution of commercialized vice in the city, *Publications of the American Sociological Society,* 20, 164–76, reprinted in Theodorson, *op. cit.,* pp. 50–6.
Shaw, C. R. and McKay, H. D. (1942) *Juvenile Delinquency and Urban Areas,* University of Chicago Press, Chicago.
Wirth, L. (1928) *The Ghetto,* University of Chicago Press, Chicago.
Zorbaugh, H. W. (1929) *The Gold Coast and the Slum,* University of Chicago Press, Chicago.

Case studies of English and Welsh cities include:
Castle, I. M. and Gittus, E. (1957) The distribution of social defects in Liverpool, *Sociological Review,* 5, 43–64 (reprinted in Theodorson, *op.cit.,* pp. 415–29).
Giggs, J. A. (1970) The socially disorganized areas of Barry, in H. Carter & W. K. D. Davies (eds.), *Urban Essays: Studies in the Geography of Wales,* Longman, London, pp. 101–43.
Giggs, J. A. (1973) The distribution of schizophrenics in Nottingham, *Transactions Institute of British Geographers,* 59, 55–76.
Herbert, D. T. (1976) The study of delinquency areas: a geographical approach, *Transactions Institute of British Geographers,* New Series, 1, 472–92.
Timms, D. W. G. (1965) The spatial distribution of social deviants in Luton, England, *Australia and New Zealand Journal of Sociology,* 1, 38–52.

An interesting observation on the geographical literature on crime is made by:
Pahl, R. E. (1975) Spatial and social constraints in the inner city, *Geographical Journal,* 141, 386–7.

The geography of physical illness and mortality is discussed in:
Howe, M. (1979) Death in London, *Geographical Magazine,* January, 284–9.

On the problems of ethnic minorities, see:
Commission for Racial Equality (1978) *Five Views of Multi-Racial Britain,* CRE/BBC, London; especially the papers by Rex, Little and Huddleston.
Dalton, M. and Seaman, J. M. (1973) The distribution of New Commonwealth immigrants in the London Borough of Ealing, 1961–66, *Transactions of the Institute of British Geographers,* 58, 21–39.
Jones, P. N. (1976) Coloured minorities in Birmingham, England, *Annals of the Association of American Geographers,* 66, 89–103.
Jones, P. N. (1979) Ethnic areas in British cities, in D. T. Herbert & D. M. Smith (eds.), *Social Problems and the City,* Oxford University Press, Oxford, pp. 158–85.
Lee, T. R. (1977) *Race and Residence,* Oxford University Press, Oxford.
Peach, G. C. K. (1975) Immigrants in the inner city, *Geographical Journal,* 141, 372–9.
Smith, D. J. (1977) *Racial Disadvantage in Britain,* Penguin, Harmondsworth.

On industry in the inner city, see:
Dennis, R. (1978) The decline of manufacturing employment in Greater London: 1966–74, *Urban Studies,* 15, 63–73.
Keeble, D. (1978) Industrial decline in the inner city and conurbation, *Transactions Institute of British Geographers,* New Series, 3, 101–14.
Lloyd, P. E. and Mason, C. M. (1978) Manufacturing industry in the inner city: a case study of Greater Manchester, *Transactions Institute of British Geographers,* New Series, 3, 66–90.
Thrift, N. (1979) Unemployment in the inner city: urban problem or structural imperative?, in D. T. Herbert & R. J. Johnston (eds.), *Geography and the Urban Environment Volume II,* Wiley, Chichester, pp. 125–226.
Wood, P. A. (1978) Industrial changes in inner London, in H. D. Clout (ed.), *Changing London,* University Tutorial Press, London, pp. 38–48.

References to housing problems are listed at the end of Chapter 8, but the following are particularly relevant:
Adams, B. (1973) Furnished lettings in stress areas, in D. Donnison & D. Eversley (eds.), *London: Urban Patterns, Problems and Policies,* Heinemann, London, pp. 354–82.
Bassett, K. and Short, J. R. (1978) Housing improvement in the inner city, *Urban Studies,* 15, 333–42.
CDP–PEC (1977) *The Poverty of the Improvement Programme,* CDP Political Economy Collective, Newcastle-on-Tyne.
Harloe, M. *et al.* (1973) The organizational context of housing policy in inner London: the Lambeth experience, in D. Donnison & D. Eversley (eds.), *op.cit.,* pp. 313–53.
Kirby, D. A. (1979) *Slum Housing and Residential Renewal,* Longman, London.

Discussions of 'levels of living', 'social well-being' and 'the quality of life' include:
Coates, B. E. and Rawstron, E. M. (1971) *Regional Variations in Britain,* Batsford, London.
Harvey, D. (1973) *Social Justice and the City,* Arnold, London, esp. Chapter 3.
Knox, P. L. (1975) *Social Well-Being: A Spatial Perspective,* Oxford University Press, Oxford.
Runciman, W. G. (1966) *Relative Deprivation and Social Justice,* Routledge & Kegan Paul, London.
Smith, D. M. (1973) *The Geography of Social Well-Being in the United States,* McGraw-Hill, New York.
Smith, D. M. (1977) *Human Geography: A Welfare Approach,* Arnold, London.

# 10

# Beyond the Fringe

## The Fringe in Context

THE urban fringe and the territory beyond provides a second context in which crucial social and spatial changes are being worked out in contemporary England. At first glance what lies beyond the fringe may appear to be totally different from what is found in the city. Surely one is 'countryside', the other 'town'; one is declining, the other growing? To some extent these observations are correct but, perhaps surprisingly, there are points of similarity between the two types of area. Fundamental social changes are occurring in each and important new features of spatial differentiation are being produced. Long accepted images of both urban and rural life are being rendered increasingly redundant with every census, indeed every year, that passes. Members of privileged social groups with good access to information and finance are exercising their right of choosing where to live in more dramatic ways than ever before. In so doing they are entering space that was formerly occupied in different ways by other social groups. Inner-city areas, undergoing the process of gentrification, lose their sense of working-class community, whilst the hierarchical and close-knit social structure, traditionally associated with rural settlements, is being replaced by various forms of social polarization. Occupation of space inside the urban fringe is becoming noticeably more differentiated not just because of gentrification but also because of the establishment of distinctive blocks of residential territory that are occupied by particular migrant groups. Beyond the fringe important aspects of spatial differentiation are also being produced and at a variety of scales. Some settlements are being invaded by newcomers but not others; and, at a finer level of scrutiny, new estates are being constructed for occupation by families with varying quantities of financial backing. For example, in the 1980s a 'village' located in the urban shadow of a great city may well comprise an estate of council housing, two private estates (one for rather more well-to-do people than the other) as well as its ancient nucleus.

The 'urban fringe' is undoubtedly an important phenomenon for the social geographer but it has proved notoriously difficult to define. This problem stems from the disquieting fact that in the industrial, and especially post-industrial, world social phenomena do not correlate neatly with spatial characteristics. A small settlement surrounded by fields may satisfy all the visual requirements for being 'rural' but the greater part of its workforce may commute to jobs in nearby cities and follow an essentially 'urban' way of life. Kurtz and Eicher (1958) examined a number of definitions relating to land use, employment, administration, journey-to-work and lifestyle and concluded that the 'fringe' was to be recognized in the farming hinterland where land use was changing from agricultural to residential functions, population densities were increasing and land values were rising. It was, in short,

178

an area of invasion. Their definition emphasized process rather than morphology and thereby provided a challenge to geographers who had habitually stressed the importance of land use, settlement morphology and central place hierarchies in their research. The present chapter will, in fact, adopt a fairly traditional geographical definition and will recognize the fringe as the outer limit of continuously built-up suburbia. (Such a delimitation does not, of course, correspond with any kind of administrative boundary.) But having done so, the following pages will concentrate on the social processes at work in what McKain and Burnight (1953) recognized as the 'limited' and the 'extended' fringes. The limited fringe, in close proximity to the city, might be expected to bear the brunt of invasion by commuters, in search of cheaper homes and/or more pleasant environments in which to raise their families. But even within the limited fringe the pattern of evolving commuterdom is conditioned by many factors other than simple distance. These include the uneven location of systems of public and private transportation (e.g. railway stations, motorway exits), spatial variations in land ownership and planning constraints, and the differing degrees of interest in particular sites that have been shown by public and/or private developers. Green Belt policies cause housing for commuters to leapfrog the designated area and be constructed at much greater distances than might normally be expected. This is most notably the case in south-east England.

There is in fact no widespread agreement on the outer limit of the extended fringe. Plotting journeys to work would afford some clarification but would not, in itself, give any clear answers since critical thresholds would have to be decided upon to separate one dispersed city system from the next. When occupation of weekend cottages, informal peri-urban recreation and driving for pleasure are included as manifestations of urban influence the spatial analyst's task assumes nightmare proportions. Problems are magnified by the fact that few data exist which capture the locational aspects of these processes over size-able stretches of territory. Of necessity, social geographers must call upon the evidence of detailed case studies but may then have to make use of surrogate measures in order to try and translate social processes into the spatial context. But each case study is unique in itself, reflecting the bias of the individual researcher and analyzing one particular situation at a specified point in time. Generalization from this kind of information is fraught with difficulty but has to be attempted *faute de mieux*.

Perhaps the most accessible surrogate measure is population change. Figure 10.1 shows that during the 1960s depopulation characterized only two really extensive stretches of territory, namely rural Wales and the northern Pennines. Small patches of rural decline were found in the South-West, the North York Moors and around the Wash but the truly important zones of population loss during that decade involved inner-city areas. The remainder of England and Wales experienced growth of population, with rates in excess of 10 per cent being typical in most of south-eastern and Midland England, and by comparison with the 1950s demonstrating accelerated growth beyond the fringe. However, one should not be misled by the pattern of net change shown in Fig. 10.1. Trends for individual settlements are concealed by the statistical average for local authority areas and, in addition, it is highly likely that the trend for one social group may obliterate a contrasting trend for another. For example, a local authority area may increase its total population but this may be caused by a sizeable influx of middle-class commuters which conceals an important decline of agricultural workers or it may result from in-migration of retired people which hides a continuing outflow of young and middle-aged wage-earners. Nonetheless, the widespread increase in population that has taken place beyond the fringe in the past quarter

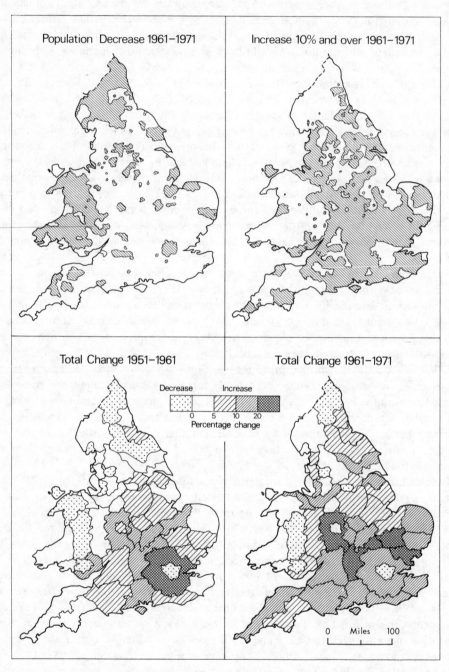

FIG. 10.1. *Aspects of population change in England and Wales, 1951–71 (after Champion, 1976).*

century stands in sharp contrast with the stagnation and decline of the inter-war years when many observers predicted depopulation as the inevitable fate of the English countryside.

To discover why this change came about it is necessary to identify the salient features that have characterized our society since World War II. The oil crisis and all its ramifications notwithstanding, a greater proportion of the English population enjoys a higher standard of living than ever before and may demonstrate its spatial preferences for residence more forcefully than in the past. Partly as a result of legislative changes, private rented accommodation is less available now than in earlier years and more families have striven to acquire a mortgage in order to purchase a home of their own. In general terms, English society has become increasingly 'middle-class', with the proliferation of clerical jobs, in what has become the post-industrial era, allowing upward social mobility. Better standards of education combined with a general evolution of the economy have made the typical Englishman an office worker rather than a factory operative. For most people the working day, week, year and, indeed, lifetime are shorter than they were a generation or so back. More time for non-work activities introduces such important themes as the possibility of longer journeys to work, weekend recreation away from the city, and retirement to the country. Social legislation relating to working hours, holidays with pay and retirement pensions has permitted increasing numbers of people to make use of their newly acquired affluence in ways that were at an embryonic stage and restricted to the truly affluent strata of society before 1945. Rates of religious observance have declined and for many people the weekend has been freed more emphatically for leisure-time pursuits. Rising rates of car ownership have afforded greater personal mobility for the average Briton than ever before. The agricultural workforce has contracted substantially since 1945 but the national population has, of course, increased and is living longer. Our society and economy and our use of space in particular are being planned and organized to an ever greater degree. These trends have affected different social groups with differing intensity but together they have forged a post-industrial society that is in many ways distinctive from its antecedents with consumption of space being not the least of these. Hardly surprisingly, less densely occupied areas beyond the urban fringe have borne a very large share of these new pressures.

## Social and Spatial Processes Beyond the Fringe: Commuting

Many locality studies undertaken in rural Britain emphasize the importance of dynamic equilibrium, whereby social and economic adjustments were muted, or else such studies have concentrated on the nature and implications of rural depopulation. Concepts such as community, reciprocity and continuity figured largely in these works which have been critically examined by Frankenberg (1966) and Bell and Newby (1971). This kind of orientation is, of course, quite inappropriate for examining what has been occurring over the past few decades beyond the urban fringe. Pahl (1965a) insists on recognizing the importance of change in the countryside and demands that social geographers should undertake process studies rather than thinking in vain of the structured communities that existed in times past but have largely disappeared from the present scene. The outer parts of metropolitan regions represent, in Pahl's words, "a frontier of social change" sweeping across whole settlements and transforming them spatially as well as socially.

Four key processes may be identified in this transformation, namely in-migration, commuting, segregation and the collapse of geographical and social hierarchies. Migrants, or newcomers, to the countryside are far from uniform in their social characteristics, ranging from well-to-do professionals, through 'spiralist' managers, to less affluent reluctant commuters. Their life-styles vary in degree from one sub-group to another but they are likely to be substantially different from those of the bulk of the old established villagers whom they may outnumber eventually. Commuting forms an essential aspect of life for the majority of newcomer wage-earners since villages are in no way the relatively self-contained 'occupational settlements' that they were in the past. The journey to work is not restricted to middle-class, white-collar residents on private estates since many people living in council housing in the countryside also need to leave their home settlements for work each day. The construction of different types of estate around old village cores has led to new forms of spatial segregation in many commuter settlements. Old established geographical and social hierarchies have collapsed as the newcomers arrived. The old terminology of market town, village and hamlet has lost all but its formal significance in those parts of the countryside in which all three levels of settlement now function as parts of the 'dispersed city'. What is more, old established social structures, with a number of distinctive layered components, have been replaced by a harsher polarization between people following middle-class or working-class life-styles.

The latter observation does not in fact contradict the point that commuter settlements contain a wide range of types of resident. Pahl recognized no fewer than eight sub-groups, each with differing problems and needs which have been perceived more sharply and examined more critically during the 1970s. For example, families with children would press for improvements in local education whilst retired folk might not be concerned about schooling but would worry about poor public transport or perhaps the closure of the local shop or doctor's surgery. Likewise, the needs of the families of car-less agricultural workers living in tied cottages or council housing would be very different from the fashionable concern for environmental conservation or preserving the beauty of the village that might emanate from the 'gin and Jag' newcomers on the private estate on the other side of the parish. As Pahl (1970) remarked, "to consider 'the village' as a sort of average of all such groups is extremely misleading. . . . There is no village population as such; rather there are specific populations which for various, but identifiable, reasons find themselves in a village" (p. 45). Nonetheless, his work in Hertfordshire in the early 1960s revealed a fundamental division along class lines which transcended more detailed sub-groupings of residents. When contact patterns, car ownership, visiting and membership of societies were examined a distinction between middle-class and lower-class people was clearly in evidence in his sample settlements, so much so that "in their relations with the outside world, the middle-class and working-class villagers moved in separate worlds" (Pahl, 1965b, p. 11). Clubs and societies were predominantly run by and for members of the middle class.

A later study by Thorns (1968) relating to Nottinghamshire produced a very similar conclusion. Like Pahl's work it recognized the diversity of people who lived in commuter villages, stressing for example that there were subtle but important variations within the rural working class between skilled and semi-skilled manual workers on the one hand and farm workers and unskilled labourers on the other. These variations derived from differences in income, working hours and conditions of work and whether one lived in tied cottages or in non-tied accommodation. Nonetheless, the two-class split was clearly in evidence. Farm workers were very definitely orientated to the village, which was "the centre of their lives" (p. 164). Many were born within a few miles of their current home. Thorns showed that they were "restricted in their outlook and their involvement outside the village" (p. 164), they formed the core of the rural working class and contrasted with the professional and managerial commuters with very wide spheres of associations and contacts, who saw the village "largely as a dormitory and a place to spend the weekend" (p. 163). In the context of south-east England, Young and Willmott (1973) have described such affluent commuters as 'regional men' who "in rural areas were more often urban, in the sense of being able to use more fully the opportunities of urban life, than many of the poorer car-less families within a mile or so of Piccadilly Circus" (p. 161).

Many commuters move beyond the urban fringe in search of the 'real England' where harmony, virtue, and deep and fulfilling relationships are believed to reside. Raymond Williams, in his study of *The Country and the City* (1973), insists that it is "difficult to over-estimate the importance of this myth in modern social thought" (p. 96) and Howard Newby (1977a) reports that for many "the English village has come to be regarded as the ideal community" (p. 13). The countryside is believed to be natural and timeless and its settlements to be the repositories of a socially beneficial way of life. Of course, Man made the countryside, just as he made the town, and the settlements he built within it contain little of any great antiquity. But these facts do little to undermine one of the most popular myths of our culture. It is a major irony that the newcomer, middle-class commuters who settled in villages in search of closely-knit, harmonious communities often destroyed the remnants of the social relationships of which they had dreamed so eagerly.

It is now over ten years since Pahl produced his provocative work on metropolitan villages. Social geographers have been jolted out of their ruts by the importance of his findings and the incisiveness of his comments. In the years that have followed further studies of commuter settlements have been completed in various parts of the country which allow a number of additional points to be made. The work around Nottingham drew attention to the importance of considering the nature of leadership in villages that were being invaded by newcomers (Thorns, 1968). In some settlements, where a farmer or a local landowner was the key personality, the social impact of newcomers was found to be less overwhelming than Pahl suggested. However, in a second type of settlement it was clear that newcomers had taken over leadership roles, whilst in a third kind of village conditions were in a state of transition and there was no obvious leadership. Enquiries in Wales showed that the two-class distinction recognized by Pahl was certainly to be found but needed to be set in a wider spectrum of social differentiation which included ability to speak the Welsh language, degree of religious observance and participation in village organizations, as well as length of residence in the settlement (Lewis, 1970).

Connell's (1974, 1978) enquiries in Surrey demonstrated not only marked social divisions in commuter settlements but also signs of antagonism between well-to-do commuters, wishing to conserve the environment and maintain the *status quo,* and council house tenants whose environment was not so comfortable and who sought change and improvement. By contrast, a study of Great Bookham, less than five miles from Connell's study area, displayed a much greater degree of cohesion and community spirit than one might have expected from the literature (Russell, 1977). In Great Bookham the range of housing types was perhaps greater than in some commuter villages, with not only a variety of house prices in the private sector but also a number of small, attractively designed council estates that were spatially integrated with other kinds of housing and whose residents were thought to be of a 'higher class' than in many areas of local authority housing in surrounding villages (Fig. 10.2). A highly active community association successfully involved all sorts and conditions of Bookhamites in a wide range of activities and there was no evidence of a middle-class takeover of clubs and societies.

To some extent it is possible to argue that more recent enquiries have demonstrated an evolution of social conditions in commuter villages by comparison with those identified by Pahl in the early 1960s. For example, many but not all council house tenants in commuter villages now own cars and hence their spatial isolation and degree of reliance on public transport is less than it was 15 years ago. But it is essential to recognize that to some degree each commuter village is unique, just as each case study is unique in terms of the selection, sampling and processing of information by the researcher and the conscious or

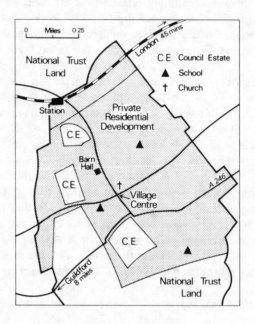

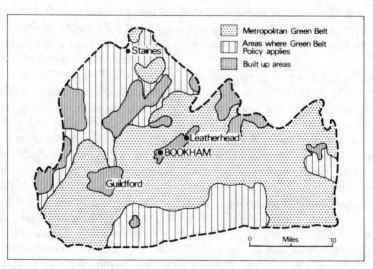

FIG. 10.2. *Great Bookham and the Surrey Green Belt country (after Russell, 1977).*

unconscious bias that he may introduce in his interpretation and explanation of the 'facts'. Thus Great Bookham was in some respects inherently different from the four Surrey villages a few miles further along the railway line that had been examined by Connell. His settlements were substantially smaller than Great Bookham and the degree of owner-occupation, cost of housing and level of rateable values were all markedly higher. It is hardly surprising that the middle-class/working-class cleavage was more acute in those rather select villages than in Great Bookham.

Each case study has added a new dimension to our understanding of commuter villages, but in order to grasp the enormity of recent social change such settlements need to be examined with reference to their past. Ringmer in Sussex has been analyzed in this light with social and economic changes being traced from 1871 to 1971 (Ambrose, 1974). In mid-Victorian times Ringmer supported a wide range of local services and half of its workforce was made up of agricultural labourers. In the late 1920s an estate of local authority houses was built half a mile away from the village nucleus and was "regarded by some as socially, as well as physically, beyond the pale. The new estate was, in fact, referred to as 'Tiger Bay' and was known, or thought, to be a very rough area".(p. 57). Between 1871 and 1961 Ringmer underwent 'organic growth' with its population rising from 1,522 to 2,208 but in the early 1960s it entered a phase of 'superimposed growth' as new estates were built and the population rose to 3,700 in 1971 and was expected to reach 4,500 by the mid-1970s. Over the hundred-year study period, family size and birth and death rates declined substantially. Power and educational opportunity was no longer the preserve of a very limited elite but was redistributed more widely through the village's social spectrum. Ringmer was no longer a relatively 'closed cell' but had become part of a larger 'open system' drawing its newcomer households especially from Brighton, Lewes and other parts of Sussex but also from the whole of south-eastern England. The newcomers differed from the old-established villagers in many respects. Newcomer households were larger and most contained young children, whilst old-established households were older and smaller, often with only two persons being left since the children had left home. There were of course differences in concern between the two groups, with newcomers supporting the local school and making the case for playgroups whilst older residents wanted improved facilities for pensioners. With the obvious exception of the nuclear family most newcomers had no close relatives in Ringmer. By contrast many old-established villagers did have relatives living close by. Newcomers had spent more years in formal education than older residents. Over 80 per cent of newcomers were owner-occupiers, whilst council housing and privately rented accommodation was much more important for old-established villagers. Rates of car-ownership were higher for newcomers and there was a slight difference in journey-to-work behaviour, with long established villagers tending to be more local in their place of work. On this point Ambrose stressed that, whilst virtually all professional workers moved out each day, a village the size of Ringmer managed to provide a fair number of jobs for manual and junior non-manual workers. But with respect to shopping, recreation and membership of clubs and societies newcomers and old-established villagers had surprisingly similar patterns of activity. The evidence did not support the notion of a newcomer, middle-class takeover of organizational life and, in spite of very clear social differentiation, residents of Ringmer did not feel their village to be as divided as one might have expected in the light of earlier case studies. As in Great Bookham, it may well be that the spatial organization of the village had a part to play in fostering social contacts. New private estates were certainly distinctive both from the old village and from council housing, but old Ringmer had a very loose morphology and there was space for new estates to be inserted relatively close to the village nucleus. In Ambrose's words "residential propinquity and work contact appear much more important than formal social organizations in conditioning the pattern of close friendship in the village" (p. 136).

In spite of so many favourable conclusions, Ambrose has his share of criticisms to raise. He questions whether social integration will continue if Ringmer grows any larger. He condemns the new estates as "socially unbalanced and aesthetically insensitive" (p. 220) and has harsh criticisms of the role of the private housing market as it benefits property developers and those able to obtain mortgages but offers nothing to large and less comfortably-off sections of our society. The Ringmer study is, in fact, entitled *The Quiet Revolution*. Ambrose argues that "a social revolution may be said to occur when radical and relatively rapid changes take place in social structures, living standards, access to opportunities and in the bases upon which authority and privilege are conferred and exercised. Changes of this nature have occurred in Ringmer, quietly but surely, primarily during the inter-war period and most of all in the last decade" (p. 218). In spite of the emergence of Britain as a welfare-state, post-industrial, middle-class society there are very many people whose access to decent housing, employment and education remain seriously limited. For Ambrose, and many other social geographers, "the quiet revolution is not yet complete" (p. 220).

### Hobby Farming and Retirement Migration

The inequalities of our society become all too obvious as other processes are probed that contribute to the re-population of territory beyond the urban fringe and the changes in its social composition. Part-time farming is a highly complex but little studied phenomenon involving many parts of England and many different types of operator. In midland and northern England industrial workers make up a sizeable proportion of part-time farmers and other notable groups include forestry workers (in north Wales and northern England) and boarding house proprietors (in the South-west). In south-eastern England the picture contains other important components, especially large numbers of businessmen who have invested in land and run their 'hobby farms' over the weekends and continue to commute to office jobs during the week.

Gasson (1966; 1967) has shown that counties such as Kent and Sussex have contained large proportions of owner-occupied, part-time holdings throughout the present century. These enterprises tend to be relatively simple; raising beefstock on permanent grass or growing cereals that are harvested by seasonal contract workers. The housing and environmental resources of areas in and beyond the Green Belt have become increasingly attractive in recent years to businessmen and to others with access to sizeable amounts of capital for investment. Green Belt legislation prevented 'desirable country properties' being constructed in close proximity to London but existing farm houses might be purchased to provide the ideal setting for realizing the dream of a secluded place in the country. Buildings have been modernized inside and preserved, or enhanced, outside. The land has been farmed as a hobby or leased in part to surrounding operators; in fact, full-time farmers have tended to retreat to more distant areas of south-east England and many are harsh in their criticism of weekend dabblers who hold on to land and hinder amalgamation and enlargement of full-time holdings. Gasson acknowledges that many hobby farmers treat agriculture as a recreation rather than a business but her comments are appreciative of the capital that they have brought into their own brand of farming and that they use in part for preserving old houses and buildings and generally enhancing the rural environment.

However, hobby farming is not a discrete phenomenon. In one respect it blends into the establishment of commuter settlements since many hobby farmers are 'regional men' who travel long distances to work four or five days each week. In another respect, hobby farming merges with the arrival of retired people who have chosen to spend their final years in the territory beyond the urban fringe. Perhaps as many as a fifth or even a quarter of part-time farms are run by people who have retired from other types of job. Finally, there exists yet another set of part-time holdings which are ancillary to the second homes located on them and which are occupied only at weekends and/or during vacations. Admittedly the proliferation of second homes does not contribute directly to an increase in the population dwelling full-time beyond the urban fringe, but it does stimulate important social and economic changes and can also give rise to local hostilities.

With people living longer and in general having become more affluent, retirement migration has emerged as a significant social trend during the 1960s and 1970s. A whole range of conditions comes into play to help explain why this should be so. Occupational and old-age pensions are widely available. Longer and more varied holidays, shorter working weeks and rising rates of car ownership have allowed more people to sample a variety of environments during their working lifetime. For some elderly folk formal retirement offers a welcome opportunity to change place of residence. Rising rates of owner-occupation mean that many elderly couples may wish to make use of the capital they have invested in property over the years by selling their highly rated suburban houses, buying smaller and cheaper properties in the countryside or along the coast and using the difference between the two sums to supplement their pensions and savings during their remaining years.

Retirement migration is often talked about and has become an important and sometimes worrying component in the life of many families, however, surprisingly little serious research has been undertaken. In a series of pioneer papers Law and Warnes (1973, 1975, 1976) analyzed available statistics and identified 'retirement areas' in England and Wales (Fig. 10.3). In order to qualify for that status an area needed to contain a proportion of over 60-year olds that was 25 per cent or more above the national mean for local authorities and had to display an increase, or a decline at less than half the national rate, in the numbers of the retirement cohort for 1961 to 1971. Coastal areas, and especially seaside resorts in the South, were particularly obvious as retirement areas in 1971 but so too were a number of inland areas, most notably the villages and small towns of the South-west and of East Anglia. On a smaller scale, the Welsh border, mid-Wales, the Lincolnshire Wolds, the North York Moors, the southern part of the Lake District and areas of rural Northumberland were each receiving quite large numbers of retirements during that decade. Each of these rural areas contained attractive scenery and lacked obtrusive industrial development but, in addition, the imposition of limits to further development in some coastal resorts plus rising costs of housing in these areas may well have deflected elderly migrants to locations in the country-side that were selected as second-best.

Retirees would seem to choose small towns and villages in which they hope a sense of community may be found as well as the housing being cheaper. The effect is cumulative, as newly retired people choose settlements to which their friends and relatives have already moved. If such a community spirit does exist or if friends and family can ease the settling-in process the move may not prove traumatic. But there are many potential difficulties to surround elderly migrants. They may well have only sampled their chosen destination during

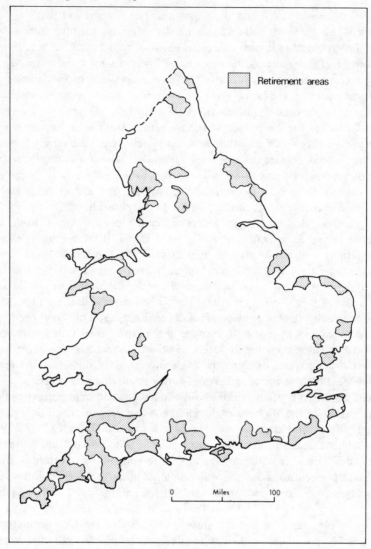

FIG. 10.3. *Retirement areas in England and Wales (after Law and Warnes, 1976).*

the summer months and have little idea of what it has to offer in the winter when the weather is bad and basic facilities for shopping or for socializing may be meagre. Retirees in small settlements may be seriously disadvantaged as they grow more infirm with increasing age. Driving may become impossible and elderly residents have to rely on public transport or the goodwill of neighbours. Of course, retired people do make use of local shops and community facilities. They pay rates but do not make use of some types of local services, especially those related to education. However, they can generate new demands for public transport and for local socio-medical services which may be at variance with the general needs of the bulk of the local population. Social services surveys undertaken after the Chronic Sick and Disabled Persons Act (1970) showed that many rural areas could not meet their various obligations relating to home help, meals on wheels, health visiting, chiropody and regular visits by general practitioners because of the high cost of providing such services in areas of dispersed settlement where income from rates tends to be low.

Retirement migration to villages and small towns can enhance population numbers and inflate the demand for local shops and for selected services, but serious difficulties can face retirees with increasing years and especially following the death of one partner. Some commentators conclude that an increase in the proportion of old people in the village or small town is socially undesirable since it may exaggerate the movement of young people away from more remote parts of the countryside. Local facilities and opportunities for young people need not decline following the arrival of retirees but where elderly people replace those of working age this serves to reduce the local labour force and creates an unattractive environment for employers. Possible job opportunities may be lost and young people may have to commute out of the area to work each day or may move away entirely. Retirement migration, of itself, is not a satisfactory alternative to retaining or installing people in the active age groups.

## Second Homes and Tourism

Neither the proliferation of second homes nor the growth of tourism makes a direct contribution to increasing the number of residents in areas beyond the urban fringe. However, both processes have assumed great importance over the past two decades as they bring more people into the countryside on a temporary basis, create seasonal demands for local services and may therefore, in an indirect way, help to support some full-time residents. In fact there is plenty of evidence for such a favourable interpretation in some parts of the country, but in other areas rural depopulation may be accelerated as demands from potential second homers inflate local house prices and help to put private accommodation beyond the reach of local people.

There is a long history of second home occupation in England and Wales but until the last quarter century it remained the privilege of a very small section of society (Bielkus et al., 1972). Ownership broadened in the 1960s but in spite of rapid increases numbers remained small by comparison with Europe and North America. In 1970 the countryside and small towns of England and Wales contained 180–200,000 'built' second homes that were either converted cottages or specially constructed leisure homes. That total had risen from an estimated 50,000 in 1955 and the 1970 figure might be inflated to 300–350,000 when static caravans were included with built second homes. Even so only about 2 per cent of households in England and Wales possessed a second home beyond the urban fringe. (The figure would be inflated marginally if urban *pieds à terre* were included). Two-thirds of our second homes are sited in coastal areas and the remainder inland. Their distribution has never been plotted but sample surveys indicate that many types of rural and coastal environment are conducive for establishing second homes. Areas with rich and varied scenery, such as the Lake District, figure prominently but so do more homely stretches of countryside such as the Weald of south-east England. Second homes are acquired for various types of use and this, together with the different declared motives, helps to explain their widespread distribution. Some 5 per cent are used only for weekend visits and these may be located relatively close to major cities, even nestling among the homes of commuters in metropolitan villages and amidst the hobby farms and retirement cottages that surround them. Sixteen per cent are used only for holidays and may well be sited in very distant locations. The remaining 79 per cent are for both weekend and holiday use and are to be found across a wide range of intermediate locations. The variety of declared reasons for acquiring a second home also require attention. Admittedly 76 per cent of the owners that were sampled declared that their prime reason for acquisition was weekend and/or holiday use but 10 per cent replied that they had acquired their property with a view to eventual retirement and that using it as a second home was only an intermediate phase.

There are no hard and fast rules about the advantages and disadvantages accruing to permanent residents from the proliferation of second homes in the countryside. On the positive side second homers pay full rates (according to the size and quality of their house) and therefore make an important contribution to the local economy without requiring expensive services such as education or health care. However, if second homes are transformed into retirement homes their occupants may well generate new and expensive demands on the facilities that local authorities attempt to provide. People spending holidays in second homes may purchase their goods and services locally but this is not usually the case for weekenders who arrive on Friday evening with enough food to tide them over until Sunday night. A few part-time jobs for caretakers or gardeners may be created but their impact is likely to be slight. Visual blight may be avoided as tumbledown cottages are restored to use as second homes, but local hostility has ensued in many cases when this has been done with the help of standard improvement grants. The 1969 Housing Act offered financial assistance for restoring and improving housing provided that the application from the householder was technically correct. The scheme was really designed to rehabilitate first homes but second homers were within their rights to request assistance and many middle-class newcomers were more aware of their 'rights' than were local residents. Some rural authorities and Members of Parliament were quick to denounce what they perceived as an abuse of the spirit of the law. Even more contentious has been the undoubted rise in house prices that has occurred in areas where second homes have become numerous. Young couples are not able to compete with newcomers in the housing market and, it is frequently alleged, are being forced to move wherever accommodation that is within their financial reach is available. That usually means a move to town. There is of course, much truth in this view but it should be remembered that rural areas need to provide employment as well as housing if they are to retain their wage-earners and unfortunately many areas where second homes have proliferated have precious little to offer by way of permanent employment.

In a report entitled *No Place in the Country* (1973), Shelter demonstrated the serious housing shortages that still afflict many residents of town and country alike and highlighted the injustice of some households having second or even third homes whilst others had no roof to call their own. Shelter did not question the right of second home ownership but argued that it should be made more difficult and expensive. A battery of increased rates, new taxes and sale charges was proposed, together with the termination of bank loans, improvement grants and tax benefits on mortgages relating to second homes. Shelter proposed that local authorities with long waiting lists for council housing should buy private properties as they came on to the market in order to prevent them being purchased for use as second homes. Plaid Cymru and many other organizations made similar proposals. In fact the turn of events subsequent to the oil crisis has dampened down the growth rate for second homes in England and Wales. Bielkus (1972) and her colleagues at Wye College forecast that numbers of 'built' second homes might rise from 180—200,000 in 1970 to 600—750,000 by 1985 and perhaps 2,000,000 by A.D. 2000. New construction would be required to absorb a great part of that demand. What has happened in the last few years is just the reverse. Numbers have remained stable or have actually fallen in some sample areas. A recent report on second homes in Scotland by the Dartington Amenity Research Trust (1977) provides explanations for the changing trend that would seem equally valid for England and Wales. Undoubtedly the general economic climate has been the main reason but, in addition, tax relief has been discontinued on second home mortgages; Capital Gains Tax has had a discouraging effect; improvement grants have been withdrawn under legislation of 1974; and parliamentary and public debate plus some hostile propaganda may have made some potential purchasers change their mind. However, it is surely realistic to interpret the current situation simply as a pause that may well come to an end if economic circumstances improve in the future. It is hard to believe that deeply ingrained cultural attitudes on the desirability of country living will be obliterated in the Englishman's mind by the state of the £ sterling.

Tourism provides a final context in which urban values have been transported into the territory beyond the fringe, along with city people who seek rest and recreation in the countryside. They have introduced new perceptions of rural resources which accentuate the worth of landscape features inherited from the past and make the case for their conservation whilst, paradoxically, also emphasizing the desirability of installing new facilities to accommodate visitors' needs. Local inhabitants may adhere to a totally different set of values, seeing land in terms of its agricultural potential rather than viewing it as scenery, wishing to uproot hedgerows and erase other redundant features which hinder the efficient operation of their holdings, and sometimes favouring the development of mining or manufacturing in areas of great scenic beauty by virtue of the new employment that will be created. But it is very easy to oversimplify complicated and even contradictory attitudes. For example, Newby (1977b) and his colleagues have shown that farmers hold a great diversity of opinions with regard to the desirability of environmental conservation. Family farmers, with a high degree of direct involvement in farm work, only moderate market orientation and frankly modest amounts of capital, tend to be much more favourably disposed towards conservation than 'agri-businessmen' for whom profit maximization and financial efficiency, rather than the art of husbandry are the key objectives of farming.

## The Challenge of Interpreting Social Change

The territory beyond the fringe provides a truly challenging environment for the social geographer. Urban derived values have been diffused widely through the mass media and by the permanent or temporary presence of city people. But not every village is a newcomers' village and every other house is far from being a second home (MacGregor, 1972). To be sure the 'occupational village', which provided local employment for most of its inhabitants as they lived in a tightly-knit community, has disappeared. But there are many degrees of change to be identified and analyzed. Some settlements, containing council housing and occupational tied cottages, may remain 'farm-centred' to a much greater degree than neighbouring settlements without these types of accommodation and in which the take-over by newcomers may be much more pervasive (Newby, 1977a). For example, Radford (1970) was able to show that two villages, at equal distance from Worcester, were at very different stages in the transition from rural to urban. Both had received large numbers of newcomers but one retained the social remnants of a traditional village whilst the other had become, more emphatically, a 'suburb'.

In spite of the undoubted general comfort of English society in the final quarter of the twentieth century, many rural dwellers continue to experience serious social problems. The rural poor are at a particular disadvantage, since difficulties deriving from their socio-economic condition are compounded by difficulties emanating from spatial isolation in parts of the country where population and services of all kinds are spread both thinly and unevenly and public transport is not only expensive but is becoming increasingly sparse. The plight of such people is often concealed by apparently favourable averages, such as those cited earlier in this chapter, which gloss over deficiencies toward the end of the statistical spectrum with respect to housing, employment, mobility and access to services of all kinds (Moseley, 1979). Associations such as the Child Poverty Action Group have moved beyond the special problems of the young in order to discuss broader issues of rural poverty and their implications for countryside planning in England. Other pieces of research have successfully exploded the romantic ethos that has often shrouded enquiries into living conditions in the countryside. Problems associated with the closure of village schools have been debated openly and official plans for rationalization have been challenged by action groups who have proposed strategies to allow some small schools to survive through functional diversification.

Geographers can no longer claim ignorance either of the social problems experienced by many country dwellers or of the fundamental reasons behind those problems, namely the differential access of members of various social groups to effective power for shaping and reshaping the geographical space in which they live. In recent years British sociologists have made a series of stimulating contributions to our understanding of rural life toward the end of the twentieth century by exposing the nature of those power relationships. As he examines deprivation and allied matters the social geographer must build on their revelations to devise an approach which blends spatial logic not only with social science but also, hopefully, with social justice. The legacies of the past, in terms of institutions, power and social structures, must be comprehended as he seeks to explain both the broad trends and the subtle details of social change. Distance, time and cost are not everything. Cultural values, changing perceptions and differences in life-style should be allotted due attention. Exceptions to general rules are worthy of examination for they may well encompass very real social problems. It is obvious that some sections of society have missed out in the post-war flush of affluence and increased personal mobility. They, the poorly paid, the elderly, the handicapped and the educationally disadvantaged, are to be found beyond as well as within the urban fringe and merit the social geographer's concern.

## References and Further Reading

The concept of the fringe is reviewed in:
Johnson, J. H. (ed.) (1974) *Suburban Growth,* Wiley, London.
Kurtz, R. A. and Eicher, J. B. (1958) Fringe and suburb: a confusion of concepts, *Social Forces,* 37, 32–37.
McKain, W. C. and Burnight, R. C. (1953) The rural—urban fringe: from the rural point of view, *Rural Sociology,* 18, 108–17.

A statement on recent population changes is by:
Champion, A. G. (1976) Evolving patterns of population distribution in England and Wales, 1951–71, *Transactions, Institute of British Geographers,* New Series, 1, 401–20.

Locality studies in the countryside are set in context by:
Bell, C. and Newby, H. (1971) *Community Studies: an introduction to the sociology of the local community,* George Allen & Unwin, London.

Frankenberg, R. (1966) *Communities in Britain*, Penguin, Harmondsworth.

Jones, G. E. (1973) *Rural Life*, Longmans, London.

Lewis, G. J. (1979) *Rural Communities: a social geography*, David & Charles, Newton Abbot.

Commuter settlements are examined in:

Ambrose, P. (1974) *The Quiet Revolution: social change in a Sussex village 1871–1971*, Chatto & Windus, London.

Connell, J. H. (1974) The metropolitan village: spatial and social processes in discontinuous suburbs, in J. H. Johnson (ed.), *op.cit.*, pp. 77–100.

Connell, J. H. (1978) *The End of Tradition: country life in central Surrey*, Routledge & Kegan Paul, London.

Lewis, G. J. (1970) A Welsh rural community in transition: a case study in mid-Wales, *Sociologia Ruralis*, 10, 143–61.

Pahl, R. E. (1965a) *Urbs in Rure*, London School of Economics, Geographical Papers 2.

Pahl, R. E. (1965b) Class and community in English commuter villages, *Sociologia Ruralis*, 5, 5–23.

Pahl, R. E. (1970) *Whose City?* Longmans, London.

Russell, G. A. (1977) Great Bookham: conflict or cohesion in a commuter village? Unpublished undergraduate dissertation, University College London.

Thorns, D. C. (1968) The changing system of social stratification, *Sociologia Ruralis*, 8, 161–78.

Various forms of settlement morphology produced beyond the fringe are exemplified in:

Giggs, J. A. (1970–73) Fringe expansion and suburbanization around Nottingham: a metropolitan area approach, *East Midland Geographer*, 5, 9–18.

Life-styles of residents within and beyond the fringe are analyzed by:

Pahl, J. M. and R. E. (1971) *Managers and their Wives*, Penguin, Harmondsworth.

Young, M. and Willmott, P. (1973) *The Symmetrical Family*, Penguin, Harmondsworth.

Cultural attitudes on the merits of living in the countryside are scrutinized by:

Newby, H. (1977a) *The Deferential Worker*, Allen Lane Press, London.

Williams, R. (1973) *The Country and the City*, Chatto & Windus, London.

The social and economic aspects of part-time farming are examined in:

Gasson, R. (1966) *The influence of Urbanization on Farm Ownership and Practice*, Wye College.

Gasson, R. (1967) Some economic characteristics of part-time farming in Britain, *Journal of Agricultural Economics*, 18, 111–20.

Retirement migration is discussed by:

Law, C. M. and Warnes, A. M. (1973) The movement of retired people to seaside resorts, *Town Planning Review*, 44, 361–76.

Law, C. M. and Warnes, A. M. (1975) Life begins at sixty: the increase in retirement migrations, *Town and Country Planning*, 43, 531–34.

Law, C. M. and Warnes, A. M. (1976) The changing geography of the elderly in England and Wales, *Transactions, Institute of British Geographers*, New Series, 1, 453–71.

Lemon, A. (1973) Retirement and its effects on small towns, *Town Planning Review*, 44, 254–62.

Second homes are studied by:

Bielkus, C. L., Rogers, A. W. and Wibberley, G. L. (1972) *Second Homes in England and Wales*, Wye College.

Coppock, J. T. (ed.) (1977) *Second Homes: curse or blessing?* Pergamon, Oxford.

Dartington Amenity Research Trust (1977) *Second Homes in Scotland*, Totnes.

Downing, P. and Dower, M. (1973) *Second Homes in England and Wales: an appraisal*, Countryside Commission and H.M.S.O., London.

Mahon, D. (1973) *No Place in the Country: a report on second homes in England and Wales*, Shelter, London.

Farmers' attitudes regarding tourism and recreation are discussed in:

Dower, M. (1973) Recreation, tourism and the farmer, *Journal of Agricultural Economics*, 24, 465–70.

Newby, H. (1977b) Farmers' attitudes to conservation, *Countryside Recreation Review*, 2, 22–30.

The spatial complexities of social change beyond the fringe are exemplified in:

Jackson, V. J. (1968) *Population in the Countryside: growth and stagnation in the Cotswolds*, Cass, London.

Lewis, G. J. and Maund, D. J. (1976) The urbanization of the countryside: a framework for analysis, *Geografiska Annaler B,* 58, 17–27.

Macgregor, M. (1972) The rural culture, *New Society,* 19, 486–9.

Radford, E. (1970) *The New Villagers: urban pressure on rural areas in Worcestershire,* Cass, London.

A case study of population decline resulting from management policies on one estate is found in:
Havinden, M. A. (1966) *Estate Villages,* Museum of English Rural Life, Reading.

Studies of deprivation in the British countryside include:
Moseley, M. J. (ed.) (1978) *Social Issues in Rural Norfolk,* Centre for East Anglian Studies, Norwich.

Moseley, M. J. (1979) *Accessibility: the rural challenge,* Methuen, London.

Rogers, R. (1979) *Schools under Threat: a handbook on closures,* Advisory Centre for Education, London.

Shaw, J. M. (ed.) (1979) *Rural Deprivation and Planning,* Geo Abstracts, Norwich.

Walker, A. (ed.) (1978) *Rural Poverty: poverty, deprivation and planning in rural areas,* Child Poverty Action Group, London.

Important sociological contributions to an understanding of power relations in the British countryside are found in:
Newby, H. (ed.) (1978a) *International Perspectives in Rural Sociology,* Wiley, Chichester.

Newby, H. (ed.) (1978b) *Property, Paternalism and Power,* Macmillan, London.

Tranter, R. B. (ed.) (1978) *The Future of Upland Britain,* 2 vols., Centre for Agricultural Strategy, Reading.

A valuable study of settlement planning with profound social implications is contained in:
Cloke, P. (1979) *Key Settlements in Rural Areas,* Methuen, London.

A very readable account of social change in rural England is provided by:
Newby, H. (1980) *Green and Pleasant Land?,* Penguin, Harmondsworth.

# 11

# Social Geography and Relevance

## Well-Being

IN the preceding chapters we have argued the importance of an historical perspective to the social geography of contemporary England. On the one hand, we have stressed similarities between past and present situations, for example in the role of successive immigrant groups, our attitudes towards them, and their segregation, both nationally and within cities. In every historical period, too, we need to consider political and economic constraints on individual mobility and residential location, and the relationships between rural and urban societies. Because political, economic and technological structures have changed since pre-industrial times, the results of constraints and the nature of rural–urban relationships have also changed, but this does not deny the essential continuity of the processes.

On the other hand, the historical perspective also emphasizes evolution and change. In particular, we have interpreted the social geography of England in terms of the process of urbanization and the development of a capitalist, urban-industrial society. We have considered the transition in the spatial structure of towns and cities from the models of Sjoberg and Vance, through Engels, Burgess and Hoyt, to the multi-dimensional structure described by modern factorial ecologists. We have explained this change in terms of both demand (the preferences of class- or status-conscious individuals and households) and supply (the behaviour of governments and institutions in the land and housing systems). In two problem-oriented chapters we have focused on the problems of contemporary urban society, as manifest in inner-city districts, and the problems that urban affluence and urban attitudes have introduced to urban fringe and rural periphery. Our emphasis has been on spatial variations at the micro-scale, especially between one part of a city and another. This is justifiable in that the urban experience is the experience familiar to at least 80 per cent of Englishmen today, more than 80 per cent when the urban way of life of many living outside towns and cities is taken into account.

Nevertheless, we would be wrong to neglect research at other scales of analysis. Studies of religious segregation within cities such as London and Liverpool have been paralleled by studies comparing levels of religious observance and denominational adherence in different regions (Gay, 1971). The analysis of ethnic communities within cities has been matched by studies of cultural and linguistic variations between different parts of Britain, as well as by studies of the distribution of immigrant groups at the macro-scale (Peach, 1968; Pryce, 1975). Intra-urban variations in health and mortality also have their inter-regional parallels (Howe, 1972). There is also a growing interest at all scales in electoral geography. Levels of turnout at elections vary from rural to urban areas, from suburb to inner city, from marginal to safe seat; and party allegiances also vary geographically (Busteed, 1975; Taylor and Johnston, 1979).

Even more wide-ranging have been recent studies of regional variations in social well-being, levels of living or the quality of life. The trend was set by Coates and Rawstron's (1971) investigation of *Regional Variations in Britain,* in which the authors presented separate discussions of such topics as the spatial distribution of personal incomes, the level of health service provision, and regional variations in the ratio of population to doctors and dentists, the importance of private education and the proportions of children going on to higher education. They recognized many of the problems that have beset subsequent studies of well-being and particularly the fact that spatial inequality is not the same as spatial injustice. For example, they observed that, relative to the size of local populations, there were more general practitioners in peripheral rural areas and in parts of the affluent Home Counties (e.g. Surrey, Hampshire) than in unattractive industrial counties like Durham, Staffordshire and Nottinghamshire and some fast-growing commuter counties to the north of London (Fig. 11.1). But they acknowledged that GPs' lists probably should be shorter in rural areas to compensate for the long distances that doctors have to travel between calls, much as rural parliamentary constituencies contain smaller electorates than those in urban areas.

Coates and Rawstron also stressed that the needs for doctors (i.e. a 'just distribution' of GPs) could not be assessed by analyzing demand in terms of current usage. In 1967 doctors issued 6.6 prescriptions per head of the population in north-west England but only 5.4 in the south-east, but it could be argued that, if it had been as easy to see a doctor in the north-west as it was in the 'doctor-rich' counties of Surrey and Hampshire, the demand for prescriptions would have been even higher. It may be preferable to estimate the demand for health services using indicators such as conditions of work, levels of pollution and housing quality in each region.

A second example of regional variations in the performance of the National Health Service reinforced this conclusion. Coates and Rawstron found that the average duration of stay in acute hospitals varied from more than 13 days in Liverpool to only 8.6 days in Oxford. From these figures it was tempting to conclude that the health service could be made more efficient if Liverpool's length of stay was reduced to that of Oxford. But it was just as likely that the inequality reflected greater needs in areas of bad housing and insufficient recreational space like Liverpool, where patients recovered more quickly if they convalesced in hospital instead of at home.

After such interesting and careful discussions of individual patterns of variation, Coates and Rawstron's attempts at explanation, synthesis or policy recommendations were disappointing, sometimes reverting to the assumption that spatial inequality *was* the same as social and economic inequity. Many of the various indices they examined told the same story: the desirability of the south-east and unattractiveness of older industrial areas in the north and midlands. They concluded that many of these spatial variations would be unacceptable to an informed, democratic society claiming equality of opportunity as a goal, but their prescription provided little other than the provision of more information. Certainly they did not envisage major structural changes in the ways in which resources were allocated in society. Any reform would be within the constraints of the existing political system.

The same is true of subsequent empirical studies of social and economic well-being. They have provided adequate descriptions and, in some cases, explanations of social patterns,

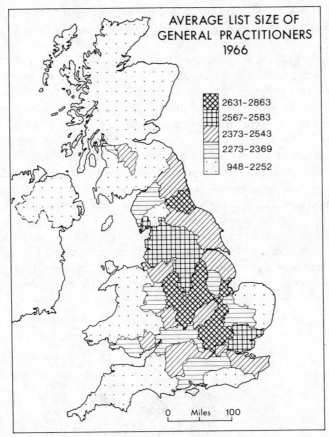

AVERAGE LIST SIZE OF
GENERAL PRACTITIONERS
1966

2631- 2863
2567- 2583
2373- 2543
2273- 2369
948- 2252

0    Miles    100

FIG. 11.1. *Distribution of general practitioners in Britain, 1966 (after Coates and Rawstron, 1971).*

but little emphasis has been placed on how conditions may be improved. In fact, there is the danger that the demand for more information, for a 'Geographical Survey' (Coates and Rawstron, 1971), or for more interest in socio-spatial reporting and management on the part of government (Knox, 1975), may hasten the Orwellian nightmare of a '1984' type of government control (Smith, 1973). It may be argued that a well-intentioned but naïve request for more information is as undesirable as it is unlikely to succeed. In the face of reductions in public expenditure, we are likely to be presented with less information, not more!

Knox (1975) took advantage of factor analytic techniques to reduce a mass of information on levels of living in counties and county boroughs in England and Wales to 6 principal components that accounted for the majority of variance in 53 original variables. The variables were carefully selected to measure different *aspects* of the *constituents* of the level of living. For example, Knox identified three *aspects* of Housing: Occupancy (the degree of sharing, level of overcrowding, and tenure), Quality (the provision of basic amenities, the rateable value of dwellings) and Levels of Housebuilding (the numbers of new houses or conversions completed by public and private sectors). Unfortunately, the information that is actually available rarely matches what is required: some data are inaccurate; in other cases we have to make do with inputs rather than outputs, measures of expenditure rather than attainment; and some *constituents* cannot be quantified at all. Furthermore, factor analysis assumes that all variables are equally important: they all contribute one unit of variance to the statistical analysis. Knox acknowledged the need to avoid a "new Philistinism" (p. 54) of quantifying the unquantifiable, but he still fell into the trap in identifying four 'diagnostic' variables that sum up different dimensions of life in England and Wales and then adding them together to produce a single map of the level of living. This procedure might be acceptable if the four variables were clearly normative, so that we could be confident that high values were 'good', low values 'bad', or vice versa. But of Knox's four diagnostics, only three — the average number of persons per room, the proportion of households without exclusive use of a fixed bath, and the percentage unemployed — are normative. The fourth, the proportion of the population aged 60 or above in each area, may depict an increasingly important dimension of British society, but it is not clear whether large numbers of old people are 'good' or 'bad' for an area.

The result of adding together scores on the four diagnostics is a map purporting to show regional variations in levels of living (Fig. 11.2). However, the addition technique has the effect of producing large numbers of 'middling' scores, all 'middling' for different reasons. Thus, Hull and Cornwall record similar, below average, levels of living, although it is unlikely

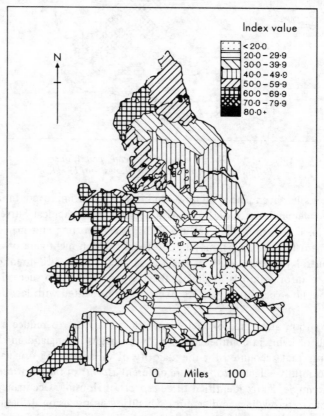

Index value

< 20·0
20·0 – 29·9
30·0 – 39·9
40·0 – 49·9
50·0 – 59·9
60·0 – 69·9
70·0 – 79·9
80·0+

0    Miles    100

FIG. 11.2. *An index of level of living in England and Wales, 1961; the heavier the shading, the worse the level of living (after Knox, 1975).*

that either the experience or the problems of life in the two areas are the same. Smith (1973) asked whether we would prefer a cancer-free society composed of illiterates or a fully literate society, ravaged by cancer. Knox's insensitive addition of dimensions as unlike as 'cancer' and 'literacy' merely ignores the question, implying that there is nothing to choose between Smith's two opposite conditions.

It is also probable that many so-called inter-regional variations are really inter-urban in origin and that the most significant differences are in the quality of inner-city environments and the extent of urban poverty. On Fig. 11.2, Cardiff and Newport appear as more attractive areas than the surrounding counties of Glamorgan and Monmouth (now Gwent). But repeating the exercise at the scale of individual local authority areas within South Wales, the inner areas of both Cardiff and Newport emerge with lower levels of living than any part of South Wales other than one or two local authorities in the eastern valleys. At this scale life in every part of Cardiff except one northern suburb is less attractive than life in south Glamorgan, to the west of the city (Fig. 11.3).

Our principal objection to Knox's study and, to be fair, one that he recognized in the conclusion to his book, is that he paid insufficient attention to the definition of a just or fair distribution. Even if we accept that Hull and Cornwall have similar levels of living, should our reaction be to direct identical amounts of aid to each area, or is one more needy than the other?

### Relevance

Our critical discussion of studies that describe inter-regional (or, as in factorial ecology, intra-urban) variations inevitably leads us to question the relevance of social geography to

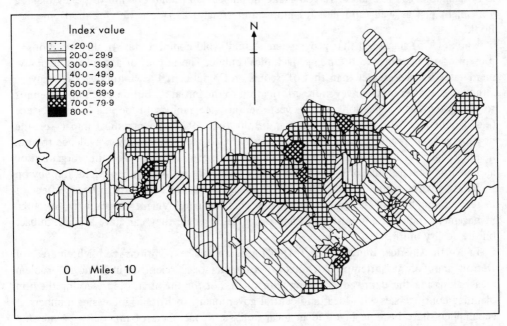

FIG. 11.3. *Levels of living in South Wales, 1961; the heavier the shading, the worse the level of living (after Knox, 1975).*

life outside the ivory towers of academe. Human geography has long been assailed for its irrelevance. Ley (1978) notes that much social science has followed the 'counter-revolutionary' role of diverting attention away from the injustices of society and towards things that do not really matter. Peet (1977) has asserted that all social science serves some political purpose, usually maintaining the *status quo* by providing partial, within-the-system solutions to problems, or by focusing attention on the irrelevant. Thus the powerful statistical armoury of locational analysis was directed at "such socially ephemeral matters as shopping behaviour and the location of service centres" (Peet, 1977, p. 10). In one sense the relevance of this kind of geography lay in its irrelevance: in being irrelevant it performed a vital diversionary role! In the field of social geography this criticism could also be levelled against ever more sophisticated applications of factorial ecology, which defined dimensions of urban structure that might not accord with the perceptions of residents or policy makers; or against analyses of decision making that assumed that individuals were free to choose where to live, work, shop or educate their children. Gray's (1975) attack on non-explanation in urban geography constituted this type of criticism.

In response to an increasing demand for social relevance, geographers began to study apparently more relevant topics. Peet described this phase as changing the topical focus of human geography yet retaining its existing research methodology. For example, the 1974 Annual Conference of the Institute of British Geographers concentrated on the theme of *Geography and Public Policy;* the Royal Geographical Society organized a symposium in 1975 on *Spatial and Social Constraints in the Inner City;* and social geographers everywhere began to measure the extent of ethnic segregation, criminal activity, mental illness and, more generally, the access to 'scarce resources' as outlined in Chapter 9 and earlier in this chapter. But the mere selection of a topic for study that also happens to be of current popular interest is no guarantee of relevancy. If you make no impact on public opinion or policy making you might just as well (and perhaps more interestingly) carry on studying the Domesday Book!

Knox (1975) suggested that geographers should avoid complex statistical abstractions in presenting their results to the non-geographical public. The impact of a map of unemployment rates will be greater than that of 'scores on Component I' of a multivariate analysis, although the latter may convey more information to the initiated. But despite some attempts to bridge the communications gap between 'serious' geography and 'popular' social science (e.g. Gould and White, 1974; Taylor and Johnston, 1979), geographical impact on the development of public opinion has been limited. Geographers have given evidence to and, in a few cases, been members of Royal Commissions (e.g. on local government reorganization and environmental pollution), but there is no evidence of a coherent geographical lobby on social or environmental issues. This is not to deny the much more significant effect of increasing numbers of geography graduates entering employment in planning, resource management, housing administration and other fields where they can have a direct impact on the quality of life.

In North America, Bunge's (1969, 1974) geographical 'expeditions' to blighted areas of Detroit and Toronto attempted to involve academic social scientists in living in problem areas, alongside the deprived, planning *with* them, not *for* them, and representing them in planning controversies with local and central government. In Britain, increasing numbers of geographers have become involved in local politics, as members of inner-city partnership committees, local councillors or organizers and advisors of community action groups.

But radicals continue to criticize geographical contributions to social and political debate, claiming that geographers maintain a 'fetishism' about the significance of space that distracts from the root cause of problems. Peet (1977) observed that, conventionally, "geographers try to find 'causes' of the problems they observe in what is the spatial distribution of the *results* of far deeper social causes" (p. 18), and Ley (1978) noted that much research has been preoccupied with symptoms rather than causes. An emphasis on spatial patterns and ecological correlations "always overidentifies local variables at the expense of overarching ones" (Ley, 1978, p. 42). For example, geographers devote their energies to explaining why crime rates are higher in X than in Y, or why area A is poorer than area B, while ignoring the reasons why crime exists at all or why any area (or, more fundamentally, any individual) should be poorer than any other. However, this fetishism of space is an inevitable and intrinsic part of geography. Of course, geographers must recognize their limitations and not claim to provide the ultimate answers to social problems, but to deny the significance of space is to deny the foundation of geography. Indeed, Peet compromised almost immediately, his attack on the fetishism of space (p. 19) being followed by the statement that "geographical variations give a strong spatial weight to social process, so much so that we can speak of *spatial processes*" (pp. 21–2).

So far we have considered what has often been designated as 'liberal' geography. Thus the first part of Harvey's (1973) *Social Justice and the City* dealt with 'Liberal Formulations', attempting to improve conditions within the existing political system and applying the existing methodology of the social sciences. But by Part Two, Harvey had undergone a conversion to more radical ways of thinking, epitomized in the heading 'Socialist Formulations'. Since 1973 many social geographers have followed him along the road to a Marxist standpoint, where theory and practice are perceived as inseparable.

In reality, practice seems no nearer to theory in Marxist geography than in more traditional schools of thought. Some absurd claims have been made for the Marxist approach. Peet (1977), after castigating the ideological, value-laden nature of conventional human geography, asserted that "for Marxist geographers the combination of the materialist perspective and the dialectical method allows the development of non-ideological theory" (p. 19). But there are few grounds for arguing that while all previous and most present geographers have been ideologically tainted, Marxists can somehow stand outside of ideology. Claims like the above led Ley (1978) to describe Marxism as "a secular religion", sharing many of the characteristics of religious belief that Marx so forthrightly condemned (Lyon, 1979). It promises "not only the accurate diagnosis of contemporary alienation but also its dissolution in experience" (Ley, 1978, p. 47).

Certainly, Marxist geographers have given the subject a much-needed jolt: much human geography, especially in the quantitative revolution, was counter-revolutionary, obscuring instead of illuminating reality; much so-called 'relevant' human geography has really been no more relevant than anything which preceded it; and much human geography has been far from human, reducing *Homo sapiens* to 'economic man', 'satisficer man' or a crude stimulus-response mechanism, reacting automatically to the sticks and carrots offered by his physical and cultural environment. But although Marxist geography is humanistic in terms of its own definition of what it means to be human, that definition is sadly one-dimensional. To quote Peet (1977) again: "Marxist geography accepts the tenet that social processes deal essentially with the production and reproduction of the material basis of life" (p. 21). Thus the essence of man lies in his labour power, his capacity for productive work. The inevitable result of this assumption is a form of economic determinism, however vociferously Marxists may try to deny it. So, from the viewpoint of humanistic geography, positivists (e.g. location analysts) and Marxists are equally reductionist: they all have a partial, economic view of man. But there is a difference. Positivists may be *consciously* reductionist, whereas Marxists believe that their's is a total view of man. For example, Alonso – for the positivists – prefaced his location theory with the observation that "the approach that will be followed in this study will be that of economics, and from this wealth of subject matter only a pallid skeleton will emerge. Both the Puerto Rican and the Madison Avenue advertizing man will be reduced to that uninteresting individual, economic man" (Alonso, 1964, p. 1). By contrast, no similar confessions of incompleteness preface Marxist analyses of the land market. Lyon (1979) has commented that the 'economic factor' became prominent simply because man was seen as maker; but life is more than labour, and even labour is more than economic activity. It is not justifiable to reduce values and ideas to incidental phenomena, the icing on a solidly materialist cake.

To the extent that in this book we have adopted a positivist approach to social relations, our defence is the same as Alonso's. We recognize the partial and incomplete nature of our presentation. Insofar as we have based our discussion on economics, whether from Marx or from Adam Smith, we would claim that at the aggregate or group level with which the book has been concerned, this approach does provide the *basis* for explanation. Moreover, as humanistic geographers have acknowledged, there is a danger of reacting against quantification and location theory by simply asserting the uniqueness of everything. We must try to integrate case studies and draw what generalizations we can, accepting that these will not be rigid laws, as the advocates of 'social physics' expected to find in the quantitative revolution.

All this debate about positivism, Marxism and humanism is important because we need to get straight our view of the world and our view of geography before we can decide how to link the two in a socially relevant human geography. It may be important, as Coates and Rawstron (1971) advocated, to act as messengers proclaiming the bad news of spatial inequalities to the uninformed, preparing the ground for social and political reform. But information is not neutral. What sort of information on what sorts of inequalities do we think that we should be spreading? How do we assess needs if some – for security, love, community, beauty – are not only impossible to quantify but also impossible to define?

Theory and action can be co-ordinated at two levels. At the level of the individual, "the structural reform within society must be matched with an even more pervasive revolution within the minds and hearts of individual people" (Buttimer, 1972, cited in Smith, 1973, p. 143). At the level of the community the role of geographical expeditions among the poor and powerless has already been noted, but there is equal reason for geographers to be involved in local government and community affairs among those – in the City or the stockbroker belt – *with* the resources to relieve poverty and the power to determine how resources are allocated. As well as informing the poor of their rights, we should be persuading the rich of their responsibilities. At which point, the social geography of England becomes inseparable from the future social geography of the world.

### References and Further Reading

Aspects of the cultural geography of Britain are discussed by:
Gay, J. D. (1971) *The Geography of Religion in England*, Butterworth, London.
Peach, G. C. K. (1968) *West Indian Migration to Britain*, Oxford University Press, Oxford.
Pryce, W. T. R. (1975) Migration and evolution of culture areas: cultural and linguistic frontiers in north-east Wales, 1750 and 1851, *Transactions, Institute of British Geographers*, 65, 79–107.

Various aspects of regional variations are illustrated in:

Coates, B. E. and Rawstron, E. M. (1971) *Regional Variations in Britain*, Batsford, London.

Gould, P. and White, R. (1974) *Mental Maps*, Penguin, Harmondsworth.

Howe, G. M. (1972) *Man, Environment and Disease in Britain*, David & Charles, Newton Abbot.

More wide-ranging analyses of the quality of life include:

Coates, B. E., Johnston, R. J. and Knox, P. L. (1977) *Geography and Inequality*, Oxford University Press, Oxford.

Knox, P. L. (1975) *Social Well-Being: A Spatial Perspective*, Oxford University Press, Oxford.

Smith, D. M. (1973) *The Geography of Social Well-Being in the United States*, McGraw-Hill, New York.

Smith, D. M. (1979) *Where the Grass is Greener*, Penguin, Harmondsworth.

On electoral geography, see:

Busteed, M. A. (1975) *Geography and Voting Behaviour*, Oxford University Press, Oxford.

Taylor, P. J. and Johnston, R. J. (1979) *Geography of Elections*, Penguin, Harmondsworth.

Examples of social concern among 'establishment' geographers include:

Institute of British Geographers (1974) Geography and public policy, *Transactions, Institute of British Geographers*, 63, 1–52.

Brooks, E., Herbert, D. T. and Peach, G. C. K. (1975) Spatial and social constraints in the inner city, *Geographical Journal*, 141, 355–87.

The theory and practice of 'geographical expeditions' is discussed by:

Bunge, W. (1969) The first years of the Detroit geographical expedition, *Field Notes*, 1, 1–9, reprinted in R. Peet (ed.) (1977) *Radical Geography*, Maaroufa Press, Chicago (1978, Methuen, London), pp. 31–9.

Bunge, W. (1974) Regions are sort of unique, *Area*, 6, 92–9.

Alonso's classic study of economic man is:

Alonso, W. (1964) *Location and Land Use*, Harvard University Press, Cambridge, Mass.

Finally, on ideology and social science, see:

Gray, F. (1975) Non-explanation in urban geography, *Area*, 7, 228–35.

Gregory, D. (1978) *Ideology, Science and Human Geography*, Hutchinson, London.

Harvey, D. (1973) *Social Justice and the City*, Arnold, London.

Ley, D. and Samuels, M. (eds.) (1978) *Humanistic Geography*, Maaroufa Press, Chicago; esp. D. Ley, (1978) Social geography and social action, pp. 41–57.

Lyon, D. (1979) *Karl Marx: A Christian Appreciation of His Life and Thought*, Lion, Tring.

Peet, R. (ed.) (1977) *Radical Geography*, Maaroufa Press, Chicago (1978, Methuen, London), esp. R. Peet (1977) The development of radical geography in the United States, pp. 6–30.

# Index